ALL THINGS MADE NEW

Biblical Abbreviations

OLD TESTAMENT

Genesis	Gn	Nehemiah	Ne	Baruch	Ba
Exodus	Ex	Tobit	Tb	Ezekiel	Ezk
Leviticus	Lv	Judith	Jdt	Daniel	Dn
Numbers	Nb	Esther	Est	Hosea	Ho
Deuteronomy	Dt	1 Maccabees	1 M	Joel	Jl
Joshua	Jos	2 Maccabees	2 M	Amos	Am
Judges	Jg	Job	Jb	Obadiah	Ob
Ruth	Rt	Psalms	Ps	Jonah	Jon
1 Samuel	1 S	Proverbs	Pr	Micah	Mi
2 Samuel	2 S	Ecclesiastes	Ec	Nahum	Na
1 Kings	1 K	Song of Songs	Sg	Habakkuk	Hab
2 Kings	2 K	Wisdom	Ws	Zephaniah	Zp
1 Chronicles	1 Ch	Sirach	Si	Haggai	Hg
2 Chronicles	2 Ch	Isaiah	Is	Malachi	Ml
Ezra	Ezr	Jeremiah	Jr	Zechariah	Zc
		Lamentations	Lm		

NEW TESTAMENT

Matthew	Mt	Ephesians	Eph	Hebrews	Heb
Mark	Mk	Philippians	Ph	James	Jm
Luke	Lk	Colossians	Col	1 Peter	1 P
John	Jn	1 Thessalonians	1 Th	2 Peter	2 P
Acts	Ac	2 Thessalonians	2 Th	1 John	1 Jn
Romans	Rm	1 Timothy	1 Tm	2 John	2 Jn
1 Corinthians	1 Cor	2 Timothy	2 Tm	3 John	3 Jn
2 Corinthians	2 Cor	Titus	Tt	Jude	Jude
Galatians	Gal	Philemon	Phm	Revelation	Rv

ALL THINGS MADE NEW

Homily
Reflections for
Sundays and
Holy Days:

Cycle B

HAROLD A. BUETOW, PHD JD

ALBA·HOUSE   NEW·YORK

SOCIETY OF ST. PAUL, 2187 VICTORY BLVD., STATEN ISLAND, NEW YORK 10314

Library of Congress Cataloging-in-Publication Data

Buetow, Harold A.
  Homily reflections for Sundays and Holy Days / Harold A. Buetow.
     p.   cm.
  Includes bibliographical references.
  Contents: Cycle B — All things made new.
  ISBN 0-8189-0728-2
  1. Church year sermons. 2. Catholic Church — Sermons. 3. Sermons,
American.
  BX1756.B826H66   1996
  252'.6 — dc20   96-20679
                                                      CIP

Produced and designed in the United States of America by the
Fathers and Brothers of the Society of St. Paul,
2187 Victory Boulevard, Staten Island, New York 10314,
as part of their communications apostolate.

ISBN: 0-8189-0728-2

Printing Information:

Current Printing - first digit   1   2   3   4   5   6   7   8   9   10

Year of Current Printing - first year shown

1996   1997   1998   1999   2000   2001

TABLE OF CONTENTS

INTRODUCTION TO CYCLE B:
ALL THINGS MADE NEW

The Foreword and Preface in Liturgical Cycle A, which volume is entitled *God Still Speaks: Listen!*, contains information on homilies and how to use these books. Cycle A's Introduction deals with the fact that God still speaks to us, our obligation to listen, and the results of listening. Cycle C, *Ode to Joy*, contains an Introduction that points out a fundamental aspect of Christianity: Joy. This Introduction to Liturgical Cycle B, *All Things Made New*, emphasizes another often forgotten aspect of Christianity.

Foundations

As indicated in the homily for the Sixteenth Sunday in Ordinary Time in this volume, the word "new" has at least two meanings. One is in the order of time. Thus a widget — car, refrigerator, television set — off an assembly line is new. But each is exactly like the thousands of other widgets before it. The other meaning of the word "new" is in the order of quality: bringing into the world an item that did not exist before. That is our meaning here.

When the Book of Revelation spoke of "a new heaven and a new earth" (Rv 21:1), it was revealing a dream deep in Jewish thought. Then newness was shown from Jesus' birth to his resurrection. At Jesus' birth, astrologers recognized a star as new. In this brilliant new star was God breaking into His own order and announcing something special. Matthew marks some of the beginning of Jesus' ministry, a furtherance of "the dawning of the ages" (Mt 4:12). "He has done all things well," the crowds said, alluding — probably unconsciously — to God when He looked at all His creation and called it good (Gn 1:31). The implication was that he was bringing about a new creation.

In giving his mission the night before he died to spread the love of

God to the world, Jesus *breathed* on the apostles (Jn 20:22). This was a sign of the new creation, of the new life as the Spirit is breathed into those who are being sent forth. The action of Jesus breathing on the apostles may seem a strange procedure to us, but it was reminiscent of the first creation when God breathed his Spirit into a living being (Gn 2:7). From the Jewish Scriptures the apostles were familiar with God doing this. There were many dramatic examples.

Two examples are especially noteworthy. One was when God took the creature Adam, formed from dirt, and breathed on him, giving him life (Gn 2:7). Another was the mystical experience of Ezekiel being led by the Spirit into a plain in Babylon and having a vision of a whole field full of the long-lifeless unburied dry bones of thousands who had fallen in battle. In one of the most unusual and dramatic scenes in all literature, the breath of God — which Ezekiel summoned from the four winds — brought the bones to life and they stood upright, a vast army. (Ezk 37:1-14; Cycle B — Pentecost Vigil Mass).

A new day for the human race came with the resurrection of Jesus, the most momentous occasion since the spanking newness of the days of creation. It was so unique that, when during his life Jesus spoke of it, the apostles did not know what "rising from the dead" meant (Mk 9:10, Second Sunday in Lent, Cycle B). That is truly "Gospel," or "Good News." It is "news" because it represents something that is completely unheard-of: The disaster of death has been turned into the triumph of life. It is "good," because it concerns not only Jesus, but all those who hear it.

This brings happiness to the world. When Jesus' followers sing, "Jesus Christ is risen today," we do not mean only, "Jesus Christ was risen once upon a time." We mean that the risen Christ is all around us, in the eyes and faces of those sitting beside us, in the bread and wine of the altar, in the newly baptized, and in the people we meet and for whom we do good things in Jesus' name all the time. Through us, he walks the earth today teaching, healing, touching, suffering, dying, and rising.

It was the first Pentecost Sunday on which the newness most showed itself to the world. This volume is named after the title of the homily for that Sunday in this Cycle B, *All Things Made New*. Pentecost means many things, all of them having to do with commemorating God coming to meet the human race. But it's been humorously said that some people are so spiritless that, had they been alive at the first Pentecost, they would have arrived with fire extinguishers to put out the tongues of fire.

The second creation, like the first, was the start of something big.

The Spirit of God continues to breathe over the universe. Through his Spirit God creates, vivifies, propels people to leadership, and stimulates religious enthusiasm — in short, makes all things new. The power of Pentecost is in the hands of those who choose to love and forgive and share the peace that is borne from above. As with Ezekiel's dried bones coming to life, and the apostles' fear in the Upper Room being turned to joy, and the wind and the fire of the Spirit making it possible for ordinary mortals to confess Jesus as Lord before hostile audiences, God's intervention shakes the world.

New Outlook on Death

It has overcome even death. The seventeenth-century Italian painter Salvator Rosa painted "L'Umana fragilità." It depicts a mother, an infant, and Death, who is represented by a winged skeleton. As the mother looks on passively, Death is forcing the baby to scrawl these words on a piece of paper: "Conception is sinful, life is suffering, death inevitable." For moderns, Woody Allen perhaps synopsized this barren summary of people's lives when he said, "It's not that I'm afraid to die, I just don't want to be around when it happens."

But Christians have what Isaiah promised: a new hope, a new light. For them, though Jesus died a death that was reserved for the lowest and most vicious criminals, he now sits at the right hand of God. Imagine the excitement at Corinth or Thessalonica when the Christians there received that message. Jesus had conquered death (1 Cor 15:22) and made it possible for all to defeat sin, vanquish death, and free humankind (vv. 24-28). Suddenly death need not mean "the end," but the beginning of something new — even for the lowest slave!

Death for us is a door, not a wall: It opens into a new beginning. Someone has also compared death to standing on the seashore. A ship spreads her sails to the morning breeze or primes her engine and starts for the ocean. She fades on the horizon and someone says, "She's gone." Just at the moment when someone says, "She's gone," others, watching her coming, take up a glad shout, "Here she comes!"

New Persons

One of the most important areas of newness is in the concept of person. One basis for people being lovable is that they are made in the image of God (Gn 1:26f.). That was an explosively powerful idea when it first came to light — in ancient Egypt, in Mesopotamia, and especially in the Roman Empire, when three-quarters of the people were either slaves or descended from slaves and only one man, the Emperor, was thought to be in God's image.

Take away people being in God's image and we can legitimately become pessimistic about humankind the undocile, despondent over people the unthinking, impatient with human beings the self-seekers. Forget the love of people being based on the love of God, in fact, and it becomes possible to agree with all who ultimately hold human beings in low regard.

In the world of ancient Rome, the attitude was that it made no sense for Rome to be ruler of the world if its citizens had to do their own work. Slaves were not necessarily treated poorly, but they were not treated as persons. They were not allowed to marry, so they cohabited. Their children became as much the property of the master as lambs, kids, or colts.

Christianity came into that kind of world with the good news that *every* human being is created in God's image, that all persons are precious because all are so loved by God that He gave His only Son. An essential part of the "Good News" was that people who mattered to no one else mattered to God. For instance, in the face of haughty patrician Romans who looked down on Christians, and of some Christians who were putting on airs in the pagan city of Corinth in the first century A.D., St. Paul tells his people that, by the world's standards, they may be unimportant nonentities (1 Cor 1:26), but by spiritual standards they have Christ and are therefore all-important. Paul says that we are *all* called — called to a new creation, possessing in Christ everything that all people have yearned for.

Elsewhere, Paul let the Corinthians know that we are not God's slaves or hired help, but His children. Paul says that "whoever is in Christ is a new creation" (2 Cor 5:17). Humankind has not been the same since Jesus. We are not creatures like the clothes you are wearing, or your pet cat beside you, but a creation. Through Jesus people have become completely new: "brand new," a child might say.

In the mysterious final book of the Bible, the Book of Revelation, right after words about the New Creation — the New Jerusalem, the New Heavens, and a New Earth — comes the end of the book and the end of the Bible. It ends (Rv 22:13) with Jesus applying to himself the words used by God of Himself in the very beginning of the Bible (Gn 1:8): "I am the Alpha and the Omega." Here it means that Jesus is "the first and the last, the beginning and the end": complete in every way, timeless, and with full authority. And St. Peter tells us (1 P 1:39) that our life is patterned on the death and resurrection of Jesus in an unbelieving world.

God's saving action begins in a big way with new birth through Baptism. Through Baptism, one becomes filled with newness of life. This life of sanctifying grace is called new because it is vital, liberated, emancipated. When you think about it, the entire New Testament is about the new birth emphasized in this passage.

Our new birth is a birth to many things. It is a birth to true *hope* (1 P 1:3), a hope which draws its life from Jesus' rising from the dead. Sophocles encapsulated the contrasting despair-filled pagan viewpoint for all time when he wrote: "Not to be born is best... but once a man has seen the light [of life] the next best thing, by far, is to go back ... where he came from, quickly as he can." Our rebirth is also a birth to an *inheritance* (v. 4). That inheritance is the heavenly kingdom. Best of all, we're reborn to *salvation*. In the New Testament, salvation can mean many things: deliverance from danger, emancipation from sin, release from the shackles of individual limitations, freedom for personal growth. All our rebirth is a cause for rejoicing (v. 6).

Paul in his major theological treatise, his letter to the Romans, in one of the most beautiful chapters in the entire Bible, says essentially the same thing. He says we who are baptized, by reason of the presence of the *Spirit* within, enjoy a new relationship to the *Father*: that of children, and heirs through *Christ*. Thus we enjoy an intimate relationship with the persons of the Triune God.

These revolutionary and far-reaching principles of the sacredness of people were fraught with dangers: that Christian slaves who had fellow-Christian masters might presume upon their situation, for example, or that they might revolt. It is true, of course, that Christian principles of the special sacredness of persons apply particularly to those people who are society's outcasts.

Among them are those whom the Jewish Scriptures call the *anawim* — those who trust in God rather than in their own power or efforts. The New Testament highlighted their preëminence. When Mary visited Elizabeth, she declared that God has "lifted up the lowly" (Lk 1:52). When Jesus preached in the synagogue at Nazareth, he commented from Isaiah to the effect that God "has anointed me to bring glad tidings to the poor" (Lk 4:18). When John the Baptist sent a delegation to ask whether Jesus was God's chosen one, part of Jesus' answer was, "the poor have the good news proclaimed to them" (Mt 11:5). When Jesus announced his "beatitudes" in the Sermon on the Mount, the first he declared "blest" were the poor (Lk 6:20).

Another segment of the populace for whom social justice is only beginning to catch up with the best in the Christian heritage is women. Throughout history the story of Adam and Eve in Genesis has unjustifiably had a more profoundly negative impact on women than any other Biblical story. It has led writers to depict Eve as subordinate and inferior to Adam, because she was created after and from him, and as weak, seductive, and evil, the cause of Adam's disobedience.

The best of the tradition, however, teaches that woman completes the creative process begun with the creation of the first man. When the woman is created to be Adam's "helper" or "helpmate," the Hebrew expression does not have the pejorative sense carried by the English words. The same Hebrew word is often used to describe God, and today might be expressed better by the word "companion."

All the expressions in Genesis — rib, bone of my bone, woman, man — indicate the unity of nature of man and woman, a unity unlike any other. The term "rib" is particularly significant. As some rabbis said, the woman was created not from the man's feet to be beneath him or stepped on, nor from his head to be above him, but from nearest his heart to be alongside him, equal to him, and loved by him, and from beneath his arm to be protected by him.

At the end of the process of Adam and Eve's discovery of the completion of each in the being of the other came the first human words recorded in the Bible — and they are a love song. A most touching part of that song is the three-times repeated term of endearment of the man for the woman, "this one": *"This one... is bone of my bones and flesh of my flesh; This one shall be called 'woman,' for out of 'her man' this one has been taken"* (Gn 2:23).

When (Mk 1:2-16, in the Twenty-Seventh Sunday in Ordinary Time in this Cycle B) the Pharisees questioned Jesus about divorce, they spoke in a specific context. Jesus, going back to "the beginning of creation" (Mk 1:6), concluded, "Therefore what God has joined together, no human being must separate" (v. 9). In the divine "joining together," God ratifies the mutual love of persons; their sexual union serves as a pledge of exclusive fidelity to each other. So Jesus struck a blow for women by recognizing women's culture of intimacy, close relationships, and emotional attachment to persons.

Other teachings and actions of Jesus show his elevation of women: his admitting them to companionship, for example, when that was against the custom, his dialogue with the Samaritan woman, his love for Mary Magdalene, the woman with menstrual problems, the woman taken in adultery, and a host of others.

Adding to Jesus' new elevation of the position of women, St. Paul presents something new in all the world up to that time. It is an ethic of *reciprocal duties* between husband and wife: The words "one another," for example, are repeated three times (Col 3:9, 13, 16). At that time under Jewish law a woman was a thing, the possession of her husband: A man could divorce his wife for any or no reason. In Greek society — the society of the culture of the time — a respectable woman had to lead a life of seclusion: She was never to be seen on the streets alone, even for marketing, and she was in complete servitude to the man. Under both the Jewish and the Greco-Roman societies, there was a double standard and no reciprocity: All the privileges belonged to the husband, all the duties to the wife.

Another concept of newness of persons has to do with children. Under the Roman law of the time parents were dominant, especially the father, whose *patria potestas* gave him the power to make his child work like a slave, sell his child into slavery, condemn his child to death, or do whatever else he wished. Under Jesus' dispensation, children are to obey their parents (Gn 3:20), yes, but *in the Lord*.

St. Mark describes people bringing their little children to have Jesus touch them (Mk 1:13, in the Twenty-Seventh Sunday in Ordinary Time, Cycle B). Jesus was the kind of person with whom you would do that — he cared for everyone, including children, and, because he radiated sunshine rather than gloom, children were attracted to him.

The principle of the sacredness of persons resulted in new relationships and conditions: democracy, for example. Democracy — "government of the people, by the people and for the people," in Abraham Lincoln's definition — is not only a form of government, but a spirit. It consists largely in assumptions — one person about another, one nation about another. In our civilization these assumptions are Christian.

The United States is not Christian in any formal religious sense: Its citizens transgress Christianity's precepts freely. But it is Christian in the sense that the basic teachings of Christianity are in its bloodstream. The central doctrine of its political system — the inviolability of the individual — is inherited from two millennia of Christian insistence. Applications of Christian ideals are manifest in the arguments that politicians use in public, in the popular ideas of good taste, and in the laws and manners of the people.

New Values

From the very beginning, Christianity's values were topsy-turvy from the rest of the world. A king, Jesus was born in a stable. The shepherds to whom his announcement came first, aside from Mary and Joseph, were looked down upon by their contemporaries. In his adult life, Jesus, though he lives in heaven, had nowhere on earth to lay his head; though he will return in the clouds, he entered Jerusalem on a donkey; though he gives life to all creatures, he gave himself up to be killed on a cross; though angels served him, he served us; and, though he was rich, he emptied himself (*kenosis*) and made himself a poor slave.

When he taught, he turned people's perceptions upside-down by saying, "Many who are first will be last, and the last will be first" (Mt 19:30). The haughty Pharisees resented his being in the company of the outcasts of society. People of that time thought that God blesses with riches those He loves, and the world still looks upon rich people as "first."

Christian faith entails leaving behind everything that is less than God in order to be able to accept the God who contains all things. Faith in Jesus gives his followers a new set of values: giving instead of getting, serving rather than ruling, forgiving and not avenging. We are grateful for life given by God without cost, friends provided without price, eternity promised without merit. We have the insight that our worth is not measured by what we own but by what we share, and that we have the opportunity to grow in the lasting wealth of love. We see that wealth is not necessarily a sign of God's favor, and that poverty can be.

No matter what prioritization Christians make of their values, preëminent among them is love. Jesus, in his final meal with the apostles, telling them he was leaving "a new commandment" (Jn 13:34), spoke of love. What is "new" about that? Two big things. For one, Jesus extends love to *all* people without distinction, as he had shown with his story of the Good Samaritan (Lk 10:29-37). Secondly, Jesus' commandment is new in the ideal it strives to emulate: Our love should be as he has loved us (v. 34). There can be no greater love than "to lay down one's life for one's friends" (Jn 15:13). As proposed in Cycle B's homily for the Thirty-First Sunday in Ordinary Time, *Something New for Your Love*, those areas of newness are important.

St. John makes one of the greatest statements about God in the whole Bible: "God is love" (1 Jn 4:8). That statement is not only beautiful, but answers many questions. It explains creation: Why did God create our world, many aspects of which we have messed up?

Because God is love.

It gives insight into free will: God who gave us this most precious gift does not take it away, even when we use it against Him because God is love.

It gives us an appreciation of divine providence: Had God been only intelligence or law and order, He would have created the world and left it to its own laws and devices.

But God is love.

It helps understand redemption: Had God been only justice, He might have left humankind in its sin.

But God is love.

And it puts into perspective the world beyond the grave: Had God been simply creator, He might have left people to die forever.

But God is love!

The chief way God revealed His love to us, though, is not by having brought about creation, or giving us free will, or establishing His providence over us, or accomplishing our redemption, or providing a world beyond the grave — but by sending His only Son into the world (1 Jn 4:9). And He did that in order that through His Son we might have life.

And Jesus is our life. For the writer of the letter to the Colossians, it meant a great deal to say that (Col 3:4). Sometimes we say of a person, "music is her life," or "sports are his life," meaning that such a person finds the meaning of life in music or sports. To say Christ is our life is farther reaching. We are to "put to death" all the evils in our nature that are "earthly" (v. 5), take off our "old self" (v. 9) and "put on the new self" (v. 10). This gradual growth into Jesus' life includes the realization that it is possible to spend less and enjoy more, to live simply so that others may simply live, to reject greed and grow rich in God.

New Vision of Law

In civil law, a covenant is a specific kind of contract between two or more persons. In religion, a covenant is an agreement between God and humankind, or between God and a specific people like the ancient Israelites through the mediation of individuals. The earliest historical covenant in the Bible was that between God and Noah. The glorious symbol for that was the rainbow. Originally a sign of peace, the rainbow embraced a renewed humankind, all living creatures, and the inanimate world. Later, the rainbow would serve as a sign of God's majesty: Ezekiel used it to describe "the likeness of the glory of the Lord" (Ezk 1:28) and the Book of Revelation indicated that around the throne of God is "a rainbow as brilliant as emerald" (4:3).

Next was the covenant with Abraham, the symbol for which was circumcision. In the next covenant in the Bible, that with Moses, the symbol was Sabbath observance sealed with a sacrifice, a religious act of worship offered to God, in which blood — the life — of animals was offered to God. As Moses sprinkled the blood on the people, he said, "This is the blood of the covenant which the Lord has made" (Ex 24:8). At the Last Supper, when Our Lord was establishing a New Covenant (or testament; see Hebrews 9:15, as in the Cycle B homily on the Solemnity of the Body and Blood of Christ), he modified Moses' words only slightly: "This cup is the New Covenant in my blood. ..." (Lk 22:20; see also Mt 26:28; Mk 14:24; 1 Cor 11:25). The outward sign of the covenant with Jesus is Baptism.

Jesus' New Covenant — new testament — is in some ways basically the same as the old: Both are to help humankind, both are God-centered, both involve the people of God, and in both the response is shown in obedience to God's law. But the New Covenant will be different from the old in many ways. As promised by the prophet Jeremiah (Jr 31:33), it is not inscribed merely on tablets of stone or in a book as with the old covenant, but on human hearts, so that people's commitment will be interior. Our New Covenant gives hope and life and strength, because it is a relationship of love, a relationship between the heavenly Father and His children. It tells people what to do, makes it possible for them to do what they are supposed to do, encourages them to do it, and gives them the means and the strength to do it.

Jesus brought his newness also to attitudes toward the practice of the Mosaic law. One example is *kosher*, a long list of unclean animals which could not be used for food, and rules about cooking. Jesus said that these are not what defile people: that people are defiled from within, never from without (Mk 7:15). But Jews had suffered and died for the opposite position. They treasured their memory from about two hundred years before of a widow whose seven sons refused to eat pork (2 M 7). With their mother's encouragement, her sons were killed horribly — by having their tongue cut out, their extremities chopped off, being fried alive, being scalped — all before the eyes of their mother.

Other aspects of his law the early Christians found as difficult as we do, a law that in two thousand years the world has proved itself not sufficiently ready to keep. Jesus says, for example, "offer no resistance to one who is evil" (Mt 5:39). And he gives four examples of the Christian spirit in this matter. We are to meet the physical violence of someone who strikes us on the cheek by offering the other cheek as well (v. 39). Against litigiousness, he advised putting Christian generosity above legal rights (v. 40). Those who are forced into labor for foreign powers, Jesus advised going beyond the call of duty (v. 41).

The Jews believed in love of God and of neighbor. The last seven commandments in their Decalogue constitute essential elements of relations with other people — but with a very important difference: In the codes of the other Near Eastern peoples, violation constituted only a crime against one's fellow human beings; in the Jewish Scriptures, it is a crime against God — an entirely new orientation.

Jesus' greatest commandment is to love God wholeheartedly (Mt 22:37; from Dt 6:5), and his second like the first: "You shall love your neighbor as yourself" (Mt 22:39; from Lv 19:18). The novelty of Jesus' answer does not consist in quoting these two texts: Both are in the Jewish Scriptures. Jesus' novelty consisted in putting both texts side by side with *equal weight*, rescinding the rabbinic "heavy" designation for the first commandment and "light" designation for the second. Thus he put an intimate bond between love of God and love of neighbor. *This* was new. Also new was a completely new interpretation of "neighbor." In the time of Leviticus it meant Israelites only. For Jesus, the word has the widest meaning possible: It includes every member of the human race.

To illustrate that, Jesus told the story of the Samaritan among robbers. When he asked which of the three passersby (a priest, a Levite, and a Samaritan) "was neighbor to the robbers' victim" (Lk 10:36), the "scholar of the law" to whom he addressed the question could not even bring himself to say the despised word "Samaritan": He answered that it was "[t]he one who treated him with mercy" (v. 37). In Leviticus, the neighbor was one who was to be loved, such as one who lives nearby or is a countryman. Jesus' new definition of neighbor is *one who loves.* Jesus' admonition to "go and do likewise" is a date to be remembered in the history of humanity! The human race grows in sensitivity. Just as we look back at some practices of people and call them barbarous, we, too, shall be looked upon by future generations as insensitive in many ways.

In truth, the second precept is the manifestation of the first. Love of God issues forth in proper love of ourselves and other people. Many warm people who do not believe in God love themselves and other people properly. But it is really only when we love God that human beings become deeply lovable — not with sentimentality, but with commitment. There is an intimate connection between our love for God and our relationship with our neighbor. It is only in and through the proper love we bear for self and one another that we *actualize* our love for God. Thus in our everyday lives we taste and touch eternity.

New Symbol

God's Suffering Servant in Isaiah is an entirely new concept. Whereas traditional Jewish wisdom was that God inflicted suffering only on those who deserved it, the idea that the righteous might suffer for others was revolutionary. Through his suffering, Jesus learned and grew (Heb 5:8) to the point of being able to accept suffering not with resentment but with reverence.

Jesus said that whether anyone wants "to come after me" (Mt 16:24) is voluntary, but once people accept, they must know that God then expects an ascent of one's soul, an ascent that begins with saying "no" to self and "yes" to God. The highest point of our ascent arrives when we take up our crosses, whatever they may be, out of the joy that follows upon love. Jesus was not speaking in romantic poetic metaphors: At the time he spoke these words, the cross was the symbol of ultimate degradation.

The cross was the depth of Jesus' humiliation. From that nadir, Jesus' upward movement began: "God... exalted him and bestowed on him the name that is above every name" (Ph 3:9). The apostles went to preach the cross everywhere — not as though conducting a funeral, but raising toasts!

As indicated in the homily for the Fourth Sunday of Lent in Cycle

B, people's attitudes to the cross have not changed. Many prefer to believe in the kind of Jesus *they choose* instead of looking at the Jesus *God sent*. But God does not work in our ways, but according to His own will, and that includes the mysterious message of the cross. The cross, though considered foolishness by the world, is a wisdom. To understand that wisdom leads to living not only in the letter of God's law but, even more importantly, in its spirit, which is love.

New Organization

The New Testament is the written record of the testimony of our brothers and sisters banded together in a fellowship called Church, a society established by Jesus. Through this institution, Jesus presented a wonderful new prospect, never present before: The human race organized for the pursuit of an altogether new ideal. This Church — a word used in no other Gospel than Matthew's — would be an *organization* with Peter as its first head, as well as an *organism* working quietly for good within society like leaven in bread or seed in the earth.

Through his ascension Jesus ceased to be present in his Church in one way in order to be present in another — a way that is more profound and intimate. He is present when people gather, two or three, in his name. It was to make one family out of humankind that Christ died. The Church is his mystical body: He is the vine, we the branches (Jn 15:1-10). Just as Jesus is the fullness of the Father, so the Church is the fullness of Jesus (Eph 1:23). Everything that makes God God abides in Christ Jesus!

To the present day the Church remains the same community of forgiven sinners in which we keep faith with our heavenly Father and with Jesus in the Spirit. The Church, at times as vacillating as Peter, as stubborn as Thomas, as irascible as Paul, and always as faithful as the mother of Jesus, the Beloved Disciple, and Mary Magdalene, continues to proclaim saving truth generation after generation. We have inexpressible joy in having a faith membership in a Church that is still learning, communal, praying, and overall happy.

Mary

Jesus' Blessed Mother has opened a window for us on the radical transformation — newness — possible through the power of Jesus. She embodies our rebirth, our new life. Here, a human being is the source of divine life, nurturing and bringing it to birth in herself and then in others.

Mary is the preëminent model for humanity, growing into the full image of God — receptive to God and creative in sharing the bringing of the Good News to the world. She is the model, not only for women, but also for men. She is the new human being whom God points to as His image, in being fully human, heartwarmingly compassionate, and, because completely sinless, totally free. Her holiness should not make her distant from us: To the contrary, it is holiness, not sinfulness, that is normal.

Conclusions

In biblical times, it was common for people to receive a new name to mark a new stage in their life and growth: Abram became Abraham when he accepted God's promise, Sarai became Sarah when God promised her a son, and Jacob became Israel when he entered a new relationship with God. In the New Testament, Simon became Peter when he came to follow Jesus.

Jesus, too, received a new name. What required that was the fact that the crucifixion resulted in his final redemption of humankind, and thus brought about a new relationship between Jesus and the Father and between Jesus and us. So whereas the Father initially "bestowed on him the name that is above every other name" (Ph 2:9), Jesus' new name is *Lord*.

No name could go no higher or further than St. Thomas's confession of "my Lord and my God!" (Jn 20:28). St. Paul's statement that "Jesus Christ is Lord!" (Ph 2:11) means that Jesus is the master of all life, a cosmic influence over all creation. This statement was the early Church's first creed, and it remains the essence of the Christian creed ever since. Christians give Jesus an obedience, a love, and a loyalty they can give no one else. At his name, "every knee must bend" (Ph 2:10) — not in broken submission to might and power, but to the influence of love.

Today it is legal to change our name as often as we want, so long as there is no intent to defraud. Some advocate choosing a new name at age seven, eleven, sixteen, and twenty-four and, for women, at forty-five, or when her last child has grown and left home, whichever comes first.

If it were the custom to change our name when we thought we had become a new person, would you have been able to change your name yet?

ALL THINGS MADE NEW

FEAST OF THE IMMACULATE CONCEPTION
Gn 3:9-15, 20   Eph 1:3-6, 11f.   Lk 1:26-38

Sin: What It Means to Be Without It
Rediscovering Innocence; Saying "Yes" to God;
Making Room for Jesus in Our Lives

We're celebrating today not Jesus' conception, nor the virgin birth of Jesus, important though we hold both of these to be. We come together to celebrate the first moment of Mary's existence — her conception in the womb of her mother St. Anne — from which moment Mary was free from all sin. In short, we're celebrating her Immaculate Conception, the title under which our nation is dedicated to Mary.

But what is our picture of this sinless person? A hand-wringing nursemaid? A weak emotional dependent who doesn't let her son grow up, as in Renaissance paintings? An interfering mother whose power, as suggested by some prayers and holy pictures, sometimes appears stronger than God's? One who overshadows or stands in the way of Jesus? A woman collapsing at the foot of the cross?

For a complete picture of Mary, none of these is sufficient. The fuller picture of Mary is of one who, like us, was a person in pilgrimage on this earth and who because of her openness to God was ever growing. Like us, her complete faith also involved the chalice of suffering, the daily trials of life, the uncomfortable human condition.

There are other annunciations in Scripture: in the Book of Genesis, for example, and in the Book of Judges; to John the Baptist in Luke's Gospel; and to the shepherds in the hills of Bethlehem. The pattern in all of them is that there's a messenger from God, the person is afraid, the angel says don't be afraid, the message is given; the person objects; and the answer is a sign.

The beautiful story of the Annunciation to Mary, as told in today's Gospel, is unique. It's a favorite for painters. It's full of suspense. The angel's greeting went way beyond the normal Hebrew mode of address, which was "shalom," or "peace." The angel's greeting is so important that it's been translated in many ways: "Hail, favored one," "Greet-

---

Note: This homily is mostly on Genesis; Cycle A is mostly on Luke, Cycle C mostly on Ephesians.

1

ings, most favored one," "Rejoice, O highly favored daughter." A result of the Church's Spirit-guided reflection on these words was something that Mary didn't know: that she was always in grace. And, as the Spirit hovered over the "chaos in the beginning" to bring about the world of creation, so does he hover now over a virgin to bring out the *new* creation.

The angel told Mary that, through the power of God, she could become a mother. But she wasn't married, and at that time to be an unmarried mother was considered a scandal because it was an offense against God and a betrayal of all who loved the unfortunate woman. Any woman considered so unfaithful as to become pregnant outside marriage could be brought outside the town walls and killed by stoning.

Mary, if she accepted God's call, would risk putting herself beyond any hope of security. She would have to take a huge step into the dark. She would have to accept the pain, show the trust of letting go, and be radically open to God. Mary knew all this and still said "yes." That took more than ordinary courage. If we think about it, we realize that all of us have annunciation stories of our own.

One of the most telling verses in the Annunciation story is that (almost identical with Isaiah 7:14) in which the angel told Mary that she will name her son. To name something correctly enables us to identify it. The name that Mary will give her son will be Jesus (v. 31). The name, from *Jeho* (the Lord) and *Shua* (Savior), is the root of the name Joshua, from which in turn comes the name *Jesus*. He is Lord of all creation and people's savior from evil. The name confronts us immediately with the doctrine of sin and grace.

The tremendous drama of the origins of the *original* sin is in the excerpt from the Book of Genesis in today's First Reading. We must remember, of course, that the Book of Genesis is not an attempt to explain how the world began in the language of science. It's an unparalleled study of the central problems of human life, especially the struggle within every human being between goodness and evil — questions older than strict science. It's the heart of the matter of living.

The great history of the covenant offered by a saving God begins at the very moment when Adam and Eve broke their commitment to their Creator. Nothing essential has changed from Genesis to today concerning sinners. In the garden, the human race enjoyed intimacy with God. When Adam, the first man, disobeyed, God called him (v. 9).

Adam didn't immediately respond, his excuse being that he was naked (v. 10). His nakedness was a powerful symbol for Adam's sense of being unprotected, exposed, and self-conscious in his guilt. The only thing right that can be said about Adam's excuse was that he had an awareness of propriety before God. This propriety is repeated later in the Scriptures (Ex 20:26), where the Law pointed out that a worshiping encounter with God demands proper dress. (That prescription is no less true today than when it was written.)

When God accused him of sin (v. 11), Adam blamed it on the woman God had put there with him. When God confronted the woman (v. 12), her excuse was that the serpent had tricked her into it (v. 13). Snakes seem to have been hated from the beginning of the human race. To the sacred author, the snake went beyond popular mythology and symbolized the power of evil, and the author attributes the snake's natural characteristics to God's condemnation for his being bad (v. 14). Though we may smile at such naïvetè, is the situation essentially any different from today? Buck-passing seems to be another result of sin.

People's excuses for committing sin still consist, in one way or another, of passing the buck. We have only half-joking bumper stickers that say, "The devil made me do it!" We have psychologists who say that what we call "sins" are only irrepressible inner urges uncontrollably bursting out. We have sociologists who claim that what we call "sin" is a term for what happens because of deprived childhoods and unenriched lives. And we're only too happy to latch on to any excuse that we can pass off as quasi-respectable.

Genesis next has God state more precisely the relationship between sin and people. Sin is real and, although sometimes explainable by exculpating circumstances, doesn't admit of self-indulgent excuses. But Genesis says that God puts enmity between sin and the woman (v. 15). The Church interprets "*the* woman" as being Mary. In this, Mary's immaculate conception and continued sinlessness are one with the sinlessness of Jesus. Mary is what Eve would have been if Eve hadn't sinned. She's also what we would have been, if there were no Original Sin. In all this, the Book of Genesis is what the Church has called the proto-evangelion, which means something like the "pre-Gospel" or the foreshadowing of the Gospel: the promise of redemption even at the moment of the human race's first fall from grace.

Mary's submission to God's will is the creative submission of the liberated human being who — being unattached from all other than

God and therefore not subject to any human being — is free to serve God. Mary's sinlessness, however, must be understood in the wider context of love, self-giving, sensitivity, and readiness to take risks. And risk-taking is inherently failure-prone: Otherwise, it would be called sure-thing-taking. In the current context, it's the self-forgetting submission to God of people like Abraham and Moses, who left the safety of familiar structures to embark into the unknown.

Mary is the forerunner of Luke's rogues' gallery: that is, women, sinners, little people whom no one would expect to respond favorably to God's revelation. She's the preëminent model for humanity, growing into the full image of God, receptive to God, and creative in sharing the bringing of the Good News of salvation to the world. She's the model, not only for women, but also for men. She's the new human being whom God points to as His image in being fully human, heart-warmingly compassionate, and totally free. But most of all she's completely sinless. Her holiness shouldn't make her distant from us: To the contrary, it's holiness, not sin, that's normal.

Genesis' analysis of the relationship between sin and the human race states that enmity between sin and Mary will continue through all generations: between the offspring of Satan and her offspring. Humankind will gain the clear victory: Jesus will strike at the serpent's head, while the serpent will strike only at Jesus' heel. Later revelation, like today's Gospel, confirm this optimistic but vague message of victory and specify the way in which the victory will come. But we're always free. They tell a humorous story that, during a heated debate in the United States Senate, one senator told another to "go to hell." The senator under attack appealed to the presiding vice president, Calvin Coolidge, concerning the propriety of the remark. Coolidge, who had been idly leafing through a book, looked up and said, "I've been going through the rule book. You don't have to."

The first woman was called "Eve" (*hawwa* in Hebrew), because this is related to the Hebrew *hay*, which means "living" (v. 20). Though the first woman is *physically* "the mother of all the living" human beings, she and her husband committed sin that introduced death. Mary, the second Eve, is the mother of all that is the *spiritual life*. Let's imitate her innocence. If we have lost our innocence, let's pray to her to rediscover it so that we can become like her, true children of God and co-creators with Him of the god-like in others. Like Mary, let's make room for Jesus in our lives.

FIRST SUNDAY OF ADVENT
Is 63:16f.; 64:1, 3-9   1 Cor 1:3-9   Mk 13:33-37

The Comings of Jesus
That's the Spirit!; Come Back to Me; Be Alert!; New Hope; Stay Awake!
The Eternal Significance of Every Minute; Grace and Peace; Be Prepared

A critic with a sense of humor once said of a play he disliked that he saw it under adverse conditions — with the curtain up. For many people, life itself is a shapeless play without any apparent plot or direction. Many of us just slide along in life. If we gave the same amount of reflection to what we want to get out of life that we give to the question of what to do with a two-week vacation, we'd be startled at how aimless are our "busy" days. Reflection upon meaningful goals of life is made difficult by such pressures of modern living as how we're going to meet payments, the rampant secularistic outlook which suggests that this present world is all there is, the political approach which says that the materially good life is all we want.

Christian teaching goes against all that. In the Church's celebration of the mystery of Christ, during the closing Sundays of the past Church year we looked forward to the final coming of Jesus. Today, as we're beginning a new Church year, we do the same, in a marvelous mixture of end and beginning. Some, however, say that the Church's real "New Year" should be at Easter time, when the Lord makes all things new in his death and resurrection. Still others observe that there really is no "Church Year" as such, but that we simply have different liturgical seasons and celebrations. In any case, there are three cycles of readings, today we begin Cycle B, and Cycle B is the year of St. Marks' Gospel. Because of the analogy with Lent, Advent acquired a penitential character. The liturgical color is the color of penitence. But in Advent we're told to rejoice. So many would like to eliminate the penitential character of Advent. Advent should be a season when we renew our hope because of the coming of Christ.

As we reflect upon the period of waiting for Jesus' first coming at Bethlehem, and as we begin to prepare for his coming now at Christmas, we also await his final coming into our lives. In other words, we celebrate his coming in history, his coming in mystery, and his com-

ing in majesty. Knowing that he has already come as a child born of
Mary gives us confidence. Amidst the overshadowing material prepa-
rations for Christmas, we begin our spiritual preparation for Christ's
coming by way of the season of Advent.

Jesus' voice, through St. Mark's Gospel, stirs us to be watchful
and alert (v. 33). The disciples had asked when the end of the world
would come. Jesus didn't get specific about time, but his central teaching is that he will return in glory to usher in the end of the world. Because no one but the Father knows the precise time of any of the end
events, it's necessary to be constantly vigilant. One thing is sure: No
matter when Jesus' second coming to planet Earth, he will be coming
to each of us at our death.

Jesus' one-line (v. 34) parable about it tells of a traveling master
who leaves his employees in charge. The moral of the story (vv. 35f.)
is that we have to be on the alert not only about the end, but about our
responsibility toward the *present*: Every moment has an eternal significance, so we should be on guard (v. 37). It's a message that's relevant to all times, but especially to our own, when some of our technological inventions remind us constantly that we live in the shadow
of eternity. Troubled societies always ask questions about the end of
the world. Ours is no exception. The fact always is that we're either
going to go to meet the Lord at death or when he appears in his glorious second coming — whichever comes first, as the warranties say.
These are fitting thoughts for Advent.

Equally fitting for the spirit of Advent are today's thoughts from
Isaiah: thoughts given to his dispirited people around the end of their
exile in Babylon of the need for a Redeemer for the human race's sinfulness. The passage opens and closes by addressing the Lord our father (vv. 63:16; 64:7), a reminder of the Exodus from Egypt, when God
had called Israel his son, his first-born (Ex 4:22). Because in this life
we're all exiles, we make Isaiah's Advent prayer our own. No matter
what one may see of sin in oneself and be disappointed, there's always
encouragement: God rescues and saves — but He *does* rescue and save.
Even if you've hit bottom, there's the encouragement that there's no
place to go but up.

When Isaiah saw Jerusalem hit bottom in ruins, he pleaded for
God to tear the heavens open and come down (v. 19); the people of
that time thought of the skies as a solid, plastic-like transparent vault,
which would need breaking through for God to come to earth. At the

same time Isaiah's prayer (64:2-7), intended to be recited by all the people, confessed their guilt and admitted that God was right to have permitted the Exile as a punishment for sin. God hasn't heaped a heavy burden of sorrow upon sinners; He's simply allowed sinners to wallow in their own responsible guilt. By ourselves, we're like withered leaves carried to and fro by the winds of our guilt. (God's welcoming attitude is well expressed by the beautiful hymn, "Come back to me.")

St. Paul in today's Second Reading also provides an appropriate opening to the season of Advent. Paul was aware of the sinfulness of the Corinthians, even the Christians among them: pride, immaturity, faithlessness, and — a very great problem — the divisions within the community. Despite his knowledge that he was going to have to deal honestly with these problems, Paul diplomatically begins his letter warmly. He opens (v. 3) with a prayer for what have become the essential blessings of Christianity: "grace" — what the nonreligious world might call "good health" or "good luck" — and "peace," the Jewish "shalom," a special kind of all-embracing well-being that can come from God alone. This includes not only harmony among people, but also the forgiveness of sins and reconciliation with God: the kind of warmth we feel at Christmas.

In this opening of his letter, Paul addresses some Corinthian Christians who were boasting of their many gifts. None seemed to understand that *gifts* are things one doesn't deserve and can't earn. Among their gifts were the wonder-causing speaking in tongues, prophecy, proclaiming wisdom, teaching, and making public God's revelations. We can think of others that have been given *to us* — music, for example, or the ability to work with one's hands, and all kinds of other talents. All of them aren't to be used for *our* gain, but held in trust for the honor of *God*.

Right up front, Paul states his own position about himself. Some Corinthians had had doubts about whether Paul was a true apostle, because other preachers were more dynamic than he. He reminds them that the very gifts they had from God were proof that his preaching had been effective (vv. 6f.). Paul's reference to waiting for Jesus' full revelation (v. 7) is an excellent expression of the Advent spirit. Part and parcel of Paul's teaching is that the Lord will come in glory at the end of time. Until that time, all are to rely on God's gifts of faith, grace, and peace.

The Advent theme continues as Paul speaks of the "day of our

Lord Jesus Christ." The Jewish Scriptures had often used the phrase, "The Day of the Lord." Paul and the other early Christians looked upon that day as the time when the Lord would return in his full glory; it would also be a day of judgment. Meanwhile, reminiscent of the spirit of encouragement in Isaiah, Paul reminds us that through all our problems and difficulties God is faithful, and has called us to fellowship with his Son (v. 9). That fellowship is very intimate: It means the life-giving union that exists among us faithful that arises from our union with Christ.

We can't call ourselves Christian and live our lives without a purpose. We wait for the comings of Jesus — in everyday living, at Christmas, at our death, and at the end of the world. We're going to be held accountable for the eternal significance of every moment. All waiting involves some tension, even if it's simple waiting on a street corner for a friend. When waiting involves the very meaning of life, temptations can intrude themselves. In that respect, we're no different from the ancient Israelites who were tempted to despair before seemingly insurmountable difficulties, the Corinthians who were tempted to pride over their gifts, and Jesus' first apostles who were tempted to gloat in the power of the Second Coming.

The seventeenth-century Italian painter Salvator Rosa painted "L'Umana fragilità." It depicts a mother, an infant, and Death, who is represented by a winged skeleton. As the mother looks on passively, Death is forcing the baby to scrawl the following words on a piece of paper: "Conception is sinful, life is suffering, death inevitable." At an exhibit of that painting in the National Gallery of Art in Washington, D.C., modern cynical non-believers stood transfixed before this barren summary of their lives.

But Christians have what Isaiah promised: a new hope, a new light. And our waiting for Jesus isn't a *despair-filled* tension. So we live by faith, walk in hope, and are renewed in love so that, when the last scene of the drama of our life unfolds and Jesus comes to be our judge, we shall not merely know him, but come to him as a friend.

SECOND SUNDAY OF ADVENT
Is 40:1-5, 9-11   2 P 3:8-14   Mk 1:1-8

Preparing for Christ's Coming: Repentance
What to Do about the Coming(s) of the Lord; The Opportunities Contained
in the Delay of God's Ultimate Coming; Repentance; Making a Fresh Start;
Prepare a Way for the Lord; Encouragement

People have for a long time alternatively loved and hated living in cities. One poet said that the builder of cities was Eros, the spirit of life,
but another spoke of "the hum of human cities" as torture. When people
get filled up with the dirt, corruption, and crime of cities they move
out; at other times, impressed with cities' convenience, culture, and
nearness to other people, they move back. In the long span of history,
suburbs are a relative newcomer.

It's difficult to fathom why in the time of Jesus the people left
relatively comfortable cities like Jerusalem to go out into the desert to
hear John the Baptist. Despite the stirring and spine-tingling opening
words of today's Good News, sometimes the Good News seems to have
a packaging problem. In New Testament times the "Good News," or
Gospel, had come to mean in particular political good news, one being
the visit of a king to one of his subject cities. In the ancient world such
a visit could mean pardons, the promise of new buildings, and other
benefits.

Nothing in today's Gospel looked much like good news. That
desert was one of the most abandoned places in the world. Its deep
gulches, arid limestone soil, and rocky precipices looked warped and
twisted. Its days were unbearably hot, its nights terribly cold.

John's food was locusts and wild honey. The locusts supplied his
body's need for protein, the honey its requirement of sugar. Whereas
locusts are unlikely candidates for an American dinner menu, that's in
part the result of cultural eating habits. Americans consume by the
millions less clean-living animals such as lobsters and oysters. In the
bayous of Louisiana, some people eat a stew of nutria, which is a wa-
ter-dwelling rodent. One United States cookbook on strange foods has
recipes for things like rodents, pigeons, reptiles, sharks, insects, and
fish sperm.

Locusts remain high-protein foods that nourish people in other countries. A young man in Korea, hearing of the Baptist's menu, said, "Ugh, that's disgusting! I hate honey!" Bushmen of Africa's Kalahari desert eat cockroaches. Crickets and termites are standard in other parts of Africa; termites, ounce for ounce, have twice the protein of sirloin steak. In Bali, butterflies and moths, lightly toasted, are staple fare. In Thailand and elsewhere, plump, juicy, high-protein, low-fat dragonfly larvae are considered a delicacy. In China, people eat camel hump, dog, cat, raw monkey brains, snake, armadillo, and bear paw — and make most of it taste good. In Japan, grilled snake meat is eaten; in Mexico, fried caterpillars; in Samoa, baked bat; in Turkey, charcoal-grilled lamb testicles.

John's skin was like leather, his feet strong and hard, his face emaciated and stern, his hair never cut or shaved, and his body wiry. His clothes were a loose weave of camel's hair, tied about his waist by a leather belt. No political marketer would permit John to appear in public looking like that today.

Another side of John caused some of the people to think that he was the Messiah: his remarkable austerity, which struck the imagination; the very suddenness of his appearance; his mighty voice which shook the people from their listlessness; and the fact that there had been no prophet for about 400 years. John's self-sacrificing way of life resulted in a piercing eye, a majesty of bearing, a voice of authority together with a touching humility.

John's message was present not only in his words but in his whole life: The man was the message. The time of Jesus was a time of elegance for the rich. That a messenger should make paths straight (v. 3) by filling in the valleys and cutting into the hills (Is 40:4) was the custom of kings. A herald would precede a king on a journey, to forewarn the inhabitants of his arrival so that they might thus smooth out their ill-kept roads.

John's essential message was repentance. This would be an important message of Jesus, too. Repentance doesn't mean only regret for the past or the performance of penance, but in addition a change of mind and heart, a new direction of life, and a new beginning, in keeping with the will of God. Its outward sign for both John and Jesus was baptism. John's baptism was an external sign and no more. The Jews were familiar with ritual washings like that. Symbolic washing and purifying was part of the very fabric of Jewish life, as we know from the regulations in the Book of Leviticus (11-15) and from part of the Pharisees' criticisms of Jesus. All of this is, of course, different from Jesus' Baptism, which is a Sacrament containing the Holy Spirit.

St. Mark, the first of the Gospels to be written, shows us that Jesus' story didn't begin with his birth on earth, but began in the mind of God long before. Mark reminds us that what he is presenting is the Gospel of Jesus Christ. The word "Christ" is not a surname, and it means "Anointed One" or "Messiah." To his contemporaries Jesus, whose name means "Savior," would have been referred to as Jesus the Son of Joseph, to signify whom they thought his father to be, or Jesus the Nazarean, indicating his city of origin, as later with Francis of Assisi, Catherine of Siena, and others.

Mark calls Jesus the "Son of God." These opening words are special: They fling us right into the middle of Jesus' reason for coming into this world; they make us want to read on. Mark tells us about it here in the very first verse of his Gospel, and again at the end, when the soldier who stood facing him on the cross will declare that this man was truly the son of God! (15:39).

Even in early Christianity, though, not all the disciples of John the Baptist followed his advice. As with us when things go wrong, they wondered where God was in all of this, and became discouraged because justice didn't seem to be triumphing. Many of John's followers didn't become Christians. These were a difficult problem for the primitive Church.

The vision of what can happen for those who live by God's word is contained in Isaiah, especially in passages like today's First Reading. This is the part of Isaiah that is set most beautifully to music by Handel in his *Messiah*. It's the part of Isaiah that Mark was quoting in the beginning of his Gospel in today's reading. It was written when the Exile in Babylon was about to end, and the people of Israel about to be set free from their captivity. To capture the joy and excitement of the time, the sacred writer tried to rekindle the vision of the great events of the first Exodus.

Isaiah's command in the first verse, to give comfort, sets a tone of mercy. The beautiful injunction to speak tenderly (v. 2) indicates that the prophet is to speak to the heart, like the deeply-felt words with which a lover woos his beloved. But Jerusalem at this time was in shambles, hardly able to listen to God's words — like us when we're wrapped too much in pain.

Isaiah's phrase about the glory of the Lord (v. 5) promises a wonderful manifestation of God's redeeming presence, like what we have in the wonder of the undeserved enthralling gift at Christmas. The remaining verses (9-10) move with a mounting crescendo to the point where we fear not to cry out the good news. The climax is God as both powerful conquering hero and gentle shepherd-king who is close to his people (v. 10f.), a familiar figure to the Jews. One of the most moving modern uses of this passage of Isaiah was Martin Luther King's "I Have a Dream" sermon, pleading for freedom and equality for all forgotten peoples, a true messianic expectation.

Reconciling our vision with God's sometimes seeming absence from our lives is what today's Second Reading is about. Written in the tradition of St. Peter, probably after the turn of the first century, it's the last book of the Bible to be written. Two generations had come and gone since Jesus and, contrary to expectations, the Lord hadn't returned. Many people were disillusioned.

The passage reminds us that Jesus' comings other than the first Christmas may seem like delay. We associate delay with a tactic of bureaucracy, and we don't like it whenever we're its victims. As the letter reminds us, however, time isn't the same to God as to us: A thousand years to us are as a day in the sight of God. Perhaps the author got his statement from Psalm 90, which says to God that a thousand years in his sight are as yesterday. To God, time is vertical: that is, all time is always present. To us, on the other hand, time is horizontal: that is, Saturday follows Friday, eleven o'clock follows ten, December follows November. So when we do wrong we're causing Jesus' sufferings in the past, in the present, and in the future.

And though all of our life — not God's — is a waiting, an Advent, we can't hold God to our time-table: He will come. In the case of the Lord's coming into our lives — at death and at the end of the world — it's not delay; it's God's patience. And God's patience is for our benefit: God doesn't want anyone to perish (v. 9), and we who live in the order of time have with every day an opportunity, a gift of God's mercy. The "day of the Lord" (v. 10), a phrase we find throughout the First Testament, offers a larger hope.

For us to put off hearing and acting upon John the Baptist's message of repentance, however, isn't like the patience of God; that is delay. We delude ourselves if we think that our experience is the reality, and all of these lessons a dream. Just as the earth which we think so

solid is really a group of giant plates underground, whose movements
produce the turbulence of earthquakes and volcanoes, so Advent reminds us that we don't live on firm time but on giant shifting epochs
whose transitions mark the advents of God.

Think, for example, of the consequences of unprepared-for vol-
canic eruptions. The volcano of Santorini, near Crete, in 1600 B.C.,
exploded with a force that spelled the end of the entire Minoan civilization. In the eruption of Mt. Vesuvius near the Roman city of Pompeii
in A.D. 79, many thousands of victims died. When Mount Tambora
near Java erupted in 1815, it caused summer crops in France to fail,
snow in New England in June, and fields white with frost on the Fourth
of July in the United States South.

With the explosion of Krakatoa, a 2700-foot-high volcano in
Indonesia, in 1883, the noise shattered the eardrums of sailors 25 miles
away, and the eruption set off seismic sea waves — *tsunamis* — that
swept miles inland on nearby islands and killed some 36,000 people.
In 1906, when the rocky masses of the San Andreas fault heaved violently, it distinguished San Francisco as the only United States city ever
to have been destroyed by earthquake; fire raged uncontrollably for
three days until extinguished by rain; four square miles in the center
of town were gone, many lives lost, and incalculable property damage
caused. San Francisco's 1989 earthquake was minor in comparison.
Seismologists warn that the next great rumbling of the San Andreas
fault may take a vastly greater toll.

When Mount St. Helens in Washington State in May 1980 erupted
with a force equivalent to more than 20,000 Hiroshima-sized bombs,
it blew down forests as if the trees were toothpicks, some as far as 17
miles away. The outbursts of Mount Pinatubo in the Philippines in June
1991 blasted up to 20 million tons of sulfur dioxide into the stratosphere.
Hot pumice rained from the sky, blotting out the sun. An observer said
it looked like the end of the world.

We can be certain that this present age of which the Bible speaks
will one day for all of us change into what the Bible calls "the age to
come." The character of the age to come is going to depend on what
we do in this present age. There comes a day when Christ will break
into the life of each of us. Our life is a perpetual advent for that. Let's
not delay to prepare for the coming of the Lord.

THIRD SUNDAY OF ADVENT
Is 61:1f., 10f.   1 Th 5:16-24   Jn 1:6-8, 19-28

Joy: What It Means, Where You Look for It,
and How You Get It
Great Expectations; The Fulfilled Life; Approaching Life's Central
Mystery; Preparing the Way of the Lord vs. Our Own;
Promises, Promises, Promises!; Christian Witness

Thinking people have over the ages tried to plumb the meaning of joy,
where to look for it, and how to get it. Some have observed that joy is
most intense in the years of childhood, and that some sights from the
years of youth — a meadow, a house once lived in, a familiar face —
can resurrect the joy of youth. Others have said that the deep power of
joy can enable us to see into the true life of things. Some have contrasted the whole-hearted joy of the poor with the relatively stiff joy of
the rich. The more religious-minded have said that the spelling of JOY
reminds us that "Jesus" is first, "you" are last, and "others" are in-be-
tween. One religious-minded person, Abbot Marmion, described joy
as "the echo of God's life within us."

The life of John the Baptist, despite his sacrifices and hardships,
was full of joy — if you define joy as the state of bliss over having or
expecting something or someone that you love. In today's Gospel, the
Evangelist introduces the Baptist with a contrast between the tempo-
rality of creation and the eternity of the Word: A man named John was
sent from God (v. 6). And, while we call John "the Baptist," or "the
baptizer," "the immerser," "the dipper," or "the plunger," he might with
equal accuracy be called "the witness": The Gospel says that he came
to testify (v. 7). The Evangelist puts forth witness after witness to the
truth of the claims of Jesus: God the Father; the Holy Spirit; Jesus' own
words; his works; the Jewish prophecies; people with whom Jesus came
in contact such as the Samaritan woman, the lepers, and the man born
blind; the crowds; the disciples; and — now — John the Baptist.

Today's Gospel tells of the Baptist's witness when the Jews sent
to ask his identity (v. 19). It was a time when some of the Baptist's
followers weren't becoming Christians because they were disillusioned
over Jesus' not showing all the spectacular "signs" they expected of
the Messiah. John's unconverted followers were spread throughout the

whole Mediterranean world. St. Paul encountered them, still unconverted to Jesus, at Ephesus and in Asia Minor (see Ac 18:24-19:4);
followers of John were also in Alexandria, Egypt. John, however, still
maintained his faith and his hope; from these came joy.

The first question of the religious authorities from Jerusalem was
direct: "Who are you?" (v. 19). It's a question, perhaps unspoken, which
is continually asked of us by others — and, hopefully, by ourselves
too. All their questions pertained to some of the persons expected to
return when the Messiah would come. John answered forthrightly, first
with a negative definition of himself. Because they were expecting the
Messiah, John answered that he wasn't he; because they were awaiting the prophet Elijah who had been taken up to heaven and was expected to return to prepare the way of the Lord, John said he wasn't
he, either; nor was he a prophet like Moses, expectations of whose return were also current in several circles. We, too, need to say who we're
not — to have a healthy sense that we aren't defined by the expectations of others, nor by our job, nor even by our family.

More positively, John quoted a text (Is 40:3) that every one of
the Gospels uses about him: that he was the voice of one crying out in
the desert, 'Make straight the way of the Lord' (v. 23). The roads of
the time weren't paved, or even surfaced, unless a King or a conqueror
was about to make a journey. Then, repairmen would straighten the
roads over which the Great One's litter would be carried. John's answer was startling, unique, and beautiful. Our positive self-definition
should, like the Baptist's, also give expression to our singularity, our
creativity, and our beauty.

The Pharisees' emissaries weren't satisfied with the Baptist's
answers, and asked about his authority: Why then do you baptize? (v.
25). It was a proper question. The Baptist was making Jews who already embraced the faith do what only unbelievers who were just coming into the Jewish faith had had to do: wash to be clean enough to be
one of God's people. John pointed to Christ, the one among them whom
they don't recognize (v. 26) — a remark that applies to our generation
as well. John humbly observed that he wasn't worthy to untie this one's
sandal-strap (v. 27). The unfastening of a master's sandals was a slave's
work; the rabbis had a saying that a disciple could do anything for his
master but unfasten his sandals, because that job was simply too lowly.

Today, though, John was fulfilling the words of Isaiah in today's
First Reading. This last part of Isaiah began with the prophet's uplift-

ing reference to his having been anointed with the spirit of the Lord God (61:1f.). This language always signals a monumental work of God, beginning with the very first verses of Genesis, when God created the heavens and the earth from the formless waste and the Spirit of God brooded over the waters. Here, God's mighty work is to bring glad tidings, to heal, and to proclaim liberty. The last is similar to the words from Leviticus (25:10) inscribed on the Liberty Bell in Independence Hall, Philadelphia: "Proclaim liberty throughout all the land unto all the inhabitants thereof."

The basic idea is the total salvation of God's people: bodily and spiritual, individual and social. That's the meaning of the year of favor and the day of vindication (v. 2), a reference to the "Jubilee Year" (Lv 25:8-22) when offenses were forgiven and the people rejoiced. Isaiah wanted his dispirited people to realize that, despite the hardships, cares, and worries of this crucial time, it was truly a "Jubilee Year": The people had been freed from their captivity and were under God's own care.

When in the second part of this passage we hear the voice of the people, we understand that the first recipients of the message are the *little* folk — those who rely on God because they have so few resources of their own (vv. 10f.). They sing a song of joy for salvation; they see salvation as being as ecstatic as a bride at the approach of her bridegroom, a fond image. These lines have caught the joyous spirit of those Jewish feasts on which pious men dance and sing. Closely resembling this song is the song of the Blessed Virgin Mary when the angel presented her with the news that she was to become the mother of God (Lk 1:46-55, today's Responsorial Psalm). Among other things, the song joyfully celebrates the wonder of salvation. Yet Jesus didn't heal all ills or right all wrongs; he didn't intend to. Hence his non-acceptance by many who expected a messiah who would.

Today's portion of Isaiah is the passage that Jesus chose when he gave his first sermon in his home-town synagogue at Nazareth. On that occasion, after Jesus read this passage, he rolled up the scroll, sat down, and proclaimed that the passage was being fulfilled in the hearing of his audience — by him!

St. Paul, at the end of his first letter to the Thessalonians which is today's Second Reading, reminds disgruntled worry-warts — and all Christians — that we're to be joyous. Like the Thessalonians who were discouraged because of the delay in the Lord's Second Coming, we can find reasons to find the glass of life half-empty. But Christianity is a way of life in joy: not a passive wait for Christ's coming, but an active participation in life. Paul emphasizes three pieces of good advice that summarize the *Christian* life: rejoice, pray, and render thanks. As in Paul's life, so now and always joy is the infallible sign of Christ's presence. St. Augustine said that "the Christian should be an alleluia from head to foot," and St. John of the Cross that "the soul of one who serves God always swims in joy, always keeps holiday, and is always in the mood for singing."

Because this isn't easy, we should pray without ceasing (v. 17), an exercise Paul amply demonstrates in this letter — especially in his final words in today's reading (vv. 23f.). These words stand by themselves as a perfect prayer as well as a perfect blessing for Advent. And we should in all circumstances give thanks (v. 18). Paul's "thank you notes" appear in this and almost every other letter he wrote. Even on the darkest days, there's always something to be thankful for, if we but reflect.

And reflect we must. Inspired by the questions to John the Baptist, we can reflect, for one thing, on what sort of God we worship. Is he an insurance agent ("I'll do this just in case"); a referee ("Mustn't break any of God's rules"); an accountant ("Have to have the books balanced")? Or do I really live out of the vision and attitude of a God of love revealed as such by Jesus Christ, whose birth we're preparing to celebrate?

Let's take home with us the message that we, like John the Baptist and many others in the Gospels, must be joy-filled witnesses to Jesus. In these days, that often takes courage. It also requires that we be rays of sunshine to a sometimes dark world.

FOURTH SUNDAY OF ADVENT
2 S 7:1-5, 8-11, 16   Rm 16:25-27   Lk 1:26-38

Our Duty to Be Prophets
Excitement over a Coming Birth; May It Be Done to Me according to God's
Word; Winter Festival or God Event?; Gifts of Love between God and Us;
The Good News Comes Closer; A New Creation; God Does the Unexpected

These days, everywhere you go you meet people who profess to be
speaking for God. You see them on the street corners, often sandwich-
signing the need for repentance. You meet them at social gatherings,
prophesying the possibility of the technology of our age leading to the
last things. But what is true prophecy? Today's liturgy on this last
Sunday before Christmas, recapitulating all salvation history, speaks
to that.

When St. Luke pictured God's announcement to Mary of the
coming birth of the Savior, much of what he wrote had to do with prophecy. Luke's narrative is a study in contrasts between the angel's message to Zechariah, the father of John the Baptist, and his appearance to
Mary. When Luke describes the message to Zechariah, he gives many
details; in the announcement to Mary, simply the time and the place.
When the angel came to Zechariah, it was within the gold-plated walls
of the Temple at Jerusalem; when within six months he came to Mary,
it was to a humble dwelling in Nazareth (v. 26). The angel's appearance to Zechariah involved a large crowd; his appearance to Mary was
private.

To Zechariah, the angel had delivered his pronouncement without first addressing any greeting; in Mary's case, he greeted her beautifully. In fact Mary, more than any human being in the Bible, is the
recipient of the most impressive salutations. The Church has added to
them. We call Mary not only the mother of Jesus, but the "mother" of
divine grace, most pure, inviolate, and undefiled. We call her amiable,
admirable, counselor, prudent, venerable, most powerful, merciful, and
faithful. She's the mirror of justice, seat of wisdom, singular vessel of
devotion, the tower of David. She's the house of gold, a gate of heaven,
healer of the sick, a refuge of sinners, and comforter of the afflicted.

When the angel came to Mary, she wasn't much more than a
young girl. How much was she like other girls? Poets have written about

girls, and their observations are heart-warming as well as humorous. They've called them the nicest things that happen to people. They're born with a little bit of angel-shine about them and, though it wears thin sometimes, there's always enough left to lasso your heart. A little girl can be sweeter (and badder) more often than anyone else in the world. A girl is Innocence playing in the mud, Beauty standing on its head. God borrows from many creatures to make a little girl. He uses the song of a bird, the squeal of a pig, the antics of a monkey, the spryness of a grasshopper, the curiosity of a cat, the slyness of a fox, the softness of a kitten.

A little girl likes new shoes, party dresses, small animals, make-believe, make-up, and tea parties. She doesn't care so much for large dogs, hand-me-downs, or vegetables. She's prettiest when she's provoked you, busiest at bedtime, quietest when you want to show her off, and most flirtatious when she absolutely mustn't get the best of you again. But when your dreams tumble down and the world is a mess, she can make you a king when she climbs on your knee and whispers, "I love you best of all!" Was Mary ever like that?

With Mary, the angel's greeting began by calling her God's favored one (v. 28). Honoring God with her whole being, Mary displayed what it meant for a human being to be "full of grace." The angel's statement that the Lord was with Mary, when it comes from God, implies a special prerogative. Much more intimate than God's presence to David, the Lord is literally with her. She's the new Ark, beyond all our reasonable expectations. She was to be the first human being who could say of Jesus, "This is my body, this is my blood." It's no wonder, then, that this simple girl was greatly troubled (v. 29). Unlike Zechariah, however, who was afraid at the *sight* of an angel, Mary was only troubled by his *words*. Gabriel understood Mary's perplexity, and spoke her name (v. 30) for reassurance.

He then proceeded with the promise that Mary would conceive and bear a son (v. 31). Mindful that the very first command given to people was to be fertile and multiply (Gn 1:28), Jews knew in addition that the whole purpose of their nation was to hand down their belief in one God until the Messiah would come: This meant rearing children. The childless man had his name struck out of family registers. And men wanted to have sons to pray the Mourner's Kaddish for them at death.

Mary was full of questions. "How can this be?" (v. 34), she asked. How was she to know that the child she was to conceive would be the

Son of the Most High — because, as she said, she had no relations with a man, actual or intended. The angel's answer was, in short, that everything would be accomplished by the Holy Spirit coming upon her (v. 35). This pictured the brooding Spirit sweeping over the waters of creation (Gn 1:2). It recalled also the cloud signifying God's presence that covered with glory the Meeting Tent and the Temple, and that would be present at Jesus' Baptism and Transfiguration. The same Spirit coming upon Mary brought about a new creation. By speaking of the Spirit coming upon Mary, Luke draws attention to the warmth and life of God present in this new creation as it was in the first.

When the angel added that the holy offspring to be born would be called Son of God, did Mary understand him to be announcing that her son would be divine? The First Testament was familiar with the idea of divine fatherhood. The prophets had declared Israel to be God's firstborn son, and King David, the shepherd, for one, was an embodiment of this sonship. But it would have been blasphemy for Jews to consider that God would be born of a woman, and Mary, as a Semite, wasn't in the habit of thinking in abstract terms like two natures in one person, a habit of the Western mind that would take hold later.

Indeed, there are indications that before Pentecost Mary didn't fully understand the divine nature of her son's mission (Lk 2:48-50). So she pondered him ever anew. Presently Mary, in an agreement that's a magnificent lesson to us in affirming God's plan even when we don't fully understand, assented (v. 38). Her prayer wasn't the usual one — "May God's will be *changed*" — but the greatest prayer in the world: "May God's will be *done*." If God wanted it, with faith and hope she would live with her uncertainties and fear. Would that all baptized persons, in spite of fear and doubts and uncertainties, were willing, with similar faith and hope, to let Christ be born and show the world God's love and compassion and joy!

As soon as she pronounced her words, the Son of God took upon himself our human nature. At once the good tidings were known in heaven, and little by little they were spread on earth. God's intention to express himself in the terms of humanity began to be fulfilled. Through the Incarnation, people were to know of the salvation, love, truth, justice, mercy, and other qualities of God.

Today's reading from the Second Book of Samuel and today's Gospel echo each other. The passage in the Jewish Scriptures is a famous messianic prophecy, written long after David lived. With the objective hind-sight of history, it shows David to have been Israel's ideal king, his age the golden age of Israel. He was wise and, despite his failings, loyal to God. Joseph, who was thought to be Jesus' father, belonged to the house of David. Just as Mary's relationship to Elizabeth, who was descended from Aaron the priest, showed Jesus' priestly character, so Joseph's membership in the house of David was intended to show Jesus' kingly character.

Today's passage tells of David's resolve to build a house to the Lord. He was disturbed to be living in a cedar palace while God's ark was confined in a tent. There was peace: With God's help David had defeated the Philistines, captured Jerusalem, and brought the Ark of God to the city. That Ark, which according to tradition contained the two tablets of the commandments given to Moses on Mt. Sinai, symbolized the presence of God with the Jewish people. The Ark had accompanied them on their journeys, even being carried into battle.

But God opposed the temple-palace David was proposing, and the class distinctions it would bring. So the prophet Nathan brought God's promise to build David a better house — not a house made of wood or stone or gold, but a royal house, a lineage, that would last forever. What Nathan was talking about was the establishment of a New Covenant between God and the Israelites; it's the first mention of the promise that became a basic part of Jewish hope and expectancy. This prophecy to David — this time a prophecy in the sense of foretelling the future — formed the basis for Jewish expectations of a messiah. Jesus, of David's family and town, would fulfill this prophecy. The offspring of the virgin, as promised, restored David's dynasty, which by then hadn't existed for 600 years.

St. Paul, in today's portion of his letter to the Romans, uses the word "prophecy" in both of its senses: the foretelling of the future and the duty of speaking up on God's behalf — a *forthteller*. Paul here brings his letter to an end in a song of praise that's also a summary of the Gospel. The Gospel is the revelation of the mystery kept secret for long ages (v. 25). That mystery has to do with the identity of Jesus.

Paul's idea is that God is present in history, whose central person is Jesus. Jesus is the one in whom all God's promises are fulfilled, the one to whom all nations must look for salvation. Through God's command Paul has made Jesus known not only to the Jews, but to the Gentiles as well. Jews and Gentiles hated each other. Strict Jews saw Gentiles as being immoral, unloved by God, and condemned. Gentiles saw Jews as snobbish, fanatic, pushy, and constant trouble-makers. Jews wouldn't eat with Gentiles, visit their homes, or even use money coined by them. That Paul, the strict Pharisaical rabbi, would become the apostle of the Gentiles, reconcile Jew and Gentile, and bring Jesus to the world is a lesson for all of us.

God has done the unexpected throughout salvation history. He took an obscure shepherd boy, David, built from him a royal house, and promised that his dynasty would last forever. Jesus, of that royal line, became man in order to save us. In Jesus, God reconciled Jew and Gentile. In our time, Jesus is there to help reconcile us all. These days, we contemplate the unexpected spectacle of Jesus' birth at Christmas. Every new birth is a wonder, but the newness of *this* one is an especial marvel. On this last Sunday before Christmas, it makes us straighten up, square our shoulders, and face our responsibility to let this newness enter and open ourselves to the possibilities of growth through God's creative action. Let's create the wonder of Christmas anew by saying "yes" to God at all times and bringing Jesus to the world.

CHRISTMAS
Is 9:1-6   Tt 2:11-14   Lk 2:1-14

Christmas and Becoming All You Can Be
What It Means to be "Merry"; Contrary to Expectations;
Where Bethlehem Is Today

Some Christmas cards have notes of disaffection and hints of rebellion with traditional Christmas. Many are trying to substitute the celebration of Winter Solstice instead. Stores have started selling solstice gifts. Nutcracker-scale pageants play out in the Midnight-Mass mood. The events, which celebrate the return of light after the longest night of the year, on December 21, seem to be just the ticket for those whose seasonal sentiment runs toward the pagan. No matter what faith they

---

Note: This homily is on the readings of the Night Mass. For the Vigil Mass, see Cycle A; for the Mass at Dawn and the Mass during the Day, Cycle C.

are, everybody hates dark days; there's almost a biological urge to celebrate the return of light. Proponents of having the Winter Solstice instead of Christmas favor candles and bonfires over Christmas crèches.

For some who observe the winter solstice, it's an antidote to the rampant commercialism of Christmas. They celebrate it on December 21st with a candle-lit tree, gifts, feasting, and a bonfire. Then, when everyone else is running around like maniacs, they have a few days of rest and quiet.

The American Atheist Society supports the solstice celebrations. With the diversity of world opinion, they see in it an opportunity to convert festival times to neutral, natural celebrations in which all people can participate as one. In sum, the solstice seems to offer a new Santa for a generation that wants to believe in something.

In truth, Christmas isn't simple. Whenever we long to have a Christmas as pure and as innocent as our crèche seems to be, we must keep a few facts in perspective. St. Luke reminds us that the first Christmas, the day of Jesus' birth, wasn't a holyday, but a working day. In today's terms, it was a day of ringing cash registers, the filing of IRS forms, and people standing in long lines, snarled traffic, and crowds so thick that there wasn't a hotel room to be found — all because of an arbitrary government edict from Rome. The true meaning of Christmas is that God entered the real world of flesh and blood, the rough-and-tumble workaday world of people with jobs to do, anxieties to deal with, the government breathing down their necks at tax time — and not the safe world of silent sanctuaries.

In today's part of St. Luke's narrative, he brings in the census to explain the time of Jesus' birth, because it was one of the few ways at that time to tell what year it was. The Roman Empire took up a census every fourteen years with the double purpose of assessing taxes and finding those who were liable for military service. In Palestine, though, inasmuch as military service wasn't expected of the Jews, it was only for assessing taxes. To simplify matters for Rome, everyone had to register in his own town. Joseph and his pregnant wife Mary therefore had to travel the ninety difficult miles in the rainy season from Nazareth, where they were living, to Bethlehem, Joseph's town because he was of the lineage of King David.

By mentioning Caesar Augustus, Luke makes a delicate contrast. For the Roman Empire of that time, Caesar Augustus was seen as the inaugurator of peace and the great world benefactor. There is still today preserved in Rome the altar of peace (*ara pacis*) commissioned by Augustus. On the other hand, Jesus is presented in the poverty and helplessness of babyhood as the bringer of peace to all: It's Jesus, not Augustus, who is the Savior of the world.

Even though Mary was about to give birth, there was no room for them in the inn (v. 7). Such a place was far from luxurious. It was merely a series of stalls opening to a common walled courtyard. The travelers brought their own food, the innkeeper providing only fodder for the animals and a fire to cook by. So Joseph took Mary to one of the many caves in the hillsides around Bethlehem and, when she had given birth, they placed her baby in a manger, a place where animals fed.

By mentioning the manger, Luke symbolizes Jesus as the sustenance of the world; often, throughout his Gospel, Luke refers to eating and drinking as a symbol for close friendship and union with God. The fact that this was her "first-born son" had no implication of subsequent offspring, but referred only to his preferential status. The rights of the first-born, called primogeniture, accrued to him: special authority, responsibility, and succession.

His mother wrapped him in swaddling clothes, the "Pampers" of the time, a square of plain linen or cotton cloth in the case of the poor, embroidered material for the well-to-do. Enclosing the whole body, including the arms and legs, the swaddling strips were wound round and round the infant like bandages and tied. People of the time thought this would make the child grow straight and strong. The procedure was probably a survival from the early nomadic days of the Israelites in the wilderness: At that time the bandaging not only afforded protection against cold and a support to the spine, but the confinement of the limbs in them enabled the mother to carry the infant more easily and securely while traveling.

Despite the rejection of the Holy Family, the primitive stable, the cold night, the animal stench, and the loneliness, this was the Son of God to whom Mary gave birth. Obviously, the event didn't meet the expectations of the people and their leaders, who were awaiting one who would save them in a sensational way, like Moses causing the plagues or Yahweh's mighty hand rolling back the sea when their ancestors came out of Egypt. But it wasn't only the Child who was born that night. It was a whole new value system, a completely new world, giving birth not among those operating the old order, but in splendor and light among the old order's victims.

Among those victims were shepherds, many of whom were in that region living in the fields and keeping night watch over their flock (v. 8). Bathless, they were mangy and stinking. Because their work made it impossible to keep the ritual details of the Law, such as the meticulous hand-washings, they were despised by the authorities and through them by the ordinary people.

A dictum of the rabbis had it that "a man is bound to offer three benedictions daily: that God has made me an Israelite, that He has not made me a woman, that He has not made me a boor." By "boor" they meant one who was ignorant of the Mosaic Law. There was a popular saying: "Don't let your son become a donkey-driver, a camel-driver, a barber, a boatman, a shepherd, or a merchant: for these are the trades of thieves." Shepherds were considered to be always so destitute as to be on the point of stealing, and hence untrustworthy. Evidence from them wasn't accepted in a court of justice.

On the other hand, the patriarchs had been shepherds. And David had been taken from shepherding his flocks in Bethlehem to be anointed king. "To shepherd" was often synonymous with "to rule." A passage in the Mishnah leads to the conclusion that the flocks pastured around Bethlehem were destined for sacrifice in the Temple in Jerusalem, only five miles away. And these shepherds who looked after the Temple lambs were destined to be the first to see the Lamb of God who takes away the sins of the world.

So while the census-takers were bending over their books and the soldiers were patrolling the streets of Bethlehem, the angels came to the shepherds (v. 13). They didn't go with their good news to Herod, nor even to the high priests. And because the glory of the Lord shone around (v. 9) the angels, the shepherds were struck with great fear: This was no natural light.

But it was among the lowly shepherds that the kingdom of God started. They heard the only song ever sung from heaven to earth: Glory to God in the highest and on earth peace to those on whom his favor rests (v. 14). After their song, the angels left this earth and the mysterious species that was different from them: the human race.

Today's reading from Isaiah shows the aspirations of one segment of the human race — the Jews — for Jesus' coming. The king they considered ideal was the quintessence of the virtues of the best of their ancestors together with new virtues that would solve their current problems. He would have the wisdom of Solomon, the courage of

David, the religious virtue of the patriarchs and Moses. He smashes
the yoke, the pole, and the rod (v. 3), the common images of enslave-
ment for human beings as well as animals.

Just as on the day of a king's enthronement he was proclaimed
to be an adopted son of God, Isaiah's king — whom we believe to be
Jesus — is also a "child" (v. 5), who would have God's own authority.
He is "Wonder-Counselor" (v. 7), remarkable for his wisdom and pru-
dence; "God-Hero," like God himself a warrior and defender of his
people; "Father-Forever," always devoted to his people; and "Prince
of Peace," his reign being characterized by perfect beatitude, justice,
joy, and harmony.

If we and the world are to move toward Jesus' values, St. Paul's
letter to Titus informs us that something more remains to be done. On
Christmas, although the grace of God has appeared (v. 11), we must
constantly remind ourselves that God's revelation in Christ demands
transformation of life. In opposing vice and promoting virtue, more is
needed than what the Greco-Roman society of Paul's time — the virtues Paul's letter mentions — demanded. It's important to remember
that our Savior's birth was only the beginning of a process which will
culminate in Jesus' Second Coming. To forget that is to risk sentimen-
talizing "Baby Jesus" into an unreal fairy-tale.

As the Christmas Prefaces remind us, in the wonder of today Jesus
has brought to the eyes of faith a new and radiant vision of God's glory.
In Jesus we see our God made visible and so we're caught up in the
love of the God we can't see. Today in Christ a new light has dawned
upon the world: God has become one with the human race and the
human race has become one again with God.

In wishing you a Merry Christmas, which we wholeheartedly do,
we reflect that God has done His part. But a lot remains for us to do.
This Christmas, let's mend a quarrel. Build peace. Seek out a forgotten friend. Write a love letter. Encourage youth. Keep a promise. Forgo
a grudge. Forgive an enemy. Listen. Be gentle. Laugh a little. Express
our gratitude. Welcome a stranger. Take pleasure in the beauty and
wonder of the earth. Speak our love. Speak it again. Speak it still once
again!

In the darkness of this night, the Christchild shines out as a wonderful light beckoning all of us to realize our full potential. But we can't
even begin to sing "O Come All Ye Faithful" until and unless we understand some applications to our lives. The Bethlehem to which we

come today is no longer a hillside cave, but any place where we can create the values of that cave to bring Christ anew to others.

FEAST OF THE HOLY FAMILY

Si 3:2-6, 12-14   Col 3:12-21 (Both in A, B & C)   Lk 2:22-40 [or 2:22, 39f.]

The Family as Creator
Faith and the Family; The Virtues Needed between Parents and Children

Is the family dead, as some people claim? In the place of families, do we have a collection of individuals who are concerned about their own pleasure, comfort, and identity, but who care little for anyone else, except as a means to their personal ends? Are homes now just filling stations, where individuals come because they need to eat, sleep, clothe themselves, and watch TV?

If the answer to any of those questions is "yes," it's one of the greatest tragedies of the Western world — ever! We have the ability today to make our homes and families the best they've ever been capable of being. The slowly evolving attributes of home "comfort" — privacy, intimacy, domesticity, ease, leisure, pleasure, convenience — only gradually combined over about the last 200 years to create a sense of "home" that we take for granted.

Right up to and into the Middle Ages, rooms lacked specific functions. Privacy was nearly nonexistent. Many people slept, ate, worked, and loved in one room, and beds enjoyed multiple occupancy. In order for the modern home to take shape, work and residence had to be located in separate buildings; specific functions had to evolve for specific rooms; and society had to have a high esteem for the two values of intimacy and privacy.

All of these began to occur dramatically in the Netherlands in the 17th century. The prosperous Dutch of that time removed the work space, first to a different floor, then to another building, and finally to another part of town. Interior spaces began to differentiate themselves

---

Note: Today's homily is mostly on Luke.

along with their functions, windows began to open and close, and a distinction between the public and the private was drawn.

With more light, more privacy, and more children came a stronger sense of family life. The French, a century later, took the next step forward with the production of furniture that, however perhaps overdone, was, above all, very comfortable. British and other merchants visited the Netherlands, admired what they saw, and took it home with them, along with such Dutch discoveries from the East as Chinese tea and Oriental carpets.

The industrial era brought such improvements as household gas lamps in the 1840's, electricity in the 1880's, and then many labor-saving appliances at the turn of the century. The importance of electricity can't be overemphasized; it provided the mechanical means to achieve comfort and broaden women's horizons, reaching a degree of efficiency and ease hitherto unimaginable. Electric light prolongs daytime, enlarges hospitality, encourages reading.

In view of that long development of which we're the beneficiaries, if our homes have become merely stopping places, that would be, we repeat, a great shame. The wreckers of marriage and destroyers of family used to be thought to be liquor, in vaudeville mothers-in-law, and in the movies designing women; today society itself seems to be anti-family, with its ethos of "me first."

As the basic unit of society, the family is extremely important. Everyone must come in contact with it in one way or another. Though some of the family's borderline aspects may change, its basic principles always remain the same. Because family, like marriage, is a process, not an arrived point, no family was or is ever perfect.

Today the Church recalls the birth of Jesus into a religious family and "meditates with profound reverence upon the holy life led in the house of Nazareth by Jesus, the Son of God and the Son of Man, Mary his mother, and Joseph the just man" (*Marialis Cultus*).

Today's section of St. Luke's Gospel tells of typical ceremonies in the life of a Jewish family from which we may learn today. These ceremonies took place at the Presentation of Jesus in the Temple — the ritual whereby parents dedicated their newborn child to God. The Jews knew instinctively that a good family life must be centered in a deep reverence for God and His law. Christians have made the Presentation a joyful mystery of the rosary, because it gave Mary and Joseph joy to present their child to God.

Though these ceremonies may seem strange to us today, behind them lies a recognition of what many have lost sight of: that a child is a gift of God and that, of all God's gifts, there is none for which people shall be held more accountable. One ceremony to show acknowledgment of this was the Redemption of the First-Born. The Jews believed that every first-born male, of cattle as well as humans, was sacred to God (Ex 3:2). In recognition of God's gracious power in giving human life, they had a ceremony whereby parents could for a certain sum symbolically buy their son back.

The other ceremony was Purification after Childbirth. After giving birth, a woman was held to be ritually unclean — for 40 days if she had given birth to a son, for 80 if a daughter. At the end of this time, she was to offer two gifts to God in the Temple. One was a lamb, in thanksgiving for the birth of her child, the other a young pigeon, which was to remove the ritual uncleanness. If a family couldn't afford the lamb, they were permitted to offer another pigeon instead (Lv 12:8). This offering of two pigeons came to be called the Offering of the Poor. Luke's "Gospel of the Poor" mentions (v. 24) that this was the offering of Mary and Joseph. It showed that they were lower middle class at best, having no luxuries, sacrificing to make ends meet, accounting for every penny spent, and knowing the insecurity of life.

Every one of Luke's introductory three verses (vv. 22-24) mentions "the law." This is a part of his theme that Jesus is the fulfillment of the Law and the Prophets of the Older Covenant. Reflection and discussion of their Scriptures led the majority of Jews to believe that they were God's chosen people. To lead them to the greatness they thought they deserved, many looked to the coming of a great champion from heaven, or a king from David's line, or some other power. Some few, however, didn't go along with dreams of armies or power, believing instead in a life of prayer and alertness to discern God revealing His plans in His own good time.

The devout Simeon was one of these. He was the quiet man, the man who listens. As a result of listening to the Holy Spirit, he came into the Temple (v. 27). He held the little bundle, whom he recognized as the Messiah, the salvation of God, in his arms; then he uttered a prayer that told the Lord that he was ready to depart this life in peace, his words echoing the prophecies found in Isaiah's "Book of Consolation." Isaiah had seen the universal outreach of God's mercy, and now

Simeon began by blessing God for sending salvation to the whole world
(v. 30f.) and not only to the frontiers of Israel.

Mary and Joseph in their loneliness had been astonished that the
shepherds should come, and now they gasped to think that this stranger
not only knew their child, but knew something of his future (v. 33). In
fact, Simeon proceeded sadly to give his mother a summary of Jesus'
fate (vv. 34f.). He predicted that Jesus would receive much opposition.
It was hard for Mary to believe that this baby in her arms would be the
downfall of anyone, but the full story would prove it to be true: People
who have heard of Jesus are judged by their reaction to him, and many
— scandalized by his humility, poverty, and death on the cross —
wouldn't follow him.

That Jesus would be for the rise of many, Mary found easier to
believe. As it would turn out, Jesus would extend the helping hand that
many people needed to lift them up out of a life of sin into a new life
of goodness. Just as there is no such thing as neutrality in values, there
is no neutrality on Jesus: One either surrenders to him or is at war with
him. By one's stand one lays bare one's heart (v. 35). Capping it all,
Mary herself would be pierced with a sword: She too would have to
make a decision about whether to follow her son.

Luke, continuing his penchant for balancing scenes and presenting counterpoints between men and women, points to another of "The
Quiet in the Land": Anna (v. 36). All we know about her is here. She
was a widow (v. 37), which meant that, at least because of the death of
her husband, she had known sorrow. Widowhood is, unfortunately, a
part of family life. Modern widows have commented that typical of
early widowhood is loss of self-esteem, rejection by married friends
who feel uncomfortable socializing with a single woman, and worries
about finances. Some widows say that initially they're so exhausted
by grief that they can hardly get out of bed in the morning.

Sorrow can have one of two effects on us: It can make us hard,
bitter, and resentful, or more understanding, kinder, and more sympathetic. It can take away our faith, or make our faith more solid. Which
side of these alternatives happens will depend on what one thinks about
God — whether He's a tyrant who sends sorrows with no apparent
reason other than His own pleasure, or a loving Father who permits us
to be tested to show who we are. To Anna, God was a loving Father.

Anna was eighty-four years old (v. 37). Age can do worse than
sap one's bodily strength: It can take away our heart, so that we be-

come grimly resigned to the way things are. It can also give us wisdom and humor and other virtues. With regard to humor as being essential to a family, in a cartoon a wife turns to her husband whose face is buried in the newspaper and says: "The marriage counselor told me to compliment you more often. ... Hey, nice elbows!"

Here again, how we develop will depend on how we think of God. If we conceive Him to be distant and remote, we despair. If He's intimately connected with our life, He gives us hope. Anna, despite her age, hadn't stopped hoping. Luke tells us how she managed to stay like that: She was in constant contact with the Source of all strength through prayer. That's a better prescription for a "fountain of youth" than all the exercise and diet manuals on the market. Her prayer life gave her the same values as Simeon: When she came on the scene she gave thanks to God first, and then spoke to others about the child (v. 38).

Through today's Gospel, we've seen Mary and Joseph's trust, faith, understanding, patience, love, and respect toward God and, through Him, toward one another. Nazareth can teach us family life in ways that are simple yet full of hidden meaning. Here we can learn who Jesus really is. We can sense the conditions and circumstances that affected his life on earth: the places, the tenor of the times, the culture, the religious customs. Here we can learn the importance of spiritual discipline for all who wish to follow Jesus and to live by the teachings of his Gospel. We learn from the family's silence and, in our time's cacophony of strident protests and conflicting claims, try to appreciate its great value. The silence of Nazareth should teach us how to meditate in peace and quiet, to be open to the voice of God's wisdom. The Holy Family's communion of love and its sacred character can teach us that the formation received at home is irreplaceable.

Christian love within marriage is a sharing of life together with a deep respect for the other person, a continued concern for their need, a growing understanding of ways to help them, and a genuine appreciation of help received from your partner when you yourself need healing. A real understanding of loving within the family reveals a depth of love which spills over into the world outside the home.

Children need the virtues of the family if they're to develop fully. Good mothers today, like Mary, suffer as well as take pride in their children. There's much truth, but not infallibility, in the words of the anonymous poet, who wrote:

If a child lives with criticism,
    He learns to condemn.
If a child lives with hostility,
    He learns to fight.
If a child lives with ridicule,
    He learns to be shy.
If a child lives with shame,
    He learns to feel guilty.
If a child lives with tolerance,
    He learns to be patient.
If a child lives with encouragement,
    He learns to have confidence.
If a child lives with praise,
    He learns to appreciate.
If a child lives with fairness,
    He learns justice.
If a child lives with security,
    He learns to have faith.
If a child lives with approval,
    He learns to like himself.
If a child lives with acceptance and friendship,
    He learns to find love in the world.

Parents should prepare their children, from an early age, within
the family circle, to think and act in accord with proper attitudes on
family life. Children should exercise the same virtues toward their parents and each other that they expect from them — trust, understanding, humility, love for one another, kindness, the emptying of self which
is the essence of the Christian life, and respect — plus reasonable obedience. Little by little, and most of all by example, parents should teach
their children to go beyond the confines of the family and take an interest in other people and in church and civic community activities. Thus
both parents and children can benefit the entire human family.

SOLEMNITY OF MARY, MOTHER OF GOD (JANUARY 1)
Nb 6:22-27   Gal 4:4-7   Lk 2:16-21
(All A, B, and C)

Happy New Year!
The Motherhood of Mary; God's Adopting Us; The Humanity of Jesus;
Mary as Mother of God; Mary's Spirituality; Mary the Ponderer

Today's solemnity has been called by many names. It's primarily the
Octave Day of Christmas, and as such has as its central celebration the
mystery of the Incarnation. Secondly, we celebrate the circumcision
of Jesus on the eighth day and thus his submission to the Law. Thirdly,
the time of circumcision is the occasion for giving a child a name; he's
called Jesus, a name far above all others and means savior. Another
theme of this day is World Peace. Today, of course, we celebrate the
solemnity of Mary, Mother of God. Finally, the feast, occurring on the
first day of the civil year, is an occasion when people look back on the
past and wish each other well for the year to come. Does that mean
that when someone wishes us a "Happy New Year," because it's a civil
and not directly a Church celebration, good Catholics should flip back,
"Thanks, but I have other plans"?

Actually, the extending of wishes for a "Happy New Year" goes
back to the religious notion of blessing. A blessing in this sense is the
verbal expression of a wish that good befall someone. As with a curse,
it rests on a belief in the power of words: the power of a blessing to
give life and happiness, and the power of a curse to bring misery and
death. This isn't to be confused with superstition or magic: Blessings
come truly from God.

A blessing recognizes that since the fall of Adam the world has
contained a tension between good and evil. A blessing therefore com-
prises two elements: the expulsion of Satan's power — evil — and
God's taking possession. The actual formula is a prayer to the Lord —
for example, Isaac's blessing of his son Jacob: "May God give to you
of the dew of the heavens [a]nd of the fertility of the earth abundance
of grain and wine. ... Cursed be those who curse you, and blessed be

Note: This homily is mostly on Numbers. For Luke, see Cycle A; for Galatians, Cycle C.

those who bless you" (Gn 27:28f.). Because the ancients considered blessings to have almost a physical effect, Isaac couldn't withdraw his blessing of Jacob even after he discovered that Jacob had tricked him to get it.

For the ancient Hebrews, the common verb in their language for "to greet" often meant "to bless." When a Jew blessed another person, that blessing was considered a petition to God; when he blessed God, it was an expression of praise and gratitude. In addition to people blessing one another, certain individuals possessed special authority to call down God's blessings: a father, upon his children; a king, upon his subjects; and priests, upon the people.

The blessing in today's First Reading, perhaps one of the best-known sections of the entire Torah, is a priestly blessing upon the people, derived from Moses's brother Aaron and his priestly descendants. The blessing is threefold, and is so beautiful that it's an integral part, not only of Jewish services, but of many Christian ones as well. It reads: "The Lord bless you and keep you! The Lord let his face shine upon you, and be gracious to you! The Lord look upon you kindly and give you peace!"

The request that "the Lord let his face shine upon you" is most interesting. Developmental psychology has shown that very early in life the baby shows a unique interest in faces or even shapes that resemble faces. Nature has programmed the child to engage with its caregivers and evoke a response from them. This process is a first stage in the child learning to interact with others. The baby Jesus' gazing on the face of Mary taught him how to become "a man like us." The later stories that tell of Jesus' ease in relating to the wealthy as well as prostitutes are, on a human level, rooted in this initial socialization process. God's face shining upon us raises us to new heights.

So the blessing first recognizes people's dependence upon God. Secondly, it wishes that God give the blessing's recipients a sign of divine pleasure. Thirdly, it wishes "peace," that precious gift of not only internal tranquility, but of prosperity and happiness as well.

The place of blessing in the New Testament is well known. As one example, Jesus ascended to the Father while blessing his disciples (Lk 24:51-53). And the two aspects of First Testament blessing — the calling down of God's bounty upon people and thanksgiving returned to God — find their perfect realization in the words of the Eucharistic Prayer that say to God of Jesus at the consecration of the bread, "he gave you thanks and praise." Those words accurately describe the double aspect of the perfect blessing.

In the Christian tradition going along from the New Testament, we find many beautiful blessings. At the end of Mass, the priest always blesses God's people before sending them into the world to love and serve the Lord. And our ritual contains blessings of water, houses, medals, lights, bread, ships, automobiles, and all kinds of other things. As in the First Testament, the Church's blessings often use gestures as well as words, like putting one's hands on the head of a person being blessed or using the sign of the cross and holy water. The Church's blessings plead for continued help in all the ups and downs of life. What has become known as the "Irish Blessing" is particularly beautiful: "May the road rise to meet you. May the wind be always at your back. May the sunshine warm your face, and the rain fall softly upon your fields. And until we meet again, may God hold you in the palm of His hand."

Other peoples have devised their own New Year customs and timing. Rosh Hashanah for the Jews, around September or October, is a time of self-examination and penance that commemorates the creation of the world and the Jews' responsibilities to God. Chinese New Years' Day (Tet) is celebrated in February or March; it's a time of great partying and firework displays. The Chinese symbolize their blessing, usually for long life and happiness, with the red and green colors that you see in all the Chinatowns of the world.

Even in our Western tradition, New Year's Day hasn't always been January 1. The names of our months indicate that the year used to begin on March 1. September means the seventh month, October the eighth month, November the ninth month, and December the tenth month. We still add compensatory days during leap year in February, because originally that was the last month of the year.

But whenever we celebrate and whatever our customs, the key is newness: a time when we can psychologically — and spiritually — put the old to rest and start afresh. For Christians, that newness comes more properly at Easter, when we bless the new holy oils, the new fire, and the Paschal Candle, and renew our baptismal vows. But as long as we can separate our celebrations from drinking too much at New Years' Eve parties, and football and parades to the exclusion of the renewal of our spirit on the occasion, January 1 is just fine.

It is, then, uniquely fitting that we extend our blessings for a

"Happy New Year." We remind ourselves, however, that every Christian who gives or receives a blessing must have true interior dedication and sincerity; the people who *receive* blessings might be better described as *participants* in the prayers of blessing rather than as mere recipients. While the external participation of the recipients of blessings is often materially slight (perhaps no more than saying "Amen"), that's no indication that active participation in receiving blessings is of minor significance.

The ideal combination of the active and the contemplative in living the life of blessing is Mary. When she said "yes" to God at the Annunciation, she, though blessed, didn't know the full story — that would be only gradually revealed to her — but she walked in trust. At the revelations of the shepherds in today's Gospel, though the others were active in amazement, Mary kept all these things, reflecting on them in her heart (v. 19). This calls to our minds incidents in Hebrew history: Jacob ponders the dreams of his son Joseph (Gn 37:11), Daniel ponders the message of the angel and the vision of the Son of Man. Whenever any important event happens in the Bible, there's pondering, a marveling at the mysterious goodness of God.

With these thoughts on blessings before us, we extend the prayer that you will be blessed with a "Happy New Year." We join with the Church in one of her blessings for this occasion (adapted from Solemn Blessing #3: "Beginning of the New Year"):

May our heavenly Father, the giver of every good gift, grant you his grace and every blessing and keep you safe throughout the coming year.

May He grant you unwavering faith, constant hope, and love that endures to the end.

May He order your days and your work in his peace, hear your every prayer, and lead you to everlasting life and joy.

THE SOLEMNITY OF THE EPIPHANY OF THE LORD
Is 60:1-6   Eph 3:2f., 5f.   Mt 2:1-12
(All A, B, and C)

Christ's Followers: Universal
Christ, Light Dawning Amid Darkness; The Divinity of Christ;
Manifestations of Christ; Ecumenism

People sometimes live in isolation. Take, as one example, dialects: The reason they exist is that people have lived in regions or valleys away from the rest of the world for so long that they develop their own way of talking, and sometimes even of thinking. It's only occasionally that people, especially youth, run away from their isolating situation.

Improper isolation can be present in religion, too. Some people think of their way to God as being the only way, an inside track, exclusive. The Solemnity of the Epiphany of the Lord, which we celebrate today, teaches that we shouldn't be narrow in our thinking about other people.

"Epiphany" means "manifestation" or "showing." Originally, the word "epiphany" referred to the visit of a king to the people of his provinces. Courtiers would insure a good attendance by throwing coins to the populace along the way; the king's visit was accompanied by a great parade, and he usually gave a banquet to which citizens were invited. He declared amnesty for political prisoners and did everything he could to insure the people's loyalty. We have remnants of all that in what we call "pork barrel" politics.

As a Christian festival, Epiphany is shot through with references to those whom people considered outsiders and therefore unacceptable to God. It's a day for emphasizing the glory of the Lord, and several events to do this used to be celebrated on this day: the baptism of Jesus and the wedding feast at Cana, as well as the coming of the Magi. At Jesus' baptism, his glory is shown by the voice of the heavenly Father and by the descent of the Holy Spirit; at Cana, Jesus worked the first of his signs and manifested his glory; and the coming of the Magi emphasized that God's Son became flesh for Gentiles as well as Jews.

Note: For other homily ideas, see Cycles A and C.

All together, the signs and symbols of this feast call us to look with wonder at the breakthrough of eternity into our passing world.

An example of God's epiphany is today's reading from Isaiah, which is a lyrical description of the new Jerusalem. It's hard to avoid the prophet's sense of excitement and exuberance here at the thought of God involving Himself with His people. The promised return of the Jews to Jerusalem from the Babylonian exile had begun. The work of rebuilding the city and restoring the Temple had started, but things weren't going well. The people needed two things: discipline to maintain their identity, and encouragement. Isaiah provided discipline by stressing observance of the Law: such rites as, for example, circumcision, keeping the Sabbath, and minding the dietary laws. From this time on, the study of the Scriptures and conduct based upon the Mosaic Law will provide a sense of community and identity in Judaism that will grow.

At the same time, the author encourages the people by telling them that Jerusalem will be a gathering place for all the nations of the world, and God's presence among the Jews will be so bright that even the Gentiles shall walk by the light of the Jews (v. 3). The Jews shall have the riches of the sea and the wealth of nations (v. 5). Caravans (v. 6) will come from Midian and Ephah and Sheba bearing gold and frankincense. Some of the popular elements of the Magi story come from this passage.

The international showing of Jesus begins in St. Matthew's Gospel with the Magi, or astrologers as they're sometimes called because they were stargazers. They represent all people to whom God showed Himself in Jesus. Although God's showing Himself in Jesus to all people is Matthew's purpose in having the Magi kneel in awe and wonder before the mystery of Jesus, we don't know how many Magi there were, or anything else about them. Perhaps the story is "midrash," a poetic and mystical meditation on a mystery in the light of the Scriptures. It's often impossible in midrash to separate what's poetic meditation and what's factual history. What we must remember is Matthew's purpose: to reveal that God showed Himself in Jesus for all people. He also wants to show the contrast and irony in Gentile leaders traveling hundreds of miles to honor the Messiah, and Jewish leaders but five miles away caring nothing for him.

For Matthew, it was a mystery of light: Star-gazers follow a star and find a baby through whom God will light up the world. Epiphany is therefore a festival of light — a celebration of the light of Jesus in the darkness of the world. It's difficult in this age of electricity to appreciate the symbolism of light, but for biblical people light was the fullest expression of God's work in the world. Just as light can't be self-contained, pouring through every crack, it's the nature of God to be manifest and to show intense life. St. John of the Cross says that Christ is "like an abundant mine with many recesses of treasures, so that however deep individuals may go they never reach the end or bottom, but rather in every recess find new veins with new riches everywhere." Here, the one whom the universe can't contain is enclosed in a tiny body.

Light as a symbol of God plays an important role in the Bible, from the Book of Genesis to the Book of Revelation. In the First Testament, God calls Moses from the burning bush and leads the Jews through the desert by a pillar of fire; Moses's face shines after he meets with God on Sinai. Many of the prophets have visions of light before they take up their calls. In Isaiah, Israel is to be a Light unto the nations. In the Second Testament, right at the beginning of St. John's Gospel the Word is the source of life, and this life brings light to the human race — the light that lightens every living creature in the world. White light was the mark of Jesus' Transfiguration. Jesus calls himself "the Light of the world" (Jn 8:12). And it was a light from the sky that marked the conversion of St. Paul on the road to Damascus.

Many parts of the world see in the Epiphany a solemnity of greater importance than Christmas, representing as it does the opening of salvation for people of the entire world. In Germany, the Three Kings' feast is a time of great rejoicing. In Latin countries, men dressed as the Three Kings are as common as Santa Claus elsewhere. Parents take pictures of their children sitting in the lap of the Kings; there are balloons and fireworks and presents; the Three Kings, not Santa Claus, bring the presents; and in church the Three Kings process to the manger, along with all the people carrying lighted candles.

The Magi's journey is full of symbolism. It is, for example, a symbol of the journey of each one of us. It wasn't without difficulties that the Magi came to believe in Jesus. Their trip was long and hard. It's also with great difficulties that many today struggle with their journey toward God, and we sympathize with those whose struggle is especially hard.

The Magi wondered about the road they should take, and some,

like Herod, taking no chances themselves, thought the Magi ridiculous
for taking their road; many voices invite us to take other roads, and
some ridicule us for taking the road to Jesus. The Magi recognized Jesus
in the rising of a star; we recognize him in the breaking of bread. They
returned to their own country filled with delight at having met the infant King of the Jews; we return to our homes ready to bring the Lord
we have received to those we meet.

There are those who, like Herod, hate and fear. Feeling threat-
ened by the star of the child of Bethlehem, they plot to destroy the work
of God among people. Worse, from some points of view, are those who
are indifferent. And there are those who, like the Magi, give adoration
and homage. All who, like them, come to appreciate the love of God
in Jesus will, like them, lose themselves in wonder.

The letter to the Ephesians sees Isaiah's vision as coming to fulfillment, just as Matthew saw such fulfillment in having Gentiles come
to pay homage to "the king of the Jews." We're to be so large-minded
as to welcome among us all seekers, no matter how far from us in outlook or attitude. At the heart of this letter, in fact, is a great revelation:
that God's love, mercy, and grace were meant not for the Jews alone,
but for all people: men and women, Jew and Gentile, slave and free.
Up to that time, the basic attitude of any group of people toward any
other was not the respect that we teach, but contempt, and the walls
between people were high.

In the ancient world, *religious* differences put the barriers even
higher. No Jew would dream that God's privileges were for all people.
The Holy of Holies (which became our tabernacle) and the Holy Place
(our sanctuary) at the center of attention in the Temple were surrounded
by courts into which only designated people could enter. Closest was
the Court of the Priests; next outward came the Court of Israel, for men
only; further out was the Court of the Women; and finally, on the out-
ermost rim, the Court of the Gentiles. If the Gentiles brought Temple
offerings, they had to leave them on a platform between their court and
the Court of the Women. And because the Court of the Gentiles was
much lower than the others and separated from the rest by a wall, it
was impossible from their low place to even see the Temple building.

Today, despite the notion of the poet Robert Frost that "something there is that doesn't love a wall, that wants it down," unfortunately many walls still exist. Indeed, there's evidence that ours can be
called a world of walls: the invisible walls around the ghettos of our

large cities, foreboding geographical walls in many parts of the world, racial walls, personal and religious walls that ostracize us.

We've got to be big enough not to build isolating walls between people and to make existing walls come tumbling down. In religion, where we live with other Christians, Jews, Hindus, Buddhists, Muslims, and others, we have three traditional Christian responses. One is exclusivism, which affirms that salvation has come to humanity through Jesus Christ and no other, and that salvation comes only to people with explicit faith in Christ. This approach says that, although there might be many things good, true, and beautiful in other lives and cultures, Christians shouldn't confuse human virtue with the faith needed for salvation.

Another response is inclusivism (from Karl Rahner), which seeks a way to express the salvation of people of other cultures. This position states that the many peoples of the world who have never been effectively evangelized are "anonymous Christians" who will be saved by using the "lights" that were given them. Once the Gospel is effectively proclaimed, these other lights will no longer be necessary.

A third position, pluralism, which isn't really acceptable to the committed Christian, says that Christianity is only one of the ways to climb the mountain of salvation. People of other religious traditions can equally well climb their own mountain to the goal.

No matter what our views, we should communicate with people of cultures and religions different from ours. Through that communication, we will come to see what is good and common in traditions, and learn from one another. While the dialogue might begin with bitter recriminations, as we listen to one another we come to respect one another's insights and become transformed.

The Magi had a vision they followed. A people without a vision is doomed to die. The need for broadening vision in the minds and hearts of *all* people are in the areas of life's meaning, of fullness of life, and of all-embracing love — all of which can be found at their deepest level where the Magi found them: in Jesus.

BAPTISM OF OUR LORD
Is 42:1-4, 6f   Ac 10:34-38 (both in A, B, and C)   Mk 1:7-11

Reasons for Baptism
Jesus' Successive Revelations of Himself; Listening vs. Hearing,
Seeing vs. Understanding; God's Revelations about Jesus; Did Jesus Need to
be Baptized?; The Meaning of Our Baptism; Baptism as a Sign of Initiation

It's fitting that we celebrate today the feast of the Baptism of our Lord
soon after his birthday, even though many years intervened between
the two. Our focus changes from the Christmas child Jesus to the adult
Jesus, and a new beginning. Jesus' baptism was the moment when he
passed from the relative obscurity of village life in Nazareth onto the
public stage of his mission of proclaiming God's kingdom. Up to now,
few people knew who he was. At his baptism, many people came to
know his identity, and he would start to show people how to live.

Baptism is meant as an acknowledgment of sin, and Jesus was
sinless; as an expression of repentance, and Jesus didn't have to repent; as an offer of forgiveness, and Jesus had no need of forgiveness;
and as the way we become children of God, and Jesus was already
God's Son. So wasn't Jesus' baptism — even though the merely ritualistic baptism of John — too much like sham play-acting for an all-
holy and sinless Jesus? Even John the Baptist was reluctant to perform
it. He preached on the theme of one mightier than himself, the strap of
whose sandals he wasn't worthy to loose (v. 7). John recognized that
the baptism he performed was only a symbolic one with water, while
the baptism to be established by Jesus would be with the Holy Spirit
(v. 8).

Water rituals are known throughout the gamut of world religions,
and they were especially common in the ancient Near East, notably Iran
and Babylonia, as symbols of ritual or spiritual purification and the gift
of new life. Even today, the Japanese say that their tea ritual, important to them, requires good water, good tea, and good spirit.

But why did Jesus submit to being baptized? For many reasons.
For one, he was indeed baptized for the forgiveness of sins — not his

Note: This homily is mostly on Mark. For mostly Matthew, see Cycle A;
    for mostly Luke, Cycle C.

sins, but the sins of others. His baptism brings about his solidarity with us in our sinful condition. In the dark days when Nazism spread across much of Europe and overpowered the Danes, Hitler ordered the king of Denmark to issue a decree whereby all the Jews in his country would publicly identify themselves by wearing a yellow arm band with the Star of David on it. The king knew that anyone so identified would be rounded up and sent to the death camps. He also knew the danger of disobeying Hitler's orders. So when he issued his decree, he wore a yellow arm band with a Star of David on it, although he wasn't Jewish. The people immediately knew what to do. The next day, everyone in the country — Jew and Gentile alike — wore the required arm band. Solidarity with those condemned resulted in life for all.

Jesus was the Suffering Servant of whom Isaiah spoke, who bore the sins of all people. When he was baptized, the voice of the heavenly Father was almost verbatim a quotation from the first line of today's reading from Isaiah: The Gospel expression "beloved son" means the same as Isaiah's "chosen one." This was the Suffering Servant of whom the Father approved. When the voice came, it came from heavens that were ripped apart — not simply "opened" — to indicate the great cataclysm that took place at Jesus' baptism: It was one of the greatest introductions of any prophet in the Bible.

In addition to telling us that Jesus is the Suffering Servant of the Lord, this passage (plus other Scripture readings) tells us more about who Jesus is. He's the Anointed of the Lord or Messiah (Christ), the Son of God, the Lord of all, the redeemer or healer of the world, the Prophet who's to come into the world, the one who ushers in the end of the ages. None of those names exhaust the titles of Jesus. He's also Lamb of God, Leader of Life, Firstborn of the Dead, Head of His Body the Church, King of the Universe.

Another reason for Jesus' being baptized is on a more natural and human plane. Up to this time, no Jew had ever wanted to submit to baptism, even a ritualistic one like John's. That was because no Jew thought of himself as being on the low level of the rest of people: The Jews considered themselves to be, after all, children of Abraham and by that fact assured of salvation. When people wanted to become converts to Judaism, they were considered to need baptism — because those Gentiles were tainted by sin and had to be washed clean.

But now things were different. John had begun a startling movement of Jewish acknowledgment of sin and of repentance for it. The size of the crowds coming out into the desert to John showed that the Jews, as perhaps at no other time in history for them or any other people, were searching for God. Jesus saw this movement, and was happy to undergo John's baptism to signify that he identified with it (v. 9). One of the good things about that was the nature of the identification. It's easy for one to identify with a movement that's for one's benefit: a prosperous social club, for example, or a popular political movement. But it's far better when one identifies with a cause that's beyond oneself and benefits others more than oneself.

Through Jesus' baptism the early Church could argue against the followers of the Baptist who hadn't converted to Christ: After all, the Spirit descended upon Jesus, not John; the voice spoke of Jesus, not John. Then the Baptist's followers would unmistakably recognize that Jesus was hereby invested as God's Suffering Servant. So whether Jesus did or didn't do what some people's preconceived notions expected, he certainly *was* the one whom God had sent. Contrary to expectations of a Messiah of power, Jesus is the Lamb who took upon himself the sins of the world and died for them.

Some time ago, on a Christian mission in Southern Sudan, a group of children came for instruction for baptism. The instructions began on Ash Wednesday and ended with baptism on Holy Saturday. On Ash Wednesday, the Maryknoll missioner gave them a newborn lamb to be in their care. The lamb stumbled awkwardly at first, but soon playfully charged at the children, who fed it milk from a bottle.

All through Lent, the lamb grew to be more gentle and accepting, innocent, trusting. The lamb, always with the children, was never troublesome or demanding. When the children sat in a circle, the lamb played within it. A strong bond grew between the lamb and the children. Toward the end of Lent, the catechists explained how they would have their Holy Thursday Eucharist, which would be followed by a special community meal; and they announced that their little lamb would be the paschal lamb. On Holy Thursday morning, there were special prayers by which the lamb took on their sinfulness. Then a catechist slaughtered the little lamb. They watched as even in its last moments the lamb seemed to trust them. The meal was well prepared, and the children ate the meat because meat came so seldom to their table. But there was a mood of quiet sadness; and there was tremendous awareness of Jesus the Lamb of God.

Jesus' baptism turned out to be a moment when God showed Jesus

His approval (vv. 10f.). In St. Mark's Gospel, the descent of the Spirit and the voice from the heavens were inner experiences of Jesus which he makes public in this account. The voice said, "*You* are my beloved Son" (v. 11). This statement is the focus of our attention even more than Jesus' baptism, because it tells us who Jesus is.

The reference pulls together many First Testament threads. It alludes, for example, both to today's First Reading (v. 1), attesting that Jesus is the unique Son of God. Isaiah says that Jesus would be sent to open the eyes of the blind, to bring out prisoners from confinement, and from the dungeon, those who live in darkness (v. 7).

The voice from heaven refers also to the early Christian usage of one of the Psalms (Ps 2:7), which sees the sonship there spoken about as prophetically fulfilled in Jesus' resurrection. The allusion is also to God's command to Abraham that he take his son Isaac, his only one, whom he loved, and offer him up as a holocaust (Gn 22:2). That strikes a note of poignancy, and elicits the same gasp of fright which makes God's command to Abraham so memorable. Here, even more than with Abraham's son Isaac, God's uniquely beloved one is set on a mission for which only God can provide.

Those are among the reasons why Jesus was baptized. Now, why are we baptized? Why did the Christian movement early on choose baptism as its sign of initiation? Today's First and Second Readings both help to answer. In Isaiah's terms, we're in many ways blind, prisoners, and in darkness. We must recognize our blindness before we can be cured of it, our confinement before we can be freed, and our imprisonment before we can come to the light. Baptism helps in that process.

But our baptism isn't only negative, calling for repentance in preparation for judgment. Today's reading from the Acts of the Apostles, a passage from St. Peter's last great discourse, presents the classic proclamation of the Gospel for non-Jews at that time, and follows the outlines of other speeches of Peter and of Paul. By this time, the message was beginning to consist of four basic units: Jesus' baptism by John, his Galilean ministry, his Judean ministry, and his passion-death-resurrection. Jesus' baptism was important enough to be included.

Jesus is God's gift to us. He didn't come, as some think, to stay the anger of a vengeful God; he came because God loves us. God was with him, as the voice from heaven at his baptism said. He brought it

about that God is also with us: Through our baptism we receive the
spirit of adoption which makes us children of God, a second birth that's
an ongoing transformation of our first. Our baptism incorporates us, in
a special way, into Jesus.

Is our baptism real to us, alive, and dynamic — or is it something we take for granted? St. Louis IX, King of France from 1226 to
1270, on several occasions spoke of the importance of the anniversary
of his baptism rather than that of his birth or coronation as king. Baptism, he said, was the beginning of a life that would continue in everlasting glory.

Has our second birth brought a realization that we have the potential for transformation? Such a transformation means conversion.
And conversion means a new vision. And a new vision of what is possible in Jesus begets mission. And mission means a search for Jesus'
values, a perhaps painful awareness of the gap between our *proclaimed*
values and our *lived* values. The waters of baptism don't save auto-
matically. The waters coming from the rock at Moses's command in
the desert saved, but the waters of the flood brought death. Would our
heavenly Father be able to say of each of us, as He did of Jesus, "You
are my beloved child; with you I am well pleased"?

SECOND SUNDAY IN ORDINARY TIME
1 S 3:3-10, 19   1 Cor 6:13-15, 17-20   Jn 1:35-42

Answer When You're Called
Life is Relationships; Sex, the Church, and God; Speak, Lord,
Your Servant Is Listening; Here I Am, Lord; God's Invitations; Vocation

Light can mean many things. A light at a home door can signify a
welcome to guests as well as a warning to potential burglars. A light-
house can give guidance to ships. A forbiddingly snowed-in nightscape
painting can be made warm and attractive by adding a cottage with a
light in a window. A light can even symbolize the presence of the Lord.
In the Older Covenant, for example, Aaron set up the lamps to burn
before the Lord regularly (Lv 24:3), a reminder that the Lord was

present in His sacred dwelling-place. The Church continues the custom with the sanctuary lamp set near the tabernacle where the Eucharist is reserved.

In a winsome story that took place about eleven hundred years before Christ, it fell to the young Samuel, like an altar server, to keep the lamp burning in a local shrine at Shiloh, a town about twenty miles north of Jerusalem. (This was not, of course, the Temple at Jerusalem, which wasn't yet built or even imagined). Samuel was the boy born of Elkanah and Hannah in their old age. When he was born, Hannah sang a song of praise to God. The Virgin Mary's *Magnificat* showed that she was familiar with Hannah's song of gratitude and praise. Hannah promised to have her first-born (she ended up having five children) reared near God. In the circumstances of today's story, Samuel was sleeping in the Holy Place where the Ark was kept.

On this particular night, just before dawn Samuel fell asleep. When the Lord called (v. 4), Samuel in his drowsiness and youth had no way of recognizing the voice as that of the Lord (v. 7). When he finally recognized the voice, he eagerly answered in the words given him by Eli: "Speak, Lord, for your servant is listening" (vv. 9f.). That's a bit different from many modern prayers, which often say, "Listen, Lord, for your servant is speaking!" Samuel's attitude, like the attitude of all who are close to God, was that of today's Responsorial Psalm: "Here am I, Lord; I come to do your will." Samuel was the one who would anoint Israel's first king, Saul, and her next and greatest king, David, from which line Jesus would be born.

Jesus' first disciples — John, Andrew, and Simon Peter — responded to God's call as readily as Samuel did. The first time they met Jesus, John and Andrew were with the Baptist, who was then their teacher, at another holy place — the spot at the Jordan River where the people had long ago crossed over into the Promised Land, the place where the ancient poems said God would arrive.

The Baptist, seeing Jesus go by, for the second time in two days uttered a statement that was full of mystery and full of suggestion: "Behold (or "Look!") the Lamb of God" (v. 36). "Behold" ("Look!") is an exclamation of revelation that causes spectators to pause and take notice, and is used in John's Gospel at key moments. The day before today's passage, the Baptist had used the word. Pilate would point to the scourged Jesus and proclaim, "Behold — look at — your King!" And from the cross the dying Jesus would say, "Behold your son" and "Behold your mother."

John the Baptist pointed to Jesus in the figure of a Lamb. Because an animal is alive as we are, yet unknown, people have sometimes used it to express divine traits. The ancient Egyptians couldn't understand the cat — who can? — and for hundreds of years looked upon it as divine. As for the lamb, in southern countries it's the animal most used for nourishment. It was also the usual sacrificial offering, particularly in the liturgy of the Older Covenant. That's why its image is so suggestive of the Savior, as one who surrendered himself into the hands of people, to be consumed upon the sacrificial altar.

When John and Andrew heard the names of the passing one — Lamb, Rabbi, Messiah — they understood enough to follow Jesus (v. 37). Like youths leaving home for the religious life, it was undoubtedly a struggle for the two to leave the Baptist. For the Baptist's part, one of his many good qualities was his complete lack of jealousy, and he let them go. We can imagine the Baptist's feelings as he watched his companions fade into the distance.

The two followed Jesus respectfully, a distance behind. Jesus turned and asked them what they were looking for (v. 38). After all, John and Andrew could have been legalists, looking for exotic discussions about the Mosaic Law. They could have been opportunists looking for power. They could have been Zealots looking for allies to overthrow Rome. They could have been men of prayer looking for God's will. Or they could simply have been bewildered men looking for sympathetic guidance.

Through history, people have come to Jesus for a variety of reasons. In Jesus' time, they were looking for the end of the world, for the final battle between the forces of good and evil, for the triumph of justice, for the final victory of God. People still come to Jesus looking for a variety of things: a security blanket, an escape from problems, an insurance policy, a prescription to enable them to live without bother.

John and Andrew began their answer with the most complimentary title they could think of: Rabbi. The word wasn't mere flattery, however: They immediately followed it by asking where Jesus stayed. They wanted more than a superficial relationship. Jesus' answer was a kind invitation, as God had given Samuel: "Come, and you will see" (v. 39). The invitation wasn't only to talk, but to hear what he could reveal to them; not only to look *at* something, but to look *into* it. They accepted. Jesus took them to the place where he was living — perhaps a cave — and they stayed with him that day.

The occasion was so memorable to the Evangelist that he even adds the time of day at which he met Jesus: four in the afternoon. Indeed, John's association with Jesus affected the Evangelist so deeply that it would color everything he wrote. He would disclose the nerve-center of Jesus' life to be in prayer: communion and intimacy with his heavenly Father. He would write that through Jesus we know what God is like and what people can become. To understand our communion with God, he would use his favorite image of "light."

Simon Peter's brother Andrew (v. 40) is one of the most attractive characters in the New Testament. For one thing, he was always content to play second fiddle to Peter. For another, he simply couldn't keep good news to himself, and seemed to delight in introducing people to Jesus. The New Testament mentions him only three times. In one (Jn 6:8f.), he brings to Jesus the boy with the five loaves and two fish. In another (Jn 12:22), he and Philip bring inquiring Greeks to Jesus. In today's passage, the first thing he did was seek out his brother Simon and bring him to meet Jesus (vv. 40f.). And what a meeting that was! The Evangelist even records that Jesus *looked* at Simon (v. 42) — a special, intense, concentrated look of love that sees not only what's on the surface, but a person's inner depths. For once in his life Simon seemed too overwhelmed to make any remarks.

Jesus changed Simon's name to Peter. In the ancient world, almost everybody had two names. One was in his native language, by which he was known to his family and close friends. The other was in Greek, the language of culture and commerce, by which he was known in the business world. For the ancient Israelites, a change of name often denoted a change of relationship with God: The person was considered to be getting a fresh start. What insight and vision it took to change Simon's name to Peter! The name meant Rock, with all its connotations of solidity and stability — nothing to do with the "Rocky" movies — qualities which, in the beginning at least, no one who knew Peter would attribute to him.

But when God looks at people, He sees not only what they *are*, but also what they can *become*. We, too, are constantly being invited to new beginnings, in ways that are best known to ourselves. In general, it's a call to perfection: to holiness, to emptying self, to serving, to personal virtue — all after the model of Jesus.

It's also a call to specifics. Today's passage from St. Paul's first letter to the Corinthians mentions, as one specific, sexual morality.

Though the letter was written to Corinth, a port city famous for its open sexual immorality, the problems of Corinth are still with us. We need practical advice on living the Christian life in the midst of moral depravity, especially all-consuming sex.

Paul could have used many arguments for sexual purity from reason, but he preferred to appeal to the Corinthians' faith. He stated his position up front — that the body is for the Lord, and the Lord is for the body (v. 13). Sex involves not just the body, but the complete person. As John and Andrew recognized in today's Gospel, all of life is relationships. Life's *deepest* relationship is with God, and every human relationship reflects that one. Our bodies, being members of Christ (v. 15) and temples of the Holy Spirit (v. 19), are sacred. So sexual sinning is tantamount to sacrilege.

In today's Scriptures, there are four sentences that are applicable to all of us: "Speak, Lord, your servant is listening," from the First Reading; "Here I am, Lord, I come to do your will," from the Psalm; "You have been purchased at what a price!" from the Second Reading; and "What are you looking for?" from the Gospel. We Christians have been called by God to many personal graces. The call comes quietly, in a way similar to that of Eli for Samuel, John the Baptist for the disciples of Jesus, and Paul for the Corinthians.

Frequently we don't hear God's call because we don't listen well. May we quiet the noise of this world so that we may correct that. Even the Chinese fortune cookie says, "From listening comes wisdom and from speaking repentance." May our lives become for ourselves and others a welcoming light at our door, a guiding light, a warm light in our window — and a light signifying the presence of the Lord.

Third Sunday in Ordinary Time
Jon 3:1-5, 10   1 Cor 7:29-31   Mk 1:14-20

Good News: Announcement and Response
Repentance; Follow in Faith; God's Unlikely Choices;
Good News and its Consequences; Reform and Believe;
Change your Life; The Breadth of God's Mercy

St. Mark's Gospel is the shortest (only 16 chapters) and the most direct, crisp, clear, and energizing of all the four Gospels. It's our major Gospel study for this Church year. We start it today.

The very first line of today's Gospel, that it was the Gospel of God that Jesus was proclaiming, are tremendous words. Contrary to the news of the world, this is *good* news: godspell, or Gospel. It's full of hope. It's news that can bring people together. It's news of salvation that gives the power to conquer sin. In essence, God's good news is His Son Jesus, in whom God appears as He really is.

Jesus begins with the declaration that this is the time of fulfillment (v. 15), which means it's the period in human history for God to make good His messianic promises as proclaimed through the prophets. The kingdom of God is at hand — arrived but awaiting development, for which people must repent, believe in the Good News, and cooperate with it. If that development isn't complete today, it's because people haven't cooperated fully. Some people are sorry for only the consequences of their sins, the mess they make, not for their sins themselves: If they could sin without deleterious consequences, they'd be happy to continue sinning.

But merely abstaining from sin isn't the reform that Jesus wants. His reform is a *positive* concept. It involves a complete change of heart toward God — which is proven by one's attempt to lead a good life. When Jesus preached it to the Jews, he was calling them to turn from formalism in religion to a more sincere worship and to greater weight to mercy, justice, fidelity to the covenant, and openness to non-Jews. Repentance for the Gentiles included turning from the worship of pagan idols to worship of the one true God and, as St. Paul's letters to the Corinthians make clear, rejecting immoral behavior. For all of us, it means an acknowledgment that over the years we've allowed some unchristian attitudes and outlooks to cloud our vision.

Normally a prolonged process, conversion can also take place in a short period of time. It's personal and intimate. It's private but not solitary: It can become communal, converting other people. It takes Jesus at his word, accepting as really true what sounds too good to be true.

This conversion is typified in Jesus' first disciples, the Bar-Jona brothers Simon and Andrew and the Zebedee brothers James and John. They turned to Jesus; from then on their lives were never the same. As Jesus passed by the Sea of Galilee (v. 16), Simon and Andrew were doing what they did for a living: fishing — ordinary people doing their ordinary day's work. And it's ordinary people whom Jesus usually chooses. Abraham Lincoln said, "God must love the common people — He made so many of them."

But are there any "common" or "ordinary" people? No more than there is an "ordinary" pencil. If you look at a pencil which we so much take for granted — *really* look — you realize its state of near-perfection for its purpose. It's a mixture of engineering, business, research, and development. The lead in a single pencil might be a mixture of two kinds of graphite (from Sri Lanka and Mexico), clay from Mississippi, gums from the Orient, and water from anywhere. The wooden case would most likely be made of western incense cedar from California, the eraser container possibly of brass or aluminum from the American West, and the eraser perhaps of a mixture of South American rubber and Italian pumice stone. The pencil isn't "common" or "ordinary," and neither are people.

Jesus' invitation for these apostles to come after him (v. 17) didn't necessarily mean that this was the first time they saw him. They had probably been in previous crowds and listened to Jesus. Their joining him to become fishers of people would require abandonment of their former means of livelihood in order to preach and work for the kingdom of God. Discipleship, like every choice, entails renunciation. We have to leave behind the nets that hold our inferior hopes and values.

Those who listened to Jesus may have had a few prejudices to overcome. So do we. First, they were expecting a glorious kingdom which would follow a Herculean battle — perfection now. Although that expectation remained a problem throughout Jesus' public life, it's less so today. Second, those who listened to Jesus may have wondered, in a self-justifying way, why they should have to repent: Weren't they already members of God's people? That's a problem today, too. A third prejudice may have been to ask why we should repent: Others need it more than we. That prejudice remains with us in our bourgeois mentality: Good people are upstanding, mannerly people such as ourselves, and those who aren't of our outlook are inferior.

Much more reluctant than Jesus' first apostles to follow God's call was the disgruntled prophet Jonah, whose life goes back to the eighth century B.C. This story written about him, though, dates from four or five hundred years later; it was probably written to counteract the excessive nationalism which grew up among the Jews after the exile.

Is his story true in the sense of having actually happened? No — we don't have to go through all kinds of fancy footwork to show how a man could survive three days in the belly of a fish. Does the story present truth? Yes! In the Scriptures, we find every kind of literature — poetry, prose, history, allegory — and short stories, of which Jonah is one. It's the nature of such folk-tales (like Cinderella for children) to force us to re-examine our values. Jonah's story is still a whale of a story! It presents a good lesson in human reform and God's mercy, contains ironically humorous elements, and provides parallels and contrasts to today's Gospel. Jesus referred to this story when the leaders demanded a sign of him (Lk 11:30,32).

A previous portion of this story mentions that, when he was first called, Jonah tried to run away. A good Jew, but narrow, Jonah didn't want God to show the Gentile Assyrian Ninevite foreigners mercy. In the mind of the Jews of that time, these were the worst possible Gentiles — the epitome of barbarism. Let the dirty pagans be destroyed! Good riddance! Jonah tried to escape by boarding a ship. The ship was tossed about by a storm. When Jonah confessed to the superstitious sailors that he was their jinx, they threw him overboard. The story has it that he was swallowed by a fish; when after three days he was freed, he decided that, considering what he'd had to go through, going to Nineveh wouldn't be all that bad after all, and he went. The city's size is exaggerated (v. 3), in order to impress one with the breadth of the mercy that God would show.

The paining Jonah wasn't unhappy to announce that Nineveh would be destroyed (v. 4). Much to Jonah's chagrin and amazement, the Ninevites, from the king to the lowest peasant, repented (v. 5) — as Jerusalem never did — and God didn't carry out His threats (v. 10). God loves even Ninevites and, on a favorable response like theirs, God restores.

The critical point is: Were they — are we — willing to change? There are some people for whom we have an instinctive repugnance: rapists, child abusers, drug sellers, muggers, abortionists. On the other hand, we profess that God doesn't wish the death of a sinner but that he or she be converted and live. And we must have hope.

Hope looks for the good in people instead of harping on the worst; opens doors where despair closes them; discovers what can be done instead of grumbling about what can't; regards problems, small or large, as opportunities; cherishes no illusions, but doesn't yield to cynicism; sets big goals and isn't frustrated by small setbacks; puts up with modest gains, realizing that "the longest journey starts with one step"; accepts misunderstandings as the price for serving the greater good of others; and is a good loser because it has the divine assurance of final victory.

We see these principles also in the middle of the first century, when St. Paul wrote to the Corinthians. Paul's converts at Corinth had asked him for guidance on questions of marriage and the single life. In Corinth there were two attitudes toward sex and marriage, represented by what we may term the *libertines* and the *ascetics*. The libertines taught that anything goes. The ascetics taught the opposite — that we have to deny the demands of our body and rise above them.

Some people, reading only St. Paul's letter to the Corinthians, have concluded that Paul was against marriage, or at least allowed it only as a concession to avoid sexual sins. But the Jews — and Paul was a good Jew — glorified marriage. They considered it, in fact, a sacred duty: Avoidance of marriage was allowed only for one reason — the study of the sacred Law. Years after this letter to the Corinthians, when Paul wrote to the Ephesians, he was clear about marriage as the most precious of human relationships. In that letter, in fact, he saw the marriage union as so sacred that he compared it to the union between Christ and his Church. What Paul did *here*, in contrast, was to state that at the end-time of fulfillment of which Jesus spoke, we should develop an appropriate order of priorities.

If Paul was acutely aware of the end of the world, we often suffer from the opposite impression: that we always have time — we can always "do it tomorrow." An Hispanic facetiously asked an Irishman, "Do you have any word in your language like our word mañana?" And the Irishman answered, "Sure, an' we do, but it doesn't have the sense of urgency that your word has!"

Today's readings present a call with the same urgency as a drowning person yelling "Help!" We're called to transform ourselves according to the mind of God. We may think it unlikely that God is calling "little us" to anything very important. But today's liturgy shows the great irony in God's sending a good but reluctant Jew to pagan Ninevites, a Pharisaical rabbi to Gentiles for whom he initially had contempt, and simple fishermen to found a world religion. This is a constant theme of the Scriptures: God often selects the unlikelies in order that He may show that great things which can't be accomplished in so-called "ordinary" people by nature can be done by the wonderful power of His grace.

FOURTH SUNDAY IN ORDINARY TIME
Dt 18:15-20   1 Cor 7:32-35   Mk 1:21-28

A Day in the Life of Jesus
Teaching and Doing: Items of Love and Concern; Being a True Prophet;
A World in Need of Healing; The Desire To Be Fully Alive;
The Need to Listen; Our Call to Prophecy; Don't Harden Your Heart;
Taking Seriously Authoritative Prophecy

People find it interesting to read about "a day in the life of" famous people. Whether that's because it gives insights into how others live, or satisfies curiosity, or gives titillation, we don't know, but books on the subject sell well.

St. Mark, beginning with today's Gospel passage and going to the end of the chapter, gives us a day in the life of Jesus at Capernaum. It was a day on which Jesus taught, cured a demoniac and Peter's mother-in-law, worked many other miracles on sick people, prayed alone, and preached in a synagogue.

Jesus began in the synagogue at Capernaum by taking a Scripture text and commenting on it, as he had done at Nazareth. In Nazareth what he said had so incensed the people that they dragged him to the brow of one of the hills into which their town was built to throw him off and kill him. He didn't preach there after that because of the hardness of the people. In Capernaum, however, where he had moved his mother to live and where he made his Galilean headquarters, the people were astonished at his teaching and he taught them as one having authority (v. 22).

That Jesus taught with authority and not like the Scribes and Pharisees may seem strange to us — for, if anything, the Scribes and Pharisees seemed to speak with excessive authority. But their teaching was actually long, involved, and with excessive accommodations of Scripture texts to suit their own purposes. Jesus, on the other hand, knew the Scriptures so well that he could communicate forthrightly and succinctly not only the texts, but also the thought behind them. Whereas people of our time, in a mistaken view of freedom of conscience, have negative views of authority, the people of Jesus' time liked authority: It gave them security in the sure knowledge of God's will. So they were spellbound by Jesus' teaching.

While that makes us yearn to know more details of what he *taught*, Mark at this time is more interested in who Jesus *is* — that is, the Son of God — and in Jesus' *doings*. The setting for that is the same as for his teaching: the Capernaum synagogue (v. 23). A man "with an unclean spirit" appeared there. Although the people ascribed their more baffling sicknesses to evil spirits, Jesus never acknowledged diabolic possession as a phenomenon, but at the same time never contested statements of others about the presence of diabolic beings. When the scribes on other occasions accused Jesus of performing exorcisms by the power of Satan, they were implying that there were diabolic manifestations among the sick being brought to Jesus.

The whole scene was supercharged. There was no need for the incantations, magic, or the long rituals of others: Jesus acted with authority. The demon *cried out*, Jesus *rebuked him sharply* with the same word with which he would later calm the stormy sea, and the demon came out of the man *with a loud cry*. The demon's first shriek (v. 23f.) was a shout of defiance, his second an agonizing cry of defeat. The demon recognized Jesus' special relationship to God. Here as elsewhere in Mark, Jesus' true identity is hidden from the people but known to the reader and attested to by the demons — the kind of thing that creates suspense in a good mystery story. Accompanied by dramatic convulsions of the man, the demon came out of him.

Whether you believe that the man was literally possessed by the devil or not, the very least we must assume is that he was out of touch with reality. Some scientists might call exorcism deprogramming, catharsis, group therapy, or identification. But many scientists agree that there's more to the human condition than meets the parameters of tests and measurements. And authority over the power of evil doesn't come easily. It's gained by enormous exertion in addition to knowledge — an *intensity* of exertion that can be born only of love.

Mark records that the onlookers were amazed (v. 27), a term that his breathless, hurried style uses repeatedly of the people's reaction to Jesus. Interestingly, what the bystanders were amazed at wasn't some miraculous power, but Jesus' *teaching*. All of this showed Jesus to be one who speaks and acts for God: a true prophet!

In today's portion of the Book of Deuteronomy, Moses on his deathbed foretold that God would raise up a prophet like him (v. 15) — one who would speak on God's behalf. Though from the context it seems that Moses was referring to all the true prophets who would succeed him, this passage was understood both by the Jews (Jn 6:14; 7:40) and the apostles (Ac 3:22; 7:37) in a special Messianic sense. More than that, the apostles understood it to refer to Jesus as the Great Prophet in whom the prophetic office finds its fulfillment.

Deuteronomy tells us that a true prophet isn't one who tells fortunes for the future, casts spells, or consults spirits. A prophet's role is to comfort the afflicted and afflict the comfortable. A true prophet sees things as they really are, hears God speak, and announces God's words to His people. Jesus was such a person. Because he was like us in all but sin, he had to search for meaning in the same way we do. He did so while listening to his Father.

St. Paul was another prophet in the true sense. In today's portion of his first letter to the Corinthians, he was answering some questions which the Corinthians had posed to him. One set of questions pertained to sex and marriage. Paul's prophetic answers were in a short letter, not a huge tome, so didn't go into detail and pertained in good measure to his own times. At the time of his writing, Christians, Paul included, were expecting the Second Coming of Christ at any moment. In the light of that, he wrote that virginity was a nobler calling than marriage. He wasn't contradicting a person's freedom to marry. In fact, he wrote (v. 35) that he had no desire to impose a restraint upon them in this matter.

Would Paul's answers be true for times when there's no evidence of Jesus' immediate Second Coming? Well, it doesn't seem right to suggest that today a spouseless and childless life is free of worries. And celibacy and virginity are no guarantee of single-minded or whole-hearted devotion to the Lord. It wouldn't be proper for a family man to be as unconcerned about increasing his income as a Franciscan priest, or for a bishop to want to lead a solitary life like a Trappist monk, or for a working man to spend half his day in church like a religious sister. Nor is there, according to reports, great evidence that husbands are overwhelmingly concerned with pleasing their wives or wives their husbands. Among the married we can find some of the holiest people and among the clergy some of the most mediocre. The important thing, for everybody in all times and circumstances, is, in Paul's words, that we be devoted to God.

Not only Paul, but all Christianity, is accused today of fostering sexual repression. But a theory which turns conventional wisdom on its head suggests that, in the Nineteenth Century at least, it was religious zeal that promoted an ethic of sexual pleasure while it was "science" that fueled a passion for sexual abstinence. Nineteenth-century Catholic revivalists across the United States, says this theory, urged followers to approach sex with the innocence of children, open to sex's redemptive powers. That compelled sober Protestant moralists to include sexuality in *their* moral teachings too. But while theologians were embracing sexual passion as redemptive, many physicians and scientists were insisting on abstinence from sex, claiming that sex was physically unhealthy, depleting vital bodily fluids and leading to feebleness and vice.

Two young Americans, whose names have become household words, adapted these strictures about sexuality. For it was fear of sexuality that led young Sylvester Graham and physician John Harvey Kellogg to experiment with whole grains and cereals, believing that an increase in whole wheat consumption would decrease lust.

Graham's dry crackers were part of a diet he proposed in 1839 lectures, which also advocated vegetarianism, with the argument that meat-eaters long for and commit sins of the flesh. Similarly, Kellogg wanted to prove that sexual activity can, as he put it, "retard growth, weaken the constitution, and dwarf the intellect." His roasted corn flakes were part of his health regimen designed to reduce the force of sexual passion.

Yet people today have no one to identify as prophets as did the people in biblical times. Our churches haven't institutionalized the prophet in the same way in which they have the priest or the deacon.

We think of prophets as distant and unfamiliar people. Nevertheless, "prophecy" is naming the truth in a given situation and explaining the logical consequences of a course of action. People can reject the truth, usually by rejecting the bearer of the word. The king kills the messenger of disliked truth.

The prophet comes and names the truth. When the prophet is low-key, people might protest mildly. But when the prophet is a whistle-blower in industry, a reformer in politics, or a preacher who proclaims God's justice, the rejection can be much stronger. People don't like to hear the truth when it requires them to change who they are or how they live. So the whistle-blower gets fired, the reforming politician doesn't get elected, and the preacher is avoided. On occasion, even today, the prophet gets killed — sometimes physically, often metaphorically.

As the prophet's task is to speak the truth, people's task is to listen to it. The prophet's task isn't easy, but neither is the task of hearing the prophetic word. If we, like the man with the unclean spirit at Capernaum, sometimes find it hard to make sense of the truth of our world, let's seek help from the healing Jesus. And let's take seriously the prophesying of our Church when she teaches with authority. The Church is called to continue the teaching function of Jesus, and to teach with authority. May our days of prophesying and listening to prophecy, healing and seeking healing, be as busy as a day in the life of Jesus!

FIFTH SUNDAY IN ORDINARY TIME
Jb 7:1-4, 6f.   1 Cor 9:16-19, 22f.   Mk 1:29-39

Apostleship and Comfort
Fulfillment; Happiness Is ...; Do Nice Guys Finish Last?; Service to Others;
The Lord Heals the Brokenhearted; A Perspective on Suffering;
Whiners Aren't Winners; Depression and Discouragement

General Robert E. Lee, for four days after his surrender following the U.S. Civil War, would eat nothing. At last, at the insistence of the Southern lady in whose house he was staying, he agreed to a cup of tea. She had just enough for one cup, having lost everything in the conflict; but when she brought that in, Lee refused to drink it unless she had some, too. She went back, got a cupful of muddy James River water, brought that in, and sipped with him. Many people in the Scriptures were of the same tough, non-whining caliber as Lee's hostess.

The Book of Job, written about five hundred years B.C., was concerned with some of people's problems that transcend every period in history — like bad things happening to good people and the question of whether people can serve God selflessly, without hope of any reward. The theology that Job knew was from Deuteronomy. It said that the good prosper and the wicked suffer. Job's tradition knew nothing of heaven or hell, so God had to reward the good and punish the evil in this life. Our Christian perspective adds a new dimension.

It's been said that expecting the world to treat you fairly because you're a good person is a little like expecting the bull not to attack you because you're a vegetarian. We're no different today: Our fast food emporiums, our microwaves, and our penchant for fast pain relief show that we know what we want, we want it our way, and we want it now. We do the same with life and religion that we do with food: We rush through them all, most of the time without much thought.

Job was deprived of family, lacked worldly possessions, was racked by physical pain, and suffered mental anguish. Eliphaz, the first of his three friends who tried to help him explain his miseries, had come up with the standard clichè that Job was suffering because he must have done something wrong. Although Eliphaz must be given credit for offering the ministry of presence, standing by an alienated human being and being willing to listen and empathize, Job (understandably) didn't like his answer.

Today's reading is part of a soliloquy in which Job bemoaned his state, which is in reality the whole wretched human condition. Life is cruel like the drudgery of those in slavery (vv. 1f.), boring as with the work of a hireling, and swifter than a weaver's shuttle (v. 6) that moves quickly back and forth in ceaseless activity. The days of work and the nights of worry are all too long. Life is so without substance as to be like the wind (v. 7). He vividly compares human life to three proverbially wretched states of life: forced military service, the life of a day laborer working only for the wages necessary to life, and simple slavery with no letup. Job, though steadfast and loyal, was impatient. His human friends had failed to explain life, and he took for granted that his divine friend wouldn't, either.

In today's Gospel, Jesus shows himself a divine friend. Although the disciples Simon, Andrew, James, and John hadn't known Jesus long, they had already begun to tell him their troubles, and the first thing they did was to tell him about Simon Peter's mother-in-law being sick with a fever (v. 30). Other exorcisms and healings of the time were attempted with elaborate incantations, formulae, spells, and magical apparatus; Jesus' present healing involved only a gesture — he grasped her hand and helped her up (v. 31).

Jesus undertook his action not to enhance his attractiveness to people, nor as a painful duty; he healed because he was interested in people who needed help. As a result of his help here, although a person after a fever is usually rather tired, Peter's wife's mother waited on them. She had learned the lesson of discipleship — and did so more quickly than her daughter's husband. She symbolizes all good Christians who, like the Master himself, come not to be served but to serve.

In little Capernaum, the people heard of the cure right away. Their enthusiasm was at first kept within bounds because the Sabbath forbade all disturbances that might have the appearance of work — even carrying the sick for help. But after sunset, when the Sabbath was over, they brought him all who were ill or possessed by demons (v. 32). Of all those from the whole town who were gathered at the door (v. 33), Jesus cured only *many*. But Jesus made the point that good health doesn't necessarily enhance the quality of our life, and ill health doesn't necessarily detract from it. And in a society such as ours, in which sickness is a sign of weakness, non-productivity is scorned, and the old are asked, "What good are you?" Jesus asserts the special dignity of the ill.

But the leitmotifs in the background of the Gospel sounded two sad notes. The people had come not out of love for Jesus, but because they wanted to use him. And Jesus wouldn't permit the demons to speak, because they knew him (v. 34). The demons knew that Jesus was their enemy, without knowing his specific identity. This is St. Mark's first use of "The Messianic Secret" — that is to say, Jesus didn't want his identity as Messiah known because the people saw him as healer, miracle worker, and magician almost, and were missing the real meaning of his life. So Jesus commanded silence until the rest of his story as Son of God would reveal him fully: that is, after his death and resurrection. Only then could he be seen as more than a performer of miracles — not magic tricks but victory over death, not a hero but a savior.

Early Sunday morning, Jesus went off to a deserted place, where he prayed (v. 35). Mark presents Jesus at prayer during times of stress over the true nature of his messiahship. But there seems nothing stressful here! Jesus looks, in fact, very successful! Simon and those who were with him told him that everyone was looking for him. (vv. 36f.). They were implying that Jesus should remain at Capernaum and capitalize on his popularity. In one sense, it's flattering to have everyone looking for you. In another sense, though, it can easily become wearisome: You don't have a moment's peace to yourself.

So there *was* stress! The disciples and all the people saw him as a miracle worker, none as proclaimer of the good news (v. 38). There's a hostile note even in Mark's phrase that Simon and his companions managed *to track him down* (v. 36) — the same words Mark would use later to describe the approach of Jesus' enemies. So Jesus, like all of us, had to search out the real meaning of his mission. He realized, also like all of us, that if he was going to be always giving out, he had to have time to take in.

The way to accomplish both was to communicate with his Father in prayer. And it worked. He found his mission, and he resolutely set his apostles straight: "Let us go on to the nearby villages," he said firmly, "that I may preach there also" (v. 38). We can only imagine how hard it was for a sensitive person like Jesus to decide to leave when people who loved him wanted him to stay. Yet that was the Father's will revealed in prayer, and that's what he did. The secret of the Christian life isn't only to love people, but to love them in God and to be a channel of God's love to them.

Mark concludes by saying that Jesus went into their synagogues (v. 39) — a few words for what must have taken months to accomplish. Jesus going from one synagogue to another acted not merely as a social worker with a great heart, or a reformer fighting for a better distribution of wealth. He saw the mystery of human suffering much more profoundly. Suffering, deep in human existence, and an essential part of sin and estrangement from God, is also a means of purification and return to God. Jesus didn't ignore pain, but didn't seek to avoid it.

Today's section from St. Paul shows that in his ministry he also faced suffering, here in the form of misunderstandings and — one of the most difficult hurts to bear — ingratitude from those he expected to be his friends. Because he earned his own way, not relying on servants or gifts, Paul was different, and that always causes difficulties. Paul had been telling the Corinthians of the sacrifices they must make for their religion; here he tells of his own sacrifices. By not accepting payment for his missionary work, Paul has kept himself independent.

His independence wasn't for personal advantage, however, but for service: to make him free to share the lot of the weak in order to win them for Christ. Paradoxically, his weakness became the occasion for making God's transforming power present. Paul made himself all things to all people (v. 22). He did this "to save at least some of them" — an expression in which there is much sadness, for it suggests that Paul's many sacrifices had also met the loss of many.

Paul's procedure is good psychology: Those who concentrate on their depression and discouragement become locked into their own subjectivity, whereas those who turn outward and empathize grow. Beethoven handled the violin so awkwardly that his teacher called him hopeless as a composer; Thomas Edison's teachers said he was too stupid to learn anything; Albert Einstein's teacher described him as "mentally slow, unsociable and adrift forever in his foolish dreams"; the sculptor Rodin's father said, "I have an idiot for a son"; Leo Tolstoy, author of *War and Peace*, flunked out of college; Babe Ruth hit 714 home runs, setting a record, but also struck out 1,330 times; Richard Hooker worked for seven years on his humorous war novel, *M*A*S*H*, only to have it rejected by 21 publishers before it was finally accepted, became a runaway best-seller, blockbusting movie, and highly successful television series.

Some people today, in the face of depression or what has been called "*anhedonia*" (an inability to relish life), might resort to a pharmacological prescription to lift them up. Such an easy fix, sometimes warranted, has a seductive appeal. On the other hand, the bias toward treating problems of the spirit like any physical condition can lead to seeing personhood as a mix of chemicals, impoverished human identity, and less respect for the individuality, the autonomy, and the dignity of ourselves and others. It contributes to a new tendency to see human beings less in terms of their life-stories, their relationships, and their "wholeness" as individuals.

In all the people presented in today's liturgy, we have models for ourselves when we're feeling depressed, without hope, bored, and discouraged. Job in his suffering finally turned to God for answers. Jesus, upset by everything that depresses the human spirit, spent himself to heal people. Paul viewed his salvation through the prism of his attempts to be the salvation of others.

We could do worse than to accept as a model one whom some might consider to be the least of today's cast of characters: Peter's mother-in-law. She resisted our human tendency to seek to be comforted and consoled but not to comfort and console others, to seek to be encouraged but not to encourage others. She found that the only way to experience full healing oneself is to heal others: She immediately waited on them.

SIXTH SUNDAY IN ORDINARY TIME
Lv 13:1f., 44-46   1 Cor 10:31-11:1   Mk 1:40-45

The Imitation of Christ
Continuing the Ministry of Healing; The Things
We Do in God's Name; Tough Love; Today's Lepers

Jewish kosher laws may have originated as prudent precautions about bacteria, which way back then they didn't know much about. The prohibition of eating pork, for example, was a quite sensible rule for those who knew nothing about trichinosis, but who observed people getting sick from eating pigs. Kosher laws also had rules concerning the cleanliness of such things as clothing and buildings.

The close-knit ancient Jews were the most careful, however, about human beings. A word they used for diseases of the skin was "leprosy" (*tsaraath*), which meant literally a "striking down," a "laying low." They applied it to what we know today as acne, ringworm, eczema, scabies, and psoriasis, which manifested themselves through sores, skin blotches, scabs, and face eruptions. Their fear applied also, of course, to what we know as leprosy in the strict sense of the word, or Hansen's disease, which eventually causes the sufferer to become a mass of ulcerated growths.

The numerous references in the Jewish Scriptures to forms of leprosy, as in today's passage of Leviticus, one of the First Testament books of laws, attest to the Jews' fear of the disease, particularly the danger of contagion. In view of the fact that they had no scientific knowledge of the disease, no antibiotics, no antiseptics, and no other remedies, their fear is understandable. The only safeguard known to their primitive hygiene was to demand the stricken person's isolation. The very word leper came to mean outcast. Unfortunately, the sickness came to be seen as a divine punishment. This reinforced the concept of lepers as among the "living dead." It was that context, more than the context of hygienic concerns, that Leviticus dealt with. Bodily integrity was necessary for the worship of Yahweh.

So the determination of the state of the disease among the ancient Jews belonged to the priest, not as physician but as judge and interpreter of the Law. During the diseased persons' period of uncleanness they had to remain outside the city, giving notice of their presence before the unknowing by using torn garments, long and flowing hair, covered beard if the leper were a man, and repeated cries of "unclean!" Lepers simply didn't belong in society: They had no hope of receiving love, no hope of being accepted as persons, no hope of enjoying ordinary human companionship. All of this in God's name!

In the New Testament, no disease was regarded with more terror than leprosy. The leper in today's Gospel pathetically reflects the times, and elicits sympathy. Despite the popular idea of the difficulty of healing leprosy, this leper nevertheless came to Jesus and knelt as he offered his beautiful prayer: "If you wish, you can make me clean."

What Jesus did in answer presents one of the most revealing pictures of him. Behind this leper was the Law, which plays such a large part in this story. The Law, powerless to help, tried only to protect the community by segregating the afflicted individual. What the Law couldn't do, this man was expecting Jesus to do. And Jesus knew what it was like to be an outsider: He was one of the poor, lived with the poor, and felt with the poor.

So — although a leper was forbidden to come near another person — Jesus stretched out and *touched* the man (v. 41): touched an unclean leper who was looked upon with fright if not hatred by the medical and religious authorities, who was popularly suspected of having committed some kind of terrible sin to have caused his disease, and who had gone beyond his legal rights in even speaking to Jesus! Jesus was there for him as he was for so many other outcasts. He was moved to perform a cure, as with most of his miracles, out of sympathy for the afflicted; and, as often with his other cures, he made physical con-

tact part of the procedure, probably to conceal the miraculous nature
somewhat by using familiar ceremonies. He regarded compassion and
charity as more important than ritual prohibitions.

After the miracle, Jesus, respectful of the Law and not recklessly
defying the conventions, sent the man to the priest to fulfill the prescribed ritual. That would enable the man to again enter fully into religious and social life. Because Jesus didn't want a furtherance of the
incorrect popular notions of his messiahship, he asked the leper not to
utter a word to anyone; but the leper, thinking Jesus wanted secrecy
merely out of humility, began to publicize the whole matter.

This resulted in an interesting paradox. As the story opened, Jesus
could move about freely, and the leper was cut off. As the story ended,
the situation was reversed: The leper went off cured into the company
of people, while it was impossible for Jesus to enter a town openly.
Jesus had taken the leper's place! In order to avoid superficial praise
based on false messianic expectations, he had to stay outside the towns.
But, despite all Jesus' precautions, the crowds still came, and still misunderstood who he was. God's Son would have to suffer and die and
rise before most people would wake up after the fact and declare that
this man was truly the Son of God.

History is tragically full of terrible things done to people by those
who don't know the compassion, empathy, and reaching out that Jesus
showed in today's Gospel. Around and after the turn of our century,
for example, the Freak Show at circuses, "dime" museums, amusement
parks, fairs, and carnivals made big business peaking in at those whom
people considered to be "odd." Photographers like Mathew Brady, famous for his Lincoln portraits and his chronicle of the Civil War, made
visiting cards of the freaks in P.T. Barnum's American Museum. The
Hilton sisters, who were Siamese twins, and the dwarfs Tom Thumb
and his wife Lavinia were photographed often.

As for lepers, in the Middle Ages a leper would be forced to watch
as a priest filled an empty grave to symbolize his or her death. Then
the leper was handed a bell to wear in order to warn others of his presence. Right through the early years of this century treatment of lepers
was not so far removed from the medieval treatment. In the United
States, most lepers were forced into a special hospital in Carville, Louisiana, isolated by a bend in the Mississippi River.

In the founding of this institution, the rules were inhuman. Patients were denied most civil and human rights. Marriage, dating, and

even dining alone with a person of the opposite sex were forbidden. Patients weren't allowed to vote or to marry, and outgoing mail was steamed to sterilize it. Escapees were returned in handcuffs. Young women who got pregnant weren't allowed to keep their babies or even touch them.

People who showed the early symptoms of the disease were quarantined for years, sometimes decades. Even if the symptoms disappeared — and it was possible that some people had been misdiagnosed — patients were detained for as long as seven years, to make sure. Patients who entered hospital gates left behind everything: friends, children, futures, sometimes hope. One boy arrived in his Boy Scout uniform. If people who had the disease refused to go to the hospital, the police — or bounty hunters — put them in handcuffs and brought them anyway.

One woman patient recently living in that hospital said, "My sisters hid me in the bedroom when they had company." A male patient said, "My folks didn't want me to tell anyone I was related when we found out I had the disease." One young woman, a nurse, said of the birth of her daughter, "I wanted to hold her so bad. But they wouldn't let me touch her. They took her away from me on a train. I begged them to at least let me go see her off at the train station, but they wouldn't let me." The disease damaged the nurse's eyes, but otherwise left her in good health. She said, "I thank God for my hands": She worked at the hospital as a physical therapist. The disease spared her hands, and took the thing she most wanted to hold.

The nuns and the staff in this hospital push patients' wheelchairs beneath the oak trees, make special shoes for twisted feet, and do everything possible to make life bearable. One nun, shaking her head at the false notions of leprosy, said of the hospital: "This is holy ground. I say that because there has been such suffering here."

The headstones in the hospital's still-present cemetery reflect much history. Some have only first names. Some have initials. Some are blank, except for the patient's number.

We still have lepers close by — people who, for one reason or another, are defined by their condition and not treated as people: the homeless, the unattractive, many diseased, many unborn children, the armless, the legless, the twisted body, the feeble of spirit and mind, people with AIDS (in many ways the modern lepers). We've caught ourselves furtively looking at them with a shaming mixture of sympathy and repulsion, pity and horror, relief and superiority. We boldly mark the limits of what we take to be acceptably human.

Those of us who try to excuse ourselves may need to be reminded that one of the great turning points in the conversion of St. Francis of Assisi to a life totally dedicated to God was his embrace of a leper. Reflecting on this later, he said: "What before seemed bitter was changed into sweetness of soul and body." Father Damien of Molokai is one of the best-known examples of self-sacrifice in behalf of lepers. Perhaps we need to remind ourselves also that we ourselves are often, in one way or another, inwardly leprous. We must decide what particular leprosy is calling to be healed here and now in our personal lives and in the life of our community.

In today's Second Reading, St. Paul's imitation of Christ could well be our personal program of life. If Christ becomes the principle and pattern of our transformation, in being conformed to him we must each discover and realize our own unique identities as persons, and be healed of the sinful dispositions that obstruct the flourishing of our true selves. Only the inexhaustibly rich Image of God who did things like today's miracle could constitute the principle and pattern for the transformation and fulfillment of every human person who has ever lived: No mere human being would suffice. The more we become like Christ, the more surely do we discover the best of our true selves.

Let us, like Jesus himself, ask what our heavenly Father would want us to do in the face of the unattractive or unpopular and like Jesus face the risks to do it.

SEVENTH SUNDAY IN ORDINARY TIME
Is 43:18f., 21f., 24f.   2 Cor 1:18-22   Mk 2:1-12

Awareness of Sin
Being a Person of Your Word; Forgiveness of Others; Keeping Promises;
Paralyzing Others by Failure to Forgive; Getting Rid of Sin

Home living in the time of Jesus in the Holy Land was more casual than many places today. The houses were open to the street, and anyone who wanted to gather around the doorway or even to enter the house was free to do so. The four men who brought the paralyzed man to Jesus had an easy time of lowering him from the roof. Every house had a flat roof to which people went for rest, for taking the sun, and to get away from it all in the cool of the evening. To that roof they had a stairway from the outside. The men could therefore bring the paralyzed man up the stairway to the roof, remove some of the straw of the roof, and lower him in front of Jesus.

The men who brought the paralyzed man, as well as the man himself and the others around Jesus, believed that a person's sickness, particularly a long sickness like paralysis, was brought on by sin. Jesus, knowing this, uttered as his first words to tell the man, "your sins are forgiven" (v. 5). This was a very kindly phrase, and the most important sentence of today's entire Gospel. Jesus still uses it with all who want it. But when he first said it the educated people among his listeners took offense, and wondered how Jesus could presume to speak that way (v. 7). To them he was uttering blasphemy, because only God can forgive sins. And they were right: People can forgive the wrongs done them, but only God can forgive sins. And, though God alone can forgive, the faith of others, like the four stretcher bearers, can help.

How did Jesus mean his statement? Did he mean it in the sense in which the prophet Nathan had announced that David's sins were forgiven when David had committed adultery and then repented? Or was he forgiving in the sense that he had what we call the "power of attorney"? Or did he mean it in the sense that he himself was a special person in God's sight, that he himself — because of the might of God — was forgiving sins? If he meant it in that last sense, he was indeed committing blasphemy if he himself were not God.

Any charlatan can say he's forgiving sin. Sin is, after all, invisible. One can see a person in the act of committing what looks like sin, one can hear another uttering what sounds like blasphemy, slander, cursing, or using God's name in vain, but one can't sense sin itself. Hence Jesus' question: "Which is easier, to say to the paralytic, 'Your sins are forgiven,' or to say, 'Rise, pick up your mat and walk'? But that you may know that the Son of Man has authority to forgive sins on earth" — he said to the paralytic — "I say to you, rise, pick up your mat, and go home" (vv. 9-11).

If he'd referred to himself as God, he would have been killed on the spot. As it was, what he was doing was helping to lead to his death.

And he knew it. But what he was doing his enemies couldn't immediately impute to him because he referred to himself by way of a controversial figure of speech from the Book of Daniel: "Son of Man." If his audience — especially the educated ones — knew their Scriptures as well as we think, they knew that he was referring to himself in the very special way meant by Daniel. But they couldn't do a thing about it.

What struck the audience wasn't the forgiveness of sins, because — as we said — they couldn't sense that, but that this man whom in this little town they knew to have been paralyzed for a long time was now able to walk. They were impressed by the wrong things. We frequently are, too. We're impressed, for example, by the fact that we can go to an airport and within a very short time be thousands of miles away. We're impressed by being able to press a button and with our own eyes see and with our own ears hear something that's taking place on the other side of the planet. But many of the important things that should most impress us are the things that we can't sense — like the forgiveness of sin.

If in those days people were overconscious of sin, we in our time are underconscious of it. Instead of calling wrong actions sins, we call them sociological aberrations, or abnormalities, or problems from childhood, or — to use a psychological phrase — guilt feelings. The word that we should rather use in connection with sin isn't "guilt," but "remorse," because what we have done by sin is to disturb the order between ourselves and God.

If sinfulness is widespread in a culture, it can lead to the estrangement from God of an entire society. So it was with the Jews in the time of Isaiah six hundred years before Christ. At that time, in what we heard in today's First Reading God promised the possibility of the forgiveness of the sins of the entire nation.

The estrangement that sin causes can be an estrangement not only from ourselves and from God, but also from our neighbors. That estrangement victimized St. Paul when he was to have visited the Corinthians. They were so sinfully engaged in their fights among themselves that Paul realized that, even though he had promised to come, his presence would make matters worse. So he stayed away.

The Corinthians then accused him of saying "yes" and "no" at the same time: talking out of both sides of his mouth. Paul reminded them that he was in imitation of Christ, who said "yes" when he meant "yes" and "no" when he meant "no." He reminded them also of a very important facet of God — namely, that God had, to back up his promise mentioned in Isaiah, given what we would call "money up front." This kind of promise — this "money up front" — was the presence of Jesus himself, which is the pledge of God's promises.

There are several thoughts that we should take with us from today's readings. One is an awareness of sin: a consciousness of the existence of sin in the world and in ourselves, and the understanding that — although sickness and disease may not be brought about by sin — nevertheless many of the ills of the world, many personal ills, and many ills in neighborly relationships are due to the commission of sin. Secondly, we must take the means that God has given for ridding ourselves of sin — especially the Sacrament of Reconciliation, Jesus' holy Sacrament that offers to reconcile us with God, with the Church, with one another, and with ourselves. The forgiveness of sin is a generous marvel, an activity that's proper to God alone. And finally, we should ask ourselves if we've ever been like one of the four friends of the paralyzed man in bringing another to Jesus.

EIGHTH SUNDAY IN ORDINARY TIME
Ho 2:16f., 21f.   2 Cor 3:1-6   Mk 2:18-22

Be Open-Minded
Feasting and Fasting; Religiosity and Fasting; Christianity:
Joyful, Fresh, New; Don't Be an Old Fuddy-Duddy

They say the mind is like the stomach: It's not how much you put into it that counts, but how much it digests. Although we're definitely to be open-minded enough to let many things enter, we have to be careful. On the one hand, if we're too open-minded we're like an open palm that will hold nothing. That can result in everything, including morals, being relative. On the other hand, if we're not open-minded enough, we become set in our ways, closed to the new. The result of that can be mental and spiritual death. Religious people, convinced of the absoluteness of the truths they hold dear, sometimes tend too much toward closed-mindedness.

Some of John the Baptist's disciples and the Pharisees were like that. They were accustomed to fast (v. 18), and Jesus' disciples were not. Although their Law didn't strictly require it, many observant Jews fasted twice a week: on Mondays and Thursdays. In today's Gospel, John's disciples and the Pharisees were disturbed at the possibility of departing from such customs.

Now, Jesus was not against fasting. There are, in fact, many good reasons for fasting. One is that voluntarily abstaining from food as well as other legitimate pleasures makes us less attached to things, more in control of our lives. Another is that, by giving things up, we might appreciate them the more: One who has to leave home for a while on business, for example, comes to an enhanced appreciation of the home. But the Pharisees used fasting for display — they actually whitened their faces and wore old clothes so people would know they were fasting and, they hoped, admire them.

Jesus, of course, didn't want his disciples to imitate the spirit of the Pharisees. Equally important was his use of an analogy that people at that time would have understood well: a comparison of himself to a bridegroom, a figure the Baptist had used (Jn 3:29). He was comparing his disciples to the "sons of the nuptial couch," a picturesque Semitic term for the closest friends of the bridal couple who were special guests at their friends' wedding. By their talk and songs they had to see to it that the wedding party went off with panache. The bridegroom, like most people of that time, worked hard and didn't go away on a honeymoon; he stayed home amid continued feasting and rejoicing that lasted for a week. Wedding guests, who came and went during the week, were exempt from the rules of fasting. It was supposed to be the happiest week in anyone's life. For the week the groom stayed with them, therefore, they couldn't fast.

Jesus' analogy was based on such First Testament passages as today's reading from Hosea. The main message of this prophet (who wrote in the eighth century B.C.) was that God's love for His people was as a husband's love for his wife. In today's passage, Hosea saw the Lord as once more becoming wedded to Israel, despite Israel's infidelities. The bride-price Israel would have to pay for this was that her people live in justice, love, and mercy (v. 21).

Indeed, this was Israel's covenant with God. A covenant with God is not an ordinary agreement, which is between parties on equal terms: This is a *special* arrangement between God and the human race in which

God is the principal party and people are free to accept or reject, but not to alter. In this covenant between God and His people, God would confer a special love: *hesed*, loyal adherence to His covenant partner. He would have mercy on their past infidelities. And they would have the pleasure of coming to "know the Lord" (v. 22) — not just in theory, but in an all-embracing way that would involve acknowledging God's will and obeying His Law.

Jesus, using the same metaphor, went on to teach a deeper truth: His disciples had not been with him simply to be his companions, or the "sons of the nuptial couch": He was breathing a new spirit into them. Over and against that day when the bridegroom is taken away from them (v. 20) — an ominous note — he spoke of the need to stay young in spirit, adventurous, open-minded. George Bernard Shaw said something to the effect that "the best thing is to die young — but delay it as long as possible." The early years of a man and woman in marriage — years of planning, forming, building — must give way to newness, discarding past notions when necessary, growing into the future. Complacency — sometimes masked in indignation over the new — is slow death.

Jesus taught this in two homey illustrations. One was that no one sews a piece of unshrunken cloth on an old cloak (v. 21). If one did that, when the garment got wet in the rain or the wash, and the new patch shrunk more than the old cloth, it would cause the old material to tear apart. More deeply, the illustration may also be a symbol of the whole universe, which Jesus does not merely patch up but creates afresh.

Jesus' other illustration was that no one pours new wine into old wineskins (v. 22). His was a time when there were no bottles; people used animal skins to hold liquids. The new skins, young and supple, stretched as the new wine in them continued to ferment. Old skins, being hard and dry, cracked and broke. Again there may be a deeper meaning: the wine symbolizing a new era, with Jesus as the one who dispenses the new wine at the Messianic banquet.

The Corinthians to whom St. Paul wrote in today's Second Reading were no less set in their ways than the Israelites whom Hosea addressed and the people to whom Jesus spoke. They had narrowmindedly said that Paul was always proudly recommending himself. But Paul was broadminded enough to state at the beginning of his letter (v. 2) that *they* were his letter of recommendation: The change in their persons was all he needed. Then he expanded even further, to say that they were clearly "a letter of Christ" (v. 3) — as is everybody. It's Jesus who produced whatever of good there was in the Corinthians, as of the good in everyone. It's not Paul, or anyone else, who's responsible for all change toward the good, but the Spirit of the living God, and that's sufficient. Seek Him first and all else either comes to you or doesn't matter.

Between us and God there's a New Covenant (v. 6). That covenant is new not only in point of time, but in the sense of quality and kind. While the adjective "new" implies a contrast with the "old," it doesn't mean something numerically *different*. It doesn't completely replace the old, but grows out of it and is related to it as fulfillment to promise: Jesus said he hadn't come to abolish the law or the prophets, but to fulfill them (Mt 5:17). The Old Covenant began with Moses reading it to the people and their agreeing to it. Whereas that covenant was written and therefore external, ours is of the spirit and therefore internal and of the heart.

Moreover, the former covenant killed. It killed *hope*, because for human nature to keep it was frustratingly impossible. It killed *life*, because under it one could get only condemnation. And it killed *strength*, because it could diagnose but not help. Our New Covenant gives hope and life and strength, because it's a relationship of love and Jesus came because he loved the world very much. It's a relationship between the heavenly Father and His children. It makes new persons of people. And it tells people what to do, makes it possible for them to do what they're supposed to do, encourages them to do it, and gives them the means and the strength to do it.

It wasn't that the Old Covenant was a bad thing: It was, however, only a forerunner and therefore second-best. But some Jews, like people all the time and particularly in religion, close-mindedly clung to the old. It was the same when Wordsworth's poetry came along, the Impressionists' paintings, and Beethoven's music. Let's be constantly on our guard to be open-minded in a way that will enable us to grow.

NINTH SUNDAY IN ORDINARY TIME
Dt 5:12-15   2 Cor 4:6-11   Mk 2:23-3:6

Religion Good and Bad
Keeping the Sabbath Holy; On the Spirit and the
Letter of the Law; Sing with Joy to God Our Help

People have long and often discussed true and false religions, and gotten into wars over it. Less often, we discuss good and bad religions. That's one of the themes of today's liturgy.

In today's Gospel, St. Mark tells two stories in which Jesus sent the Pharisees back to basics. The first story tells that while Jesus was passing through a field on the Sabbath, his disciples began to pick some of the grain for themselves (v. 23). On an ordinary day, this was permitted by the Law (Ex 23:25). But today was the Sabbath, and — as the Pharisees were quick to protest — doing this wasn't permitted (v. 24).

Jesus reminded them of an event in the life of David (v. 25). David, fleeing for his life, came to the tabernacle in Nob. He asked for food, but there was none except the twelve loaves that constituted an offering to God placed on a golden table in front of the Holy of Holies in the Temple. Though no one but the priests was permitted to eat this bread, David and his men in their need ate it. Although this theoretically broke the law, it was approved. Jesus' argument was that human law may rightly be dispensed, proportionate to one's need. The Pharisees should have known that Sabbath observance has more reference to social and humanitarian reasons than being only a remembrance of God's day of rest in His work of creation.

They would indeed have known this had they reflected sufficiently on today's First Reading, which provides the background to Jesus' confrontations. It's from the Book of Deuteronomy, which means "second law." The Ten Commandments are listed twice in the First Testament: first in Exodus and again in Deuteronomy. Today's portion of Deuteronomy tells of God's commandment to keep holy the Sabbath, along with a commentary on the subject.

Instead of making God's rest after creation the basis for Sabbath rest, as in Exodus, here the connection of Sabbath rest is with the fact that the Jews were once slaves in Egypt (v. 15), the Sabbath being the celebration of community in the promised land and a remembrance that God had loved Israel enough to bring the people into freedom. But pharisaic minds, now as well as then, push legalism to absurd conclusions, and lose law's original intent. For that kind of mind Jesus declares that the Sabbath was made for people, not people for the Sabbath (v. 27).

Good religion doesn't consist only in rules and regulations: A prior claim is human need, which entails personal decision-making. One of the loveliest stories about that is Henry Van Dyke's "The Story of the Other Wise Man," Artaban. Artaban set out to find the infant Jesus in Bethlehem with three gifts for this newborn King: a sapphire, a ruby, and a pearl. As he rode hard to meet the other wise men, he saw a sick traveler lying on the ground before him. If Artaban stayed to help him, he would be too late to meet his companions; they would have to leave without him. He chose to stay and help. But now, having to travel alone and not in a caravan, he needed camels and bearers to cross the desert. He had to sell his sapphire to get them, sad though it made him to have to give up this gift for the King.

He finally arrived at Bethlehem, but again too late: Mary and Joseph and the infant Jesus had gone. When Herod's soldiers came to carry out his command to kill all children under two years of age, Artaban was lodging in a house where there was a little child whom he'd come to love. When the soldiers came to the house, with the background sound of weeping mothers Artaban stood in the doorway and bribed the soldiers with his ruby. The child was saved and the mother overjoyed. But the ruby was gone, leaving Artaban sad that the King would never have this gift either.

For years Artaban wandered, looking for the King. Thirty-three years later he arrived in Jerusalem. There was a crucifixion that day, and from what Artaban heard about one of the men being crucified he thought this might be the King. He headed for Calvary, thinking that his pearl might buy the life of the condemned. Down the street came a girl running from a band of soldiers who were to sell her into slavery. Artaban hesitated, but then gave the pearl to the soldiers and saved the girl's life.

Suddenly the skies were dark, the earth shook, and a flying piece of tile hit Artaban on the head. He sank, semi-conscious, to the ground. The girl pillowed his head in her lap. As he lay dying, she heard him say, "But when, Lord? When did I see you hungry and feed you? When did I see you a stranger, and take you in? Or naked and clothe you? Or sick and come to you?" Then, in what seemed a whisper from far away, came a low and sweet voice that said, "Inasmuch as you did it to one of the least of my brethren, you did it to me." And Artaban smiled in death because he knew that the King had received his gifts.

The second incident in today's Gospel shows the two concepts of religion we've been talking about: the pharisaic concept of religion as empty ritual and Jesus' idea of religion as worship and service. According to the Pharisees' interpretation, the most that could be done in the way of healing on the Sabbath was to prevent an injury or sickness from getting worse; it mustn't be made better. But Jesus' healings were producing clamoring crowds and processions of more and more sick people, which greatly cut into the power of the Pharisees.

The man now before Jesus (v. 1) came because he was ashamed to beg. Jesus was aware that the Pharisees were there in the synagogue not to worship, but to scrutinize everything he did (v. 2). If Jesus had been more cautious, or more cold, he could easily have arranged not to see the man, or to put him off to another day. But Jesus was generous and warm-hearted. He had the man come before him (v. 3).

Then he put the Pharisees in a dilemma. "Is it lawful," he asked (v. 4), "to do good on the Sabbath rather than to do evil?" If they were to answer rationally, they would have to admit that it was permissible to do good, and to heal this man was a good thing. They would likewise have to deny that it was lawful to do evil, and that to leave this man in his wretched state when it was possible to help him was evil. So they remained silent.

And Jesus looked at them with anger (v. 5). When Jesus made a whip to drive the money-changers from the Temple, we infer his anger from his actions; the present occasion is the only place in all the Scriptures when anger is specifically attributed to Jesus. And it was caused by a hypocritical adherence to bad religion. So the Pharisees immediately took counsel with the Herodians to put Jesus to death (v. 6). The Pharisees considered the Herodians unclean, but they were willing to violate that part of the Law: They thought they had a good case against Jesus now, with witnesses. Jesus' good religion didn't exempt him from suffering.

St. Paul in today's Second Reading touchingly describes his human weakness and at the same time courage for the cause of Christ.

and that overriding characteristic of good religion: optimism. As God brought it about at creation that light shine out of darkness, so He continues to have light shine through darkness: God shines forth in our hearts in such a way that we can make known the divine glory to others. We especially see that divine glory shining through the face of Jesus (v. 6).

Like Paul, we weak followers of Jesus Christ are full of paradoxes. We suffer, but never to the point of giving up hope (v. 8). We're perplexed, but not driven to despair; persecuted by other people, but never abandoned by God (v. 9). When we're knocked down — as all people are at one time or other — it's always to rise up again. The secret of Paul's life was to so live the sufferings of Jesus that Jesus' life might be revealed in him (vv. 10f.).

The prime law of good religion is love, and proper celebration of the Sabbath is an offshoot of good religion. It's a celebration of life, a time to pause from our daily work, a time of blessing, a time for integrating leisure and work. Many people focus exclusively on work, leaving little time for the kind of listening, reflection, and presence that is the starting point of authentic celebration. In our liturgical feasts, we celebrate all the moments of our lives and form an intimate connection between life and worship.

In this our weekly celebration as a community, we place our central religious celebration at the service of human need, we offer our efforts of the past week to the Lord, and we reflect on the deeper meaning of our lives. If the Sabbath and our religion aren't all of that, they become empty, repetitive, and stifling. Let's celebrate our religion and our Sabbath in ways that are pleasing and acceptable to the teachings of Jesus.

First Sunday of Lent
Gn 9:8-15   1 P 3:18-22   Mk 1:12-15

God and the Devil
Is the Devil Real?; Progress through Tests; Living between
Two Worlds; Self-Sacrifice: Make any Sense?; A New Beginning;
Hope Amidst Temptation; Lent and Penance; The Meaning of Baptism

The vampires of fiction look and behave much like victims of what modern science calls *porphyria*. Porphyria is a rare disease which causes a lack of sufficient oxygen in the blood. Count Dracula may have been a victim of the disease. Victims are extremely sensitive to sunlight, which could pock-mark their skin horribly, cause their lips to tighten, and make their gums recede so that their teeth look as large as fangs. The victims also become hairy and disfigured. In the days before modern treatment, they could move about easily only after dark. The basis in truth for fictional blood-sucking vampires was that they were trying to alleviate the symptoms of their dreadful disease by getting more oxygen in their blood. Today an injection of *heme*, the oxygen-carrying part of the blood, relieves their symptoms.

Vampirism meets our world's attempts to symbolize evil. No rivals may be able to destroy vampires, according to the imaginative stories, but with them through the centuries is, as with all evil, a terrible ache, a tiresome boredom, and a lonely emptiness. How meaningful to our lives are evil and the devil? Are they any more real than vampires? Today's liturgy talks about that.

St. Mark begins today's Gospel by telling us that it was the same Holy Spirit who was, a short time before, gloriously present at Jesus' baptism, who drove Jesus out into the desert to be tempted by the evil one, Satan (v. 12f.). It's not incongruous for the Spirit to have sent Jesus to be tested. Tests aren't there to make us fail, but — as with an athlete or a student — to make us better and stronger. In Jesus' case, this test was to be a dramatic conflict of strength between him and Satan.

There were various reasons why Jesus' test took place. On the devil's part, he had observed the glorious scene at Jesus' baptism. He wanted to check the power of this holy man at the very outset of his work. For our Lord's part, there were equally compelling reasons why the devil would be allowed to tempt him. Just as the first Adam brought sin upon the human race by succumbing to the temptations of Satan, so Jesus, the second Adam, would redeem us all from sin by overcoming the temptations of Satan. The neutralization of the satanic power in creation, in society, and within the individual was part of Jesus' mission. Also, Jesus wanted to teach us by his example.

The desert — or wilderness, or wasteland — was the place where the people felt closest to God. In the desert, they had received God's law; in the desert they had become a covenanted people; in the desert they were fed with spiritual food and given spiritual drink. For those reasons, Isaiah said that the way of the Lord should be prepared in the desert. Recently, John the Baptist was doing just that with crowds of people. John also represented a more practical aspect of the desert: Some Jews, disgusted by the corruption of official Judaism in Jerusalem, had withdrawn from society to the desert, and lived in places like Qumran (whose caves gave us the Dead Sea Scrolls).

At the same time, the people considered the desert a place for wild beasts and the place where Satan ruled. At the time, wild beasts often symbolized demons. They certainly suggest the loneliness of the desert. The cry of the jackals, the roaming wild boars, and the prowling leopards on the cold nights of the rainy season (which this was) could certainly be suggestive of frightful evil demons such as vampires or other symbols of evil in modern art.

At his baptism, Jesus had experienced the divine world in the communication from the Father and the appearance of the Spirit; in his current test, Jesus was in the demonic world. In Jesus' test, the final battle has begun. Jesus' presence in the desert for "forty days" is an expression that occurs frequently in the Scriptures: Moses was said to have been on the mountain with God for forty days, for example, and Elijah was said to have gone for forty days on the strength of the meal the angel gave him. It means simply a considerable period of time.

But is there a devil? Does Satan really exist? We've been using the words "devil" and "Satan" interchangeably. "Satan" is from the Hebrew, meaning simply an adversary. In the Jewish Scriptures Satan sometimes means ordinary human opponents; often he's the enemy of all humanity. Satan's other title is "devil." This comes from the Greek *diabolos*, which originally meant one who searches for everything that can be said against a person, and then came to mean one who deliberately and maliciously slanders someone in the presence of God.

The last step in the development of the idea of Satan/devil took place when the Jews were in captivity. There they learned something of Persian thought. The Persians saw life as having two powers from which a person must choose: light and goodness (*Ormuzd*) and dark and evil (*Ahriman*). Put another way, life consisted of God and God's adversary. Satan came to be regarded as *the* adversary of God *par excellence*. So Satan is everything that is against God. People of modern Persia, Iran, who shout *Alahu Akhbar*, "God is great," and call America Satan, are in that tradition.

In the New Testament, the devil or Satan was behind human disease and suffering (Lk 13:16), seduced Judas (Lk 22:3), was having his power broken by the work of Jesus (Lk 10:1-19), and was destined for final destruction (Mt 25:41).

It was irrepressible pride that would lead to the fallen angels' rebellion and eventual expulsion from heaven. In the Christian tradition, Lucifer, the most brilliant of all the denizens of the heavenly sphere, vaingloriously waged war to overturn the regime in heaven. Defeated by the Archangel Michael, the angel who would be God was cast into the inferno. With him went about a third of the heavenly host, a horde of fallen angels. There's no possibility of redemption for Satan and his minions. Unlike Adam and Eve, the fallen angels were not tempted to sin but chose it out of untrammeled free will. They have no excuse for their disobedience.

Whether the devil is a person or not, he exists as the quintessence of evil in the world. From the time of Adam and Eve, who tried to pass the buck for their sin to the serpent, to ourselves who joke that "the devil made me do it," to today's screaming headlines, we don't have to be convinced of the existence of evil.

So is there a devil today? In his heyday, Satan was an attribute inside the self, and his victims felt "both goaded and guilty," both predestined to sin and responsible for their sinning. But he lost power when he became a visible being outside the self, for he was reduced to something that, especially today, educated people find it difficult to believe in. Moreover, pride, once the mark of the devil, was now not just a legitimate emotion but America's uncontested god.

Evil abhors a vacuum, and into the space vacated by Satan rushed many secular groups like Marxists (who substituted words like "exploitative classes" for "Satan") and psychoanalysts (who substituted "repression" and "neurosis"). Capitalism played a major role in the destruction of the American sense of personal responsibility: In the genius of capitalism in its full creative power and its concomitant brutality, Americans found that to be successful, or even to survive, one had to be a sinner. The weakness of the psychological explanations of evil is also evident.

Our culture is now in crisis because evil remains an inescapable experience for all of us, while we no longer have a symbolic language for describing it. For no subsequent movement has produced a metaphor for evil as seductive as Satan. The importance of metaphors is this: We can't fight what we can't name.

In searching for a revival of a sense of internal sin rather than an externalized scapegoat for evil, we find ourselves in a situation that gives a new and more literal meaning to the choice between the devil and the deep blue sea. If pride, relativism, and demagogy are the serpents in our contemporary garden, then, to paraphrase the question at the end of Shaw's *Saint Joan*, "Must a Christ perish in torment in every age to save those who are deficient?"

After his mention of Jesus and the devil (v. 14), Mark begins the story of Jesus, gradually unfolding the mystery of his identity. Jesus went to Galilee, a central place for his preaching, proclaiming the Gospel of God — the Good News of truth, of hope, of peace, of fulfillment of God's promise, of salvation. This is the time of fulfillment (v. 15), said Jesus, the period appointed in history for God to make good on His messianic promises. A new beginning was taking place. God was about to re-establish His sovereignty over the world. Nevertheless, Jesus would encounter satanic attacks again — at Gethsemane and during his passion, to mention only two examples.

Through Jesus, God gave us a New Covenant, which is there to help us. There had been covenants with God before, each with its own symbol. The sign of the covenant with Abraham had been circumcision, that with Moses Sabbath observance. The earliest covenant, however, was the one mentioned in today's portion of the Book of Genesis: that between God and Noah. Evil had been on the increase since Adam's sin and Cain's murder of his brother Abel. God sent the flood to destroy that evil age and permit a new beginning with a new creation. God's covenant with Noah assured humanity a future.

The symbol of that covenant was, as today's reading says, the "bow in the clouds" — the rainbow — which was originally a sign of peace; it embraced a renewed human race, all other living creatures, and the inanimate world. Later, the rainbow would serve as a sign of God's majesty: Ezekiel used it to describe "the likeness of the glory of the Lord" (1:28), and the Book of Revelation — the last book of the Bible — indicates that around the throne of God is "a rainbow as brilliant as emerald" (4:3).

All those covenants were between God and a chosen group of people. Jesus' covenant, however, is between God and all people. Its outward sign is, as today's Second Reading tells us, baptism. Baptism doesn't only remove Original Sin. It's also our birth into Christ — the way we become adopted children of God, heirs of heaven, temples of the Spirit, and sharers in the priesthood of Christ. Lent reminds the baptized of their side of the covenant, and prepares unbaptized adults for entry into the covenant.

The letter indicates that the waters of baptism are an antitype of the waters of the flood. The flood destroyed all people but eight: Noah and his wife, and his three sons and their wives. The waters of baptism, on the other hand, are a cleansing agent that has the power to save all who receive them. Through the waters of baptism, God offers us spiritual life, saving sinners from the flood waters of sin, despair, and disillusion that can sweep over us and destroy us (vv. 19-22).

Today's message demands a twofold response from people. They're summarized in the twofold reminder given us with ashes on Ash Wednesday. One part of our response should be a profound change in opening ourselves to the Kingdom of God, and permitting it to determine the direction of our life. The other part of our response should be that we believe in the Gospel — that we take Jesus at his word: that what sounds too good to be true is really true.

Let's act upon those responses. Let's acknowledge that there's evil in the world, and in us: We've sinned in what we've done and in what we've failed to do, in our thoughts, in our words, and in our actions. Let's accept Lent as a time of testing our attitudes, values, concerns, and life goals — testing not with a view to pass/fail, but to improve ourselves. Let's heed Jesus' call to renewal by living up to the saving waters of our baptism, and cross through the wasteland of evil symbolized by wild beasts and vampires toward the rainbow of God's peace. And let's not direct our Lenten works of piety in only a self-centered giving up of things we like — a good beginning — but let's move on to direct our prayers and actions outward, to the glory of God and the needs of our human community.

SECOND SUNDAY OF LENT
Gn 22:1f., 9-13, 15-18   Rm 8:31-34   Mk 9:2-10

The Mud and Stars of Life
The Tensions of Life; From Sight to Insight; Encouragement;
Give Your All; No Rose without Thorns; The Good from Suffering;
Models of Faith; Witness; Who Was Jesus?; God's Conflicting Demands

Life's a tension between our aspirations somewhere in the stars and our reality somewhere in the mud. And every year the first two Sundays of Lent present that whole range of human existence. Last Sunday, Jesus' temptations reminded us of the mud every human being since Adam and Eve has had to slog through. Today holds out a side of Jesus' starry transformation in glory.

To the mountain of the transfiguration Jesus took Peter because he was the appointed head of the apostles, John because he was the beloved disciple, and John's brother James who was to be the first of the apostles to shed his blood for the Gospel. They would be present at Jesus' agony in Gethsemane, too: Jesus hoped that their memory of his transfiguration might serve to safeguard against the surprise of his agony. This mixture of stars and mud was a very critical period in the life of Jesus. The great crowds and early successes of his ministry in Galilee had fallen away; his steps were now turned toward Jerusalem, the harassing center of religious life and authority; he had already predicted his death; and the rebuke he had already had to administer to Peter presaged disappointment in the apostles.

Traditions about the location of the high mountain of the Transfiguration vary between Mt. Tabor and snow-capped Mt. Hermon; perhaps it wasn't a physical mountain at all, but a theological one. The whole incident, after all, was at the theological core of St. Mark's Gospel: that is, determining who Jesus is. At his baptism, Jesus was proclaimed as Son of the Father; at his crucifixion he will be acclaimed as Son of God by the centurion; Jesus' transfiguration is between the two, and is central to who Jesus is.

Getting to know people is central to our relations with them. Sometimes we can work beside people, or live with them, for a long time without really getting to know them. Then, one day, something happens which causes them to open up, to begin to let us get close, and we discover a depth of riches which we didn't know existed. Jesus' transfiguration was like that.

Jesus' transfiguration was more than a merely external change in appearance. The Greek word Mark used, from which we get our word *metamorphosis*, means that Jesus' form was changed, as with a butterfly emerging from a chrysalis. His clothes became dazzling white (v. 3): Such brightness could come from nowhere earthly. In the Scriptures, final glory is seen in terms of white garments (e.g., Rv 4:4; 7:9); here, Jesus is revealed in the glory of the final age. The fact that Moses, the lawgiver *par excellence*, appeared indicated that the whole purpose of the Law was to prepare for Christ. The appearance of Elijah, the prototype of prophets, signified that all the prophets looked forward to the same end.

Above the altar in the church on Mt. Tabor today, the Transfiguration is depicted in gold-toned mosaic. Mosaics at the sides of the altar indicate four other transfigurations of Jesus: an ordinary-looking baby in a manger, whose birth was heralded by angels; ordinary bread and wine, which are changed into his body and blood; the lamb, slain but foretold in prophecy; and the tomb, in which he was buried but from which he rose. Behind the altar is a stained-glass window of two peacocks, which can at times look like an ordinary bird but with its tail feathers outstretched has a heavenly beauty.

The three apostles were impressed by all the glory, and wanted it to continue forever. Although it was an experience of something beyond words, Peter spoke. "Let us make three tents," he said to Jesus, "one for you, one for Moses, and one for Elijah" (v. 5). Perhaps his words were prompted by the joyful annual feast of Sukkoth, or Booths, or Tabernacles, an autumnal thanksgiving feast which marked the end of the fruit harvest. It commemorated their ancestors' living in tents after their departure from Egypt, and included a torchlight dance. One of the ways of celebrating it was to erect little huts and fill them with presents for children.

Indeed, Peter's words evidenced the comprehension of a child who, witnessing something awesome and ignorant of what it is, wants it because it shines. He hardly knew what to say (v. 6). It wouldn't, of course, occur to Peter just to say nothing. It's interesting to compare Peter here with Mary at the Annunciation. Like us when we can't let go of what we like, he wanted to stay and forget their other duties and even the other nine apostles, while she let the angel go even though she could have asked other questions. He was so awe-struck as to be afraid; she was fearful only that she do God's will.

Toward the end, a cloud came (v. 7) and covered the event. This cloud was no ordinary one, but what the Jews called the *shekinah*. That was a First Testament image to describe God's dwelling among His people: It was the way God came to the Tabernacle, it had filled the Temple, and it was what the Jews dreamed would return to the Temple when the messiah came.

The words from the cloud, "This is my beloved Son," receive their full meaning not from the wonders that were happening, but from Jesus' willingness to sacrifice himself. The heavenly voice was preparing the apostles to understand that in the divine plan Jesus must die ignobly before his messianic glory was complete: the mud before the stars. "Listen to *him*," concluded the voice, implying that Moses and Elijah were ceding their place to Jesus as *the* authoritative lawgiver and prophet.

When it was over, the apostles saw only Jesus in his humanity (v. 8). As the little group came down the mountain, the tensions between mud and stars continued. Because the apostles had been schooled in a concept of messiahship that didn't include the cross-side of the tension, Jesus strictly forbade them to tell anyone what they had seen before he would rise from the dead (v. 9). But they didn't know what "rising from the dead" meant (v. 10).

God seems to be in the habit of causing growth in people through tensions between glory and suffering. The event from the Book of Genesis in today's First Reading took place in about the eighteenth century B.C. It's a masterpiece from many points of view — literature, theology, drama — and is one of the best-told stories in the Bible, building suspense and unfolding itself as it goes along. It's about Abraham — for Jews their "founding father"; for Muslims a "friend of God," their patriarch; and for Christians a model of faith. The author of the story tells us that God put Abraham to the test (v. 1).

That test was painful. God was asking Abraham to sacrifice his son Isaac: his only son, his son who was even more uniquely precious than other sons who provided the greatest joy to every Israelite, the son whom he loved (v. 2), the son through whom God had promised that all nations would find blessing, the son who was the only hope of the fulfillment of that promise. In primitive times, humans were routinely sacrificed in tribute to various gods, and the unspeakably barbaric practice of families offering the lives of their children was shockingly commonplace.

Worse, God was asking Abraham to kill his son himself! Isaac, who had resulted from the promise of faith, now became the test of faith. God's demand, which conflicted with His previous promise, was hard for Abraham to understand. And his decision was difficult. But Abraham answered as he had always answered God: "Ready!" — the only attitude that saves.

The story invites our reflections. Two questions call for an answer. First, what kind of God could ask Abraham to sacrifice his son Isaac? Secondly, why was Abraham so ready to comply? The answers lie somewhere in the passionate love of God and the ineffable faith of Abraham. It was a precedent-shattering moment when Abraham's God rejected the practice of human sacrifice.

Although God spared the only son of Abraham, in a spiritual irony He didn't intervene to spare His own only Son. Echoing the Psalms and the prophets, very emotionally St. Paul tells us in his letter to the Romans that the all-conquering power of God's love has overcome every obstacle to people's salvation and every threat of our separation from God. That power manifested itself fully when God delivered up to death His own Son for our salvation.

Paul was echoing the First Reading, in which Isaac was spared. And his letter, to get people to think for themselves, raises similar questions with regard to God the Father and the sacrifice of Christ. Why did God act like that, sacrificing His Son? The only satisfactory reply is again to be found in the extent of the passion of God's love.

There's always tension between the stars we aspire to and the reality of our everyday life. The stars are our ideals; we can't quite succeed in reaching them. But, like seafarers on the seas, we choose them as our guides and, following them, reach our destiny. Through baptism, God has made us into His own image — but we've been made aware as well that we shall also share the cross of Jesus. During this Lent, which is in a special way our whole lives writ small, let's look into our hearts for whatever God has in store for us — mud or stars — and answer with Abraham: "Ready!"

THIRD SUNDAY OF LENT
Ex 20:11-17 (or 20:1-3, 7f., 12-17)   1 Cor 1:22-25   Jn 2:13-25

The Bottom-Line Meaning of Life
Wisdom and Law; Thank God for His Commandments; The Precepts of the
Lord Are Right; Laws — Can We Do without Them?; Laws and their Spirit;
Men like God, or God like Men?; The Beauty of God's Law; Words of Life

In our current Western world, many people are litigious. In the United
States there's one lawyer for every 600 people, compared with Japan,
where there's one lawyer for 12,000 people and where people prefer
other methods like family compromise to settle disputes. But *all* associations of people need *laws*: for recourse, to bind people together, and
to put into words and action what the group sees as not only putting
forth their wisdom and their priorities, but also as showing a certain
spirit.

In today's First Reading, we heard the Ten Commandments. As
expressed law, the Ten Commandments weren't the first code of eth-
ics written. But this code is different from any other: It involves the
reality of love. And unlike the other religions in the Ancient Near East,
the Hebrews knit closely together religious belief and moral living. The
Ten Commandments are the core of the law of the Jewish Scriptures.
They presume the special covenantal relationship between the living
God and His people, and it's this that makes them timeless. The living
God who first gave them would guide His people to a fuller understanding of their content and implications. That's clear from the fact that
Jesus repeats and re-interprets them in his covenant (e.g., Mt. 19:16-
22; 5:21-48).

The first three commandments provide direct regulations about
people's relations with their God. The last seven constitute essential
elements of relations with other people — but with another very important difference: In the codes of the other Near Eastern peoples, violation constituted only a crime against one's fellow human beings; in
our Bible, it's a crime against God — an entirely new orientation.

Proper orientation toward law is what today's Gospel is about.
Its first part (vv. 14-17) took place in the Temple precincts, and was
tumultuous. This was the time of preparation for the Passover, a feast
that Jews came from all over the world to celebrate: Rome, Greece,

Egypt, Tyre, Sidon. Jerusalem, ordinarily a small town by modern standards, for this feast would put up as many as two and a quarter million people. Although some of the people from within the Holy Land drove before them flocks of sheep destined to provide their paschal lamb, and others bulls and heifers for more costly sacrifices, this wasn't possible for the majority, who came from great distances.

An official inspector had to certify that the animals for the sacrifice were flawless. So for the convenience of the people the Temple *sold* animals. The problem was that the inspectors hesitated to certify an animal brought from outside the Temple, and the monopolistic price inside the Temple became exorbitant. The Temple priests made a tremendous profit from their cornered market.

Other arrangements involved further profits. For example, every Jew over 19 years of age had to pay the Temple tax. This was equal to about two days' wages for an ordinary laborer. The people's currencies from their many lands had graven images, mostly of Caesar, which were considered to be against the First Commandment. They were therefore unacceptable for the Temple tax, which had to be in the imageless Jewish shekels. Hence there were money-changers, and their exorbitant rates fleeced the pilgrims. It was the High Priest Caiaphas who encouraged the money-changers and sellers of animals to enter the main court of the Temple, strengthening his control of trade.

The buying and selling took place in the Court of the Gentiles. This meant that well-disposed non-Jews couldn't pray in peace in the only place allotted them. They were disturbed by the lowing of the oxen, the bleating of the sheep, the cooing of the doves, the babble of the crowds, the shouts of the hucksters, the haggling over prices, the disputes about exchange rates, and the rattle of the coins. Shameful to relate, all these procedures, which were legal but against the spirit of the law, were done in the name of religion.

It's no wonder that Jesus angrily broke the law and swung into action. God's house was being desecrated — worse than people who talk in our churches, or unresponsive ushers, or irreverential eucharistic ministers. For Jesus, the whole business was degrading to true religion. The prophets had been saying that for centuries, but Jesus felt deeply the insult to his Father's house, and was uncompromising on the point. Jesus was also deeply moved by pity for the outcasts and the poor, for whom the burdens of injustice were especially heavy. To the poor — pious victims of the system — who were dealing in doves, Jesus

(v. 16) was gentle: He didn't scatter them with his whip, as he did the leaders; he merely told them to leave.

Jesus' action was amazing when one considers the grandeur of the Herodian Temple, the fierce pride of the priests and scribes who ruled there, and the extent of the commerce carried on in behalf of the chief priests. (In fact, one estimate says that the Temple provided the livelihood of 20% of Jerusalem's population.) The Temple was the religious, social, and commercial center of the city. Jesus' deed amounted to open defiance of the Temple authorities; it was like attacking the legislative, executive, and judicial branches of government all in one. Jesus' attack made possible the charges of hostility against the Temple that sealed his fate. Many Christ-like figures today similarly seal their fates by attacking other lucrative businesses like abortion, drugs, and pornography.

Whereas the first part of this episode centered around the Temple building, the second part (vv. 18-22) centered around Jesus as God's temple, and shows the reactions of the Jews and Jesus' disciples. The Jews — by which St. John means the influential, educated, and suspicious leaders — at this time of Jesus' popularity didn't dare accuse him of wrongdoing.

So Jesus' enemies quietly asked him for a sign of his authority. The request showed that they understood the deeper meaning of what had been going on: Jesus had laid claim to an authority greater than the Temple and the religious officials charged with its functioning. Jesus' answer was, strangely, enigmatic, saying that if they were to destroy this temple, in three days he would raise it up. He was referring to his bodily resurrection. The leaders didn't understand that, but they would use it to misrepresent him at his trial. Neither did his disciples understand, at least not until after his resurrection.

The last part of the episode (vv. 24f.) relates Jesus' interaction with the people. He wouldn't trust himself to them because he knew them all (v. 24). He knew that to many of them he was a wonder-worker or magician; if he spoke to them of service, or sacrifice, or surrender to God's will, or carrying a cross, they wouldn't have understood and would have left him on the spot. Jesus' signs caused many to believe that somehow God is *with* Jesus, but they failed to see that God is *within* Jesus. To recognize that God is *within* Jesus — that *Jesus is God* — puts a special cast on the entire meaning of everything.

That's what St. Paul is saying today. Paul, a Jew living among non-Jews, had to face hostile Jews and non-Jews whose bottom-line meaning of life was completely different from his own. To all, he preached the heart of the Christian message, which included the cross. For the Jews, it was completely unacceptable that God's Chosen One could be one who had been executed as a criminal. False messiahs around that time were promising such things as, upon command, dividing the waters of the Jordan river or causing the walls of Jerusalem to fall. Those were the kinds of spectacular signs the Jews wanted from a Messiah. For Paul, this was nothing less than a lack of trust in God — people putting God to the test, instead of the other way around.

For the cultured non-Jews, too, to preach a God who'd been crucified was lunacy — but for different reasons. For one thing, for them the prime characteristic of God had to be a total inability to feel, because if God could feel anything — like compassion — it would mean that some person for that moment had influenced Him and would therefore be greater than God. For another thing, they sought wisdom, a system of ideas that provided the answers to all life's problems.

This search for wisdom had so degenerated by Paul's time that the cultured pagans looked to the surface of things rather than to the substance, and they wanted that surface to be respectable, high-brow, and attractive. Their emptiness fit Abraham Lincoln's description of Stephen Douglas's arguments as being thin as a soup "made by boiling the shadow of a pigeon that had starved to death." For such people a Christian preacher was considered low-brow, crude, and uncultured — and therefore not to be taken seriously. The cross contained no eloquence, no carefully-worded wisdom, and no respectability.

Those attitudes haven't essentially changed. Even today, many prefer to believe in the kind of Jesus *they choose*, instead of looking at the Jesus *God sent*. Most of us are attached to old habits: The miser loves his money, the influential craves power, the so-called "learned" dotes on his pride.

Yet God doesn't work in our ways, but according to His own will, and that includes the mysterious message of the cross. The cross is a sign (though not a miraculous spectacle) and a wisdom (though considered foolishness by the world). To understand all of that leads to living not only in the letter of God's law but, more importantly, in its spirit, which is love, and in an awareness of the presence of God, which gives an entirely new orientation to law.

FOURTH SUNDAY OF LENT
2 Ch 36:14-17; 19-23   Eph 2:4-10   Jn 3:14-21

Joy and the Cross
Keep Up Your Good Work of Lent; Well Begun Is Half Done; Joy in
Hardship; Happiness is…; Be a Lover; Bring Direction to Your Life

Romantic popular art is full of variants of the theme of boy meets girl,
boy loses girl, boy gets girl. But it isn't always true that love offered is
accepted. That's true of relations between people and God, too. At the
close of last Sunday's Gospel reading, for example, we were told that
many came to believe in Jesus — but inadequately, so that Jesus
wouldn't trust himself to them because he knew the fickleness of human nature (Jn 2:24f.).

Today, we read that Nicodemus, a ruler of the Jews, came to see
Jesus. He was a man of good will but, as is often the case with the intelligent, who perceive complexities and weigh arguments, he found it
difficult to make up his mind. He shared the lack of docility of those
whose business it is to teach and are less ready than humbler folk to
surrender themselves. And so Jesus, who in Galilee adapted his teaching to the simple capacity of country folk, now with this more sophisticated man of Jerusalem discussed matters of deeper import, at times
opening up views that reach right up into heaven.

Nicodemus appears three times in the Scriptures (and only in
John), each time at night. Today his caution in coming at night implies
heavy opposition to Jesus in Jerusalem. This is the only time on record
that Nicodemus actually met Jesus. The dialogue moved between existence from below and existence from above. They spoke, for example,
of God's having ordered Moses to make a bronze serpent, mount it on
a pole, and enable all who looked at it to be cured of the bites of poi-
sonous snakes as the people trekked through the Egyptian desert. In
view of the Jews' First Commandment prohibition against graven images, this was a strange story. The rabbis explained it by saying that it
wasn't the serpent that gave life, but God who commanded Moses to
act in this way. The serpent was only a sign and symbol to point to
God.

Jesus used the story as a parable of himself. He told Nicodemus that, for the salvation of the world, he himself would be lifted up. He meant this in a twofold sense: lifted up on the cross and lifted up into glory by his resurrection and ascension. The suffering and joy signified by these two images are essentially connected: no cross, no crown; no pain, no gain. Jesus told Nicodemus, and us through him, that if we look at Jesus and *believe*, that can give us eternal life (v. 15).

Jesus' offering eternal life stresses not the duration of life, but its quality. That's the highest life possible: the life of God Himself in us. It surrounds and infuses every aspect of our life with peace: peace with people because all are God's children, peace with life itself because we live in a friendly universe, and peace with ourselves because of a new insight into and humble acceptance of our weaknesses.

Jesus summed it all up by saying that God so loved the world that He gave His only Son (v. 16). God is not, as some people have supposed, a vengeful, stern, legal monarch whose mind Jesus came to change. God's whole essence is love. His love isn't only deep, but broad: It's the whole world He loves — even those who are in human terms unlovable. He even loves those who deliberately turn their backs on Him. St. Augustine said, "God loves each one of us as if there was only one of us to love." The fact that He gave His only Son to come into this world and die showed the extent of that love.

Even though God sent His Son that the world might be saved through him (v. 17), Jesus' coming inevitably provoked judgment. Some people condemn *themselves* by turning from the light (vv. 18-20). Judgment is a paradox of love. Suppose you try to elevate friends by taking them to a symphony concert, or by introducing them to an art exhibition, or by giving them a literary classic. During the concert, your friends fidget; at the art exhibition, they look around at everything but the masterpieces; when reading the book, they fall asleep. The music, the art, and the book aren't on trial, but those who react to them are. What you meant to elevate has become a judgment.

Today's First Reading gives an example of that on a national level. It tells how the people of Judah from the ninth to the sixth centuries B.C. ungratefully ridiculed prophet after prophet. Their spine-chilling punishment was that they were abandoned to the Babylonians, the walls of Jerusalem were breached, their precious Temple was torn down, the people degraded as captives, and the nation destroyed. The Responsorial Psalm reflects the awful emptiness of the people's captivity: "By the streams of Babylon we sat and wept when we remembered Zion (Jerusalem)." This terrible cataclysm of 587 B.C. would be repeated under the Romans in 70 A.D., when the Temple would be destroyed again and the city laid waste. The Chronicler's purpose in telling this pathetic part of salvation history was to show that, if the Jews were to survive their homesickness as exiles, it would only be through faithfulness to their religion. The same applies to us.

Today's Second Reading, from the "Queen of the Epistles," the letter to the Ephesians, inspires hope for those who, like the ancient Israelites, have grown indifferent to God and neglected His grace. As with the First Reading, the theme is that the survival of God's covenanted people is due solely to a free act of God's grace.

Like today's other readings, it's ideal for Lent: full of contrasts between human weakness and God's mighty power. To encourage our Lenten efforts, the passage tells us that God is rich in mercy (v. 4) and loves us so much that He brought us to life with Christ — and this even before we loved Him and when we were dead in our transgressions (v. 5). Unlike the Chronicler in the First Reading, who emphasized doing the right thing *in order to be saved*, Ephesians tells Christians to do the right thing *because we have been saved*.

God's bringing us to life with Christ meant that He reversed the ordinary deteriorating process of life to a life that is, like a fountain of youth, always renewing and generating. Sin does things to us that God can help with. Whereas sin kills innocence and not even God can give innocence back, He can take away the guilt of sin. And although sin makes people cynical, Jesus can reawaken ideals. Indulging in sin also weakens the will — but, with our cooperation, especially during times like Lent, Jesus can revive our will.

It's important to remember that sin is an offense not only against law, but against love. If you pass a red light, you can pay the penalty the law lays down by either a fine, or imprisonment, or both. Then you're free of the law. But if in passing the red light you killed a child, for the mother whose child you killed the matter is never over: You can never completely atone. Your crime was against her love for her child. The only thing that can restore your relationship to her is her forgiveness of you. It's like that with us and God. We can't *earn* God's forgiveness — we can only *accept* it (v. 9). The fact that He offers it is a matter for joy, which is one of the themes of today's liturgy.

Today as always, we should imitate God. Be a lover. God's love knows no limit. The Chronicler of Israel's history reminds us today that God had compassion on His people, even when they were unfaithful, acting shamefully, and defiling God's dwelling place on earth. In today's Gospel, we see that God loved the world so much that He sent His Son to rescue us from the exile of sin. The letter to the Ephesians reminds us that we came to life because of God's great love.

But love offered isn't necessarily accepted: Sometimes the story line isn't romance but tragedy: "Boy meets girl, boy loves girl, boy loses girl." This is true for us and God, too. It's possible for us to walk away from the love messages He sends us through our friends, our neighbors, our liturgies, and the other events of our lives. St. Teresa of Avila once wrote that if for one instant we let the love of God penetrate our hearts, then all things will become easy for us. The other side of this is that if we stay in the dark, refusing to let God's love penetrate our heart, then nothing gets easy. Saying "yes" to God's love, as with loving other people, opens us to the possibility of suffering as well as today's theme of joy. But loving God is the whole reason for our being, and — paradoxically — our joy is sometimes increased through our sacrifices.

Fifth Sunday of Lent
Jr 31:31-34   Heb 5:7-9   Jn 12:20-33

The Law of Life
Death to Sin and Ourselves; Embrace the World; Paradoxes of Life;
Your Religion: Love and Conviction or Conformity and Habit?;
Now Is the Hour; A Good Bargain: Death for Life

Many of us go through life looking for a law of life without knowing what it is. Some scientists and philosophers, like the influential Herbert Spencer, see the whole law of life as being self-preservation. Jesus would look upon that idea as a philosophy of defeat.

That's one of the messages of today's Gospel. The scene was heralded by the arrival of some God-fearing cultured Greeks (v. 20). They were always traveling and searching for new truths, for which they often went from religion to religion, philosophy to philosophy, teacher to teacher. They contrasted with the Pharisees, who preferred tradition (v. 19).

The Greeks approached Jesus through Philip (v. 21), perhaps because he had a Greek name and they thought he would be sympathetic to their request. Because Philip didn't know what to do, he went and told Andrew (v. 22). Andrew knew that no one would be a bother to Jesus, and so they approached him. Jesus' opening words were to inform them that the hour had come (v. 23). In the first act of his public ministry, when Mary had asked him to help the newlyweds at Cana, Jesus had said that his hour hadn't yet come (2:4). Later (4:21 and 5:25,28), he had said that "an hour is coming." Now "the hour has come for the Son of Man to be glorified."

But Jesus' law of life, as in this conversation, contains paradox, when all realities change meaning. That word "glorified," for example: By it the Jews meant that the other nations of the world would grovel before them; Jesus meant being crucified. They thought of conquering armies; he thought of the conquering of the cross. The first part of St. John the Evangelist's Gospel, which is called the "Book of Signs," is now ended. In it, John had given many wondrous deeds of Jesus — "signs" — which proved him to be God. Now John passes to the part of Jesus' story called the "Book of Glory."

Jesus' message here is the same as that of all Lent: the way to glory, for Jesus and for us, is death to self. Through that will come resurrection. At times we may think of Jesus' resurrection as a reward for undergoing death on the cross, and that eternal life — that is, the highest quality of life — comes *after* death. The truth is that eternal life comes *through* death — death to self — and comes *now*.

If all this seems strange, Jesus said, we should remember that this law of life already exists in nature: the grain of wheat, or any seed, when preserved in safety, is unproductive. Only when it's buried in the ground does it bear fruit, and that in far greater abundance than itself (v. 24). Our whole lives are similarly a cycle of dyings and risings: It's when we're prepared to die that our lives become the most fruitful. If we've been acting on those principles, when we meet people we haven't met in a long time and they reminisce about something unpraiseworthy that we may have done in the past, we can say happily, "That 'me' died a long time ago; I'm different now."

The meaning of life often eludes people who think they're living life to the hilt. People who love themselves destroy themselves (v. 25). Only by spending life do we save it. When St. Joan of Arc realized that her time was short, she prayed to God, "I shall only last a year;

use me as you can." If we take things easy we may exist longer, but we won't live at all. True greatness comes only by self-forgetting service (v. 26).

Then Jesus interrupted his train of thought. "I am troubled now" (v. 27), he said. This was an anticipation of his agony in the garden of Gethsemane. No one wants to die, especially at the age of thirty-three, and especially no one wants to die on a cross, not even Jesus. To Jesus, the instinct for self-preservation was very strong — so strong that the threat of death stirred the deepest fears in him. But real courage doesn't mean not being afraid; it means knowing enough about the situation to be very much afraid and yet doing what you have to do.

St. Paul of the Cross says, "The whole life of Jesus was a cross; the whole life of one who follows Jesus consists in this: to remain on the cross with him." In other words, to be a disciple means to love as Jesus loved: painfully. C.S. Lewis put it very simply: "To love at all is to be vulnerable." Once we begin to love, we open ourselves to pain as well as joy. Jesus' final courageous answer from his crisis of spirit was a wholehearted acceptance of his heavenly Father's will: "Father, glorify your name!" (v. 28) — that is, "Use me as you will."

In answer, the Father's voice indicated that He had already been glorified in the works of Jesus, and would be glorified again in Jesus' passion and resurrection: The end of the story will be triumph. Many successful stories and motion pictures have happy endings, and often the "happy" ending consists of death (or a symbolic death) endured and transcended. What God did for Jesus, He does for everybody. In times of crisis, God's voice comes to us, as it did to Jesus, if we prepare for it by prayer and fasting. God's voice may not sound like thunder, which was the way Jesus' bystanders thought of it on this occasion (v. 29), but it will be there.

As a result of Jesus' actions Satan will no longer rule this world except to the extent that people's dispositions will permit (v. 31). What must come first is that Jesus be "lifted up." Again, deliberate paradox. Jesus meant lifted onto the cross, and lifted gloriously in resurrection from the dead, lifted in his return to the glory of heaven, lifted up whenever he's glorified in one of his members who shares in his death and resurrection. The result of his glorification is life-giving: his drawing everyone to himself (v. 32). That idea left the Jews in open-mouthed amazement and disbelief.

One who also looked at paradox in the law of life was the author

of today's First Reading, Jeremiah. In love with life, he had to proclaim a message of doom and death; a devout worshiper, he had to
foretell the destruction of the Temple at Jerusalem; a loyal Jew, he had
to announce the fall of his nation if his people didn't stop sinning. In
the end, because people didn't listen, Judah was overrun by the Babylonian armies and its people taken to exile in Babylon.

Today's passage is from a part of Jeremiah that provides comfort in the midst of his gloomy predictions. Salvation history is the
record of how the Old Covenant fared: so badly that the nation was
destroyed; so badly that the Law of Moses, the Torah, became more
and more a series of strict rules which didn't necessarily have any relationship with God; so badly — and here's the comforting part — that
Jeremiah promised that there would be a new and final age in salvation history when God would bring about a "New Covenant" (v. 31f.:
the only time a New Covenant is spoken of in the Jewish Scriptures).

A covenant originally meant an agreement between two unequal
parties, freely entered into, binding perpetually, and sealed in blood.
After a covenant was entered into, it was the custom for the parties to
pass between halves of slain animals which had been laid out on the
ground. That action was a symbol of a prayer that, if the parties didn't
keep their word, may they be as these dead animals.

This New Covenant — new testament — will be basically the
same as the old in some ways: Both are God-centered, both involve
the people of God, and in both the response is shown in obedience to
God's law. But the New Covenant will be different from the old in many
ways. It will last forever. It won't be inscribed merely on stone tablets
or in a book as with the Old Covenant, but on human hearts (v. 33), so
that people's commitment will be made interior. (That doesn't mean
that the terms of the covenant will be subjective, but that God will move
all hearts by His grace so that they will want to keep the covenant.)
And it will no longer be necessary to put it into words of instruction
(v. 34): God will intervene directly. All this newness is made possible
because a "new heart" will be created in people, a "new spirit" given
them.

Consonant with these ideas on the law of life, the letter to the
Hebrews refers to Jesus' sufferings. Jesus prayed, even with loud cries
and tears (v. 7) — the kind of cries and tears that are wrung from a
person by searing pain. The prayers took place throughout his life, but
most poignantly in Gethsemane. Through his suffering, Jesus learned

and grew (v. 8) to the point of being able to accept suffering, not with resentment but with reverence. Abraham Lincoln, in the midst of his sufferings, said that if his sorrow were spread over all the human race there wouldn't be a smiling face anywhere. That was more literally true of Jesus. Because he underwent all the sufferings that try people's souls, he became the source of eternal salvation for all who obey him (v. 9). Jesus is the New Covenant, and in his love, forgiveness, concern, and compassion he lived it.

In our lives as well as in the lives of others, we have evidence of the terrible effects of going against the lessons of the law of life in today's liturgy: hatred, wars, memories of real or imagined hurts, continued grievances, the deep-rooted desire for revenge. But the gentle voices calling us higher are also potent. If we come closer to finding our higher selves through our Lenten prayer, fasting, and charity, we shall also discover Jesus' law of life: that in dying to self we live a divine life that goes way beyond a wish for mere self-preservation. We shall then find Jesus, become his friends and, like Philip and Andrew, bring others into his presence.

PASSION (PALM) SUNDAY

Is 50:4-7;   Ph 2:6-11 (both Cycles A, B, and C)   Mk 14:1-15:47 (or 15:1-39)

Humility
Jesus Christ Is Lord; Submission; Obedience; The Cross in Perspective

Near Pompeii in the vicinity of Naples, Italy, lies the famous city of Herculaneum which, like Pompeii, was buried by the eruption of the volcano Vesuvius in 79 A.D. A few years ago excavators found a body on the shore. It was the body of a young woman who died trying to protect a child from the eruption. From her bones they knew that she'd been undernourished from childhood and marked by heavy work. They

Note: This homily is on the Letter to the Philippians. For Matthew 26, see Cycle A;
    for Luke 22, Cycle C.

concluded that she'd been a slave — or a servant, there not being much difference in the ancient world between slaves and servants.

The position of slave is what our Lord took for us. On this Sunday, and during Holy Week which it starts, we're in the habit of thinking deeply and long about our Lord's crucifixion. Many non-Christians have an aversion to the crucifix, many Christians see it as an overwhelming cause for sadness, and many people of good will look at it and feel compassion for Jesus' pain as well as joy in his love.

St. Paul, in his letter to the Philippians from which today's second reading is taken, puts the event in beautiful perspective. Paul included this particular part, a hymn, to present an example to follow in the daily trials of Christian living. Despite its warnings Philippians is called the "Epistle of Joy." The short letter is so warm and cheerful that the words "joy" or "rejoice" appear about a dozen times. It's hard to envision that Paul wrote most of it from jail, and it's very moving to realize that Paul, right in the middle of the letter, breaks out into today's hymn.

The hymn is a summary of Jesus' life, especially the paschal mystery: "the Gospel in a nutshell." It traces the movement of the Son of God from heaven to earth and back to his Father: his existence before all time, his incarnation, his ministry, and his passion, death, resurrection, and ascension. The hymn begins (v. 6) by invoking faith in Jesus' divinity. Though Jesus was divine, this was nothing he exploited: It was concealed throughout his mortal life. He didn't stand on his dignity.

In becoming man, Jesus divested himself, not of his divinity, but of the *status* of divine glory that was correctly his. Not only did he become a real man, but he proffered himself without any exceptional privileges. More, he assumed the role of a servant. It all now came to a climax: He humbled himself by becoming "obedient to death, even death on a cross" (v. 8). This was the greatest expression of the hallmarks of Jesus' life, which were humility and self-renunciation. Though the Son of God, he desired not to dominate, but to serve. His kind of humility is unique.

This hymn looks to the cross not as a single moment, but as a summary of the entire mystery that is Christ. This lesson of the hymn says something about Paul, who even as he wrote was suffering for the sake of Christ. It says something about all of us who try to wear a smile of joy as we carry the tears of our crosses. From that low point on, our movement is upward. As the Father did with Jesus (v. 9), God will raise to the loftiest heights all who have been faithful. In Jesus' case, the Father responded by raising him from the dead, having him ascend to heaven, and giving him a glorious place of honor. With *all* who humble themselves before others in imitation of Jesus, God will, in accord with His promises in the beatitudes, exalt them most highly. Several times Jesus assured us that people who humble themselves will be exalted.

As a result of Jesus' humility and obedience, God also gave him a new name. In biblical times, one's name was very important. It was meaningful for Genesis to record that Adam had the privilege of naming the animals of Paradise. It was a common idea to give a new name to mark a new stage in a person's life and growth: Abram, for example, became Abraham when he accepted his new life as head of the Jews, Sarai became Sara when God promised her a son, Jacob became Israel when he entered into a new relationship with God. In the New Testament, Simon became Peter when he came to follow Jesus. What demanded a new name for Jesus was the fact that the crucifixion resulted in his final redemption of the human race, and thus brought about a new relationship between Jesus and the Father and between Jesus and us. So the Father "bestowed on him the name that is above every other name" (v. 9) — the name "Lord."

It isn't simply that Jesus' humiliation and exaltation recall the fate of the just man, or the wise and righteous person of Wisdom literature, or the Suffering Servant of today's reading from Isaiah. Jesus is God, Master and Owner of all life. The Father's voice had called Jesus his Son at his baptism and again at his transfiguration, the demons had called him the Son of God, the High Priest had challenged him on the point and took Jesus' reply for blasphemy, and the centurion had confessed to his divinity at his death. Jesus being God should result in a universal and cosmic adoration as an act of religious devotion, whereby "at the name of Jesus, every knee should bend, of those in heaven and on earth and under the earth" (v. 10).

Paul's goal is that "every tongue confess Jesus Christ is Lord, to the glory of God the Father" (v. 11). To say "Jesus is Lord" was the Church's first creed. It's simple, but all-embracing. One doesn't have to be clever and use many other words. Anyone who says that Jesus Christ is Lord has at least a good start at being a true Christian. We who assert it are prepared to give Jesus a faith, a submission, and a love that we give to no other.

And this short creed acknowledges that we have in Jesus someone to imitate — most especially in his humility and obedience. Jesus' exciting entrance to Jerusalem could have been an occasion to emphasize the triumphalistic character of the kingdom, and many of us, if we're honest with ourselves, might have wished it that way. Judas certainly did, and when Jesus didn't capitalize on the triumph of Palm Sunday Judas and others of like mind left him. Some, then and now, want him to be a worldly king, change their lives, bring them freedom. Others fear him — that he will destabilize Jerusalem, as we say today — and are afraid of the religious emotions that he awakens.

But for Jesus — and the evangelists who tell the story — Jesus' triumphal entry into Jerusalem was an occasion to highlight some religious notions. The donkey on which Jesus rode was a sign of peaceful approach, in contrast with the horse, which was used for war. Jesus came not at the head of an army, but in the middle of a group of poor and disorganized enthusiasts whose hopes he embodied. He strove to make all people learn his message of God's love, the love even of enemies, the love that can transform the most proudfully alienating situation into God's kingdom of peace and justice.

It's no accident that Philippi, to which Paul addressed his letter, was a city as proud as any individual could be. It had been founded by Philip of Macedon, father of Alexander the Great, and was shot through with the pagan pride that's the opposite of Christian humility. To heal the Philippians' prideful divisions and rivalry, Paul recommended that they be of one mind and show humility to one another. For an individual as well as for a city, humility is the only way we can be open to God's grace; anyone who has dealt with proud people knows how closed and aloof they are and how difficult to reach.

The humility expected of the follower of Christ isn't undue abjectness, self-depreciation, or low rank, poverty, or insignificance. It's not the same as humiliation, an abasement that makes one demeaned, degraded, and embarrassed. Nor is it a passive surrender in the face of suffering. Rather, humility is an active and faith-filled listening to our own role in God's plan of salvation. It's a consciousness of our true place before God — and, as with Jesus, it's a willingness to obey God's will wherever it takes us, including to the cross. Humility is one of the most difficult of virtues to achieve, and Jesus' cross was where it was achieved the most deeply.

It's legal to change your name as often as you want, as long as there's no intent to defraud. We could reasonably advocate changing our name whenever we thought we had grown enough to think of ourselves as a new person. If we did that, how often do you think you would change *your* name? Let's try to grow into a new person by imitating the example of our life-giving Savior who, though he lives in heaven, had nowhere on earth to lay his head; who, though he will return in the clouds, entered Jerusalem on a donkey; who, though he gives life to all creatures, gave himself up to be killed on a cross; who, though angels serve him, serves us; and who, though he was rich, emptied himself (*kenosis*) and made himself a poor slave.

EASTER SUNDAY

Ac 10:34, 37-43   Col 3:1-4 (or 1 Cor 5:6-8)   Jn 20:1-9
(All A, B, and C)

Hope For Those Who Have Lost It
Life over Death; Rejoice and Be Glad!; Think of What Is Above;
The Meaning of an Empty Tomb; Defying the Imagination;
The Need to Live a Risen Life; Jesus Is Lord

The happy person is the involved person. Such a one enjoys festivals of life — like birthdays, first communions, confirmations, graduations, and marriages. Such a one sees problems like poverty, racism, and hunger, and tries to solve them. But occasionally such a one is tempted to lose hope — perhaps feeling abandoned by others in the struggle for justice and misunderstood by even closest friends and relatives.

Christians see help against despair in the celebration of Easter. The resurrection of our Lord is the central mystery of our faith, our chief festival of life. It gives hope to those who've lost it. It's the day on which Jesus snatched victory from the jaws of defeat, vindicated

---

Note: Today's homily is mostly on Colossians. On John, see Cycle A; for Acts, Cycle C.

his life and teachings, and confirmed our faith. It's the most exciting event of world history. It isn't only an event that happened once in the past; it's the power of God that's seen constantly in people's inner experience of newness of life. The resurrection is a sign of God's loving interest in our world. All that we do on this day shows our joy and our hope: coloring Easter eggs, wearing nice clothes, dining together. Other Sundays are all "little Easters": They celebrate the same ideas, which are at the heart of the Christian faith.

Today's Gospel tells the story of the first Easter so beautifully that there's no need to repeat it here. From the beginning, Jesus' followers believed the scriptural accounts of Jesus' resurrection to be true. The very diversity of the Gospel stories about the resurrection precludes collusion or party line, and suggests that something very strange and unique happened in Jerusalem that first Easter. And when you consider the implausibility of the claim of Jesus' resurrection, it isn't surprising that it didn't become "big news" in Jerusalem that year. Clearly, the concept of individual resurrection was difficult even for converted Christians to comprehend.

In the few moments we have before we renew our baptismal promises, let's give some attention to a text with a new dimension of Easter, a sense of future: today's portion of St. Paul's letter to the Colossians. When Paul wrote the letter right after the middle of the first century, conditions for the Christian religion were at least as bad as anything today. Paul taught that Jesus had set us free by his death, and that Jesus alone of all creation is exalted above all creation. The fullness of the Godhead was present in Jesus. If the Colossians were going to consider "higher things" like layers of controlling spirits, Paul wants them to look even higher: all the way to the top, to Christ (v. 1). Christians are to think of what's above, not of what's on earth (v. 2). We're to live where Christ is — not only individually, but as a parish, as a community: We're a risen community, we're an Easter people, and "Alleluia!" is our song. Through baptism, we died with Christ and shared his new and risen life of the first Easter (v. 3).

How important it is for us to remember that! Early Christians stressed Jesus' resurrection and exaltation to the right hand of God, like St. Peter's speech in today's First Reading. What would have been the history of Christianity, or of the world for that matter, if Jesus had merely been put to death and not raised? He might well have gone down as a great spiritual leader like Socrates or Gandhi, but hardly the focal point for a new religion. Without the resurrection, Jesus' message about God would probably never have been preserved at all.

The conviction that Jesus' resurrection was something that really happened to a human being created a connection between the human and the divine which was unlike anything before. Both Jews and cultured Greek pagans had questions about whether the distant "God in Heaven" *really cared* about what happened to humans — or would insure justice in the world. The revolutionary idea of a real human person of flesh and blood being enthroned at the right hand of God resolved doubts about God's concern in a radical way.

And the resurrection completely changed the way people thought about *immortality*. From at least Socrates on, many philosophers had discussed the immortality of the soul. That part of the human person which had access to eternal truth, justice, and goodness must, a few argued, belong to the unchanging world of the divine, and not to the material world. But inscriptions found on ancient tombstones suggest that at the time of Jesus most people were fairly cynical about death. For the vast majority of them, death was simply the end.

For many Jews, the fact that most of their Scriptures said nothing about an individual afterlife probably carried the day. Once you had been buried, your only immortality was in the memory of your descendants and in the continuity of the people as a whole. Even Jews who expected that the righteous would be resurrected anticipated that it would come only at the *end of history*, and the period in which Jesus was executed scarcely seemed to them to be that time.

Consider the impact of Christ's resurrection on the average person. Speculation about immortality, divinization, and the afterlife had been largely the province of the educated upper classes. Rulers, philosophers, heroes — *they* might stand some chance of immortality. But Jesus was a Galilean peasant; he suffered a death reserved for the most vicious criminals. Yet the message was that he now sat at the right hand of God! Imagine the excitement at Corinth or Thessalonica when Paul came to those cities preaching that Jesus was "with God." Suddenly death needn't mean "the end," but the beginning of something new — even for the lowest slave!

Today, the real challenge for us is not only to believe in Jesus' resurrection — the facts are there — but to discover the energy that the early disciples found through their *faith* in it. While living a new life in faith is demanding, Jesus' resurrection tells Christians that in

Jesus, the one who suffered as a victim of overwhelming political and religious forces, we find God's power to save us. It evoked a powerful new symbol: the God whom we could *love* because of his crucifixion and in whom we could *hope* because of his resurrection. We have to ask ourselves the challenging question of whether we're working to forge his message of life and hope for our world. That entails involvement with the affairs of the world.

Though Paul's main emphasis throughout this passage has been on our present resurrection with Christ, he concludes with a reference to our future resurrection (v. 4). Christ will come in glory, and we with him. Thoughts about our own resurrection as well as that of Jesus give great courage. During his life, Jesus' involvement had made the crucifixion inevitable: He offended many of the upper classes like the Pharisees, he used a divine prerogative to forgive sinners, he inspired people to change, and he was a threat to the money-changers and other Temple profiteers. He raised his voice against injustice, held out hope to the oppressed, taught his followers to return love for hatred, and offered liberation even to the miserable.

In meeting the challenge of imitating that example, today gives encouragement and hope for those who've lost them. We human beings are always tempted to place our hope in someone or something other than Jesus. In the last century, people placed their hope in science: Science was going to solve all the problems of the world; instead, an amoral science gave us bigger and better wars. In the first part of this century (and to a certain extent today), people placed their hope in education; alas, our government schools have been rather godless. Political parties want us to place our hope in them and their solutions to social and economic woes; even the most partisan person must concede that politics isn't the answer. No, our hope must be based on Jesus Christ. True hope has no other real foundation.

Let's remember that our assertion of belief is supposed to be not merely an abstract intellectual consent, but a liberating and transforming experience of salvation that changes the way we live. Our faith in Jesus, if we've developed it to maturity, will lead to involvement and happiness. For all those reasons and in all those senses, we wish you a Happy Easter. As we renew our baptismal promises, let's re-examine ourselves: Do we think and live any differently because Jesus rose from death?

SECOND SUNDAY OF EASTER
Ac 4:32-35   1 Jn 5:1-6   Jn 20:19-31

Growth in Faith, Love, and Peace
Belief and Unbelief; The Spirit; Obedience; Building a Community of Love

Everybody has some kind of faith. Every year, for example, over 50 million people pass through each of the world's largest airports, having faith in disembodied voices, electronically amplified, telling them to get into cigar-shaped membranes of aluminum to be hurled by strange engines at phenomenal speeds about 35,000 feet above the earth. We passengers don't understand much of it, but are content to have faith that it will work.

Our faith in God may be equally casual. In today's Gospel, the glorified Jesus who appears in the closed room is totally different than before his resurrection, even though his wounds are evident. His greeting, "peace be with you," is more than a gesture of hospitality: It's the assurance of salvation won and given. Everybody is called upon to believe in what St. John calls, at the end of today's Gospel (v. 30), "signs." God's signs — Jesus' miracles, his words, and his public ministry — constitute part of the communication of God to people. The presentation of these is the purpose of John's Gospel, and these verses were his original conclusion.

All people are free, like Thomas in today's Gospel, to react to God's works in their own way. When Jesus had been crucified and buried, Thomas was broken-hearted: so broken-hearted, in fact, that he possibly wanted to be alone with his grief. He was like the man who said, "If I have to suffer, let me at least be like a well-bred animal, and let me go and suffer alone." This is, of course, a mistake. It's especially tragic if a Christian has to seek loneliness rather than the fellowship of a caring community. Thomas failed not only in his relationship with the risen Lord, but also in his relationship with the risen Lord's community.

Nevertheless, there's something admirable about Thomas. He had courage: When Jesus had proposed going to Bethany when the news of Lazarus's illness had come and approaching the town almost certainly meant death for Jesus, Thomas's wish had been for himself and

the other apostles to go to die with Jesus (Jn 11:16). And he was un-
compromisingly honest: He absolutely refused to say he believed what
he didn't believe. Once he was sure, he completely melted and wholeheartedly stammered, "My Lord and my God!" (v. 28). This is a sublime profession of faith, and a fitting crescendo to John's theme: John's
Gospel had begun by saying that "the Word was God" (1:1), and now
it ends by saying that John wrote in order that we may come to believe
that Jesus is the Son of God (v. 31).

So history's put-down with the phrase "doubting Thomas" is
unfair. His doubt is one of the most convincing arguments for Jesus'
resurrection; Thomas is the patron of those who have difficulties with
faith — and who hasn't? — but, as Cardinal Newman said, a thousand
difficulties don't make one doubt. Like Thomas, everybody's called
to faith. The effects of faith, like faith itself, admits of degrees. One of
its effects is love, and there's no doubt of Thomas's love for Jesus.

As John wrote the letter that is today's Second Reading, he looked
out upon the diverse backgrounds of Christians who were united at that
time: former followers of John the Baptist, Jews who had been excom-
municated from the synagogue, Jews in good standing, Samaritans
hated by the Jews, and non-Jews. John saw that a family type of love,
from which we learn all other loves, is essential: If we love God the
Father, he writes, we will also love His Son and our brother Jesus. And
from that love will flow all else: love for other people, church life, discipline, and morality.

The only proof of love is obedience (v. 3) — that is, seeking to
please the beloved and to bring the beloved joy. If we have true faith
in and love for God, his commandments aren't burdensome (v. 3).
John's letter reminds us (v. 4f.) that another effect of faith is to make
the Christian able to conquer the world. The "world" that the sacred
author means is the world apart from God, the world that we sometimes call a "vale of tears."

On the other hand, ours is a good world: a world created by the
Father, redeemed by the Son, and indwelt by the Holy Spirit; a world
graced by the presence of God-made-man. In John's view this world
can already be a foretaste of heaven. While the Christian is continually asked to perform a high-wire act, striking a balance between the
two extremes, there's no theological justification for the pucker-faced
drabness that's the hallmark of so many who call themselves Christian. On the contrary, the human being can, indeed must, love the things

of God's creation. Not to love them is an insult to their creator.

What distinguishes, or should distinguish, the Christian from unbelieving worldly people is not the degree of their relish for the good things of this world. The difference lies rather in the different importance they attach to possessions. Spiritual writers call this Christian characteristic "detachment" or "indifference" — both of them, unfortunately, words that have a bleak, negative ring. We practice detachment not because the world and the self are illusory or because love of the broken world is merely an attachment that will lead to more suffering, but because the world is only relatively good and goodness calls us to be faithful to a love affair with the absolute Good. The word "detachment" is shorthand for the very positive attitude Christians should have. In practice, it means that Christians can delight in created things without being slaves to an obsessive compulsion to possess them.

Why does faith in the resurrection have this positive result? For many reasons. Our faith gives us a defense to resist the infections of the world: infections that are shown by the world's low standards, base motives, and hateful attacks. And it gives us the indestructible hope of final victory: a victory such as that which Jesus had against a world that did its worst to him. The world hunted him, slandered him, tried him, judged him, crucified him, and buried him — but it failed to overcome him.

Today's reading from the Acts of the Apostles (sometimes called the "Gospel of the Spirit") speaks of the community established by Jesus' victory. The cultured ancient Greeks who read this passage might have been aware of the ideal form of communal sharing found in Plato's Republic, while Jews of the time who read it would hearken to Moses' foretelling of the ideal community of God (Dt 15:4). Indeed, St. Luke's description here uses the same words used to describe the ancient Hebrews as they waited at the foot of Mt. Sinai for the Law of God.

The ideal community in Luke's Acts mentions our living with one heart and one mind. The one mind means union in faith. The one heart means love. It isn't only a speculative love that's important to show faith: Today's section mentions some practical works. If we have faith, we will have a sense of responsibility for one another. We will abandon an overly possessive spirit, and we will have a real desire to share. We will develop deep personal relationships that are characteristic of true community.

We will, in short, be closer to the heavenly community pictured in Acts. That's a picture of the ideal that the Church should strive to become: one community of believers who are selfless and totally concerned for each other. Elsewhere in Acts, we know that in the early Church this didn't always happen: There were people who held out, like Ananias and Sapphira; there was squabbling between Jewish and non-Jewish Christians (which in one instance led to the martyrdom of Stephen); and there were problems about the distribution of food, which led to the appointment of the first deacons. The fact that this ideal hasn't even yet been realized shouldn't make us cynical, or discouraged, or depressed; we must constantly try to make true community happen.

In everything we do, let's try to enhance our faith's growth. Let's commit ourselves to the teachings of Christ and his Church which we're called to accept, even though, like Thomas, we weren't there when they were first formulated. If we've become jaded, let's renew our vision, rededicating ourselves to the constant attempt to make our Church and our world what they should be.

Let all of that begin with ourselves and right now, with this Mass: in the way we recite the Creed; in how we respond to the prayers; in the loving respect with which we exchange the Kiss of Peace; in our reverence at Holy Communion; in our fellowship with one another as we leave; and in our conduct as we drive out of the parking lot. Let's continue that by bringing about God's peace and love to our parish, that it may be a sign of God's love through concrete acts of loving service to the needy, the suffering, the housebound. Then let's bring our community of faith to our homes, to those individuals with whom we've had differences, and to people who are at times polarized because of painful disagreements about Church teachings. In other words, let's grow in faith and love ourselves, and then radiate them to everybody else.

THIRD SUNDAY OF EASTER
Ac 3:12-15, 17-19   1 Jn 2:1-5   Lk 24:35-48

Afterglow: Joy, Wonder, Love — and Sin
Burn with Love; Resurrection as Vindication; Realization,
Responsibility, and Repentance; Jesus at our Side

Familiarity, whether or not it breeds contempt, lessens wonder. When radios first came into use, people delighted in sitting by them and letting their imaginations roam. When television came, taverns were almost the only purchasers of the then-expensive new gadgets, and their customers got excited over sports events. The same initial excitement is true of the first airplanes, computers, and other wonderful inventions. Now we take all of them for granted.

It's like that with Jesus' resurrection. Why is it that so often Lent, the sorrowful season, is observed for 40 days while in popular practice Easter, the season of joy, is celebrated for only one day when the Church officially celebrates it for 50? The self-discipline, fasting, and confessions of Lent are supposed to lead to the special joy, thanksgiving, and celebration of the Easter season.

The early Christians considered Eastertide the most important time in the calendar. Officially, the Church still does. From the earliest centuries of Christianity through the recent past, it was the custom of many Christian churches to have parties, picnics, and feasts to celebrate the resurrection of Jesus.

Perhaps the reason for the ho-hum attitude is the lack of images to shape and motivate contemplation of the resurrection. Much of the artwork and symbols of churches have focused on Jesus' passion and crucifixion. Artists have tended to shy away from depicting the resurrection — and the few who have attempted it haven't captured its dazzling beauty, glory, joy, and humor.

When the resurrection first took place, there were all kinds of excitement. Consider, for example, the two disciples who experienced the risen Jesus on the road to Emmaus. They met the risen Lord, as do we all, in many ways. They met him through hospitality, which developed into the early Christian monks' motto, *venit hospes, venit Christus* — when a guest comes, Christ comes. They met him by way of the

Sacred Scriptures, which he explained to them. And, preëminently, they met him in the breaking of the bread that is the Eucharist.

It's understandable that at first they were startled. Then they were carried away by joy, a proper consequence of meeting Jesus; if joy is absent, there's something amiss: A joyless Christian is a contradiction in terms. Finally, they didn't even finish their meal in order to spread the good news to the apostles in Jerusalem.

There they found the eleven and a few companions all so strongly emotional that, before they had time to speak, the apostles insisted upon explaining their own experiences. The poor disciples from Emmaus! When they finally got their turn to talk, Jesus came and showed his glorified body. All in the room reacted just as we would: They were in a panic. Their age was no more disposed to believe in miracles than our own. From the sublime heights to which they had relegated God in all His majesty, they didn't mentally allow Him to deal with things mundane except to keep the world in its regular course.

Even when they began to come around, they were still incredulous for sheer joy (v. 41). It was simply too good to be true! So Jesus had them touch him and see the marks of the nails in his hands and feet (v. 39), to show that he was the same person who had died and risen. He then ate in their presence — not to show that he was restored to the normal life of growth and decline, but to prove even further the reality of his resurrection: that he was no ghost, or phantom, or figment of anyone's imagination. He showed that the Jewish Scriptures had foretold three things of the Messiah: He would suffer and die, he would rise again, and repentance would be preached to the whole world in his name. Lastly, Jesus enjoined them to preach the Gospel to all the nations, beginning from Jerusalem (v. 47).

Jerusalem was the capital city of the old theocracy, the site of the Temple of God, the religious center of the Jewish people, the place from which the prophets had foretold would issue the glad tidings of the new dispensation — and the city over which Jesus had wept when it failed to recognize his appearance as the time of God's visitation (Lk 19:44). Throughout the Gospel of St. Luke, Jesus journeys to Jerusalem. Now at the end of Luke's Gospel, the word of God is to go from Jerusalem to the ends of the earth, to the point where today about two billion people (out of earth's total population of almost six billion) profess faith in Jesus.

An example of the beginning of that process is the sermon in today's First Reading. It followed Peter's healing of a lame man; in the Bible, lameness is a symbol of sin, and Peter tells the people that they must turn away from their sins to be healed by the one whom God has raised from the dead. Peter shows the faith community's love and respect for Jesus by using great titles to describe him: "the Holy One," "the Just One," "the Prince of Life," "the Christ." He's showing that Jesus is the Son of the same God who was the God of Abraham, Isaac, and Jacob.

Peter places Jesus' death and resurrection within the larger framework of the Jewish tradition: Jesus as the first-born from the dead, the innocent sufferer who is the sole source of the salvation of all the world. The second section of the sermon (vv. 17-19) deals with an item of wonderment to the Jews, and remains so to us: an explanation of why Jesus suffered — the Scriptures had foretold it, said Peter. This would answer objections from the Jews who were expecting a victorious Messiah, a leader of the nation.

Being lost in joy and love and wonder at it all led some people to wrong-headed ideas, like thinking of themselves as incapable of sin and far removed from its consequences. It's the same today: "The more things change, the more they remain the same." So, to keep everybody's feet on the ground, today's Second Reading tells us the truth about Jesus and ourselves. The author of this "First Letter of John," if he was St. John the Apostle, was now at a ripe old age, which warranted his use of the address "little ones" or "children": Far from being patronizing, he's writing with the wisdom of age. He tells us that only Jesus, and not a snobbish elite few, can be the cause of sinlessness.

Of sin, the sacred author says that nobody escapes it. At the same time, however, there's forgiveness. In the midst of the realities of sin and human failure, Jesus is an advocate or intercessor (v. 1), a great word which the New Testament uses often of Jesus. It's a word that means many things: a comforter, a witness in one's favor, a supporter of one's cause, someone called to another's side. The idea has been beautifully summarized as "one who lends his presence to his friends." And Jesus has chosen to befriend sinners through the Sacrament of Reconciliation, which is a personal encounter with him.

Another phrase the sacred author applied to Jesus was easier for a Jew to understand than for us: that he was an offering for our sins (v. 2). *The* great aim of religion — all religion — is union with God: to enter into His presence with joy. So the supreme problem of all reli-

gion is that which interferes with union and joy: sin. Religion therefore offers offerings to God for sins. Morning and night, the Jews offered sin-offerings in the Temple. Their idea was to propitiate God, to
ask His forgiveness, and to show a people performing a ritual by which
the taint of guilt is removed. In God's second covenant with the human race, Jesus did this work for the whole world.

The section's last consideration is the heretics' claim that all that's
important is "to know God" (vv. 3-5). Now there are several ways of
thinking we can know God. One is by sheer intellectual *reasoning*. This
way makes the search for God rather like such other higher thought
processes as mathematics or metaphysics. Another way is the search
for God as an *emotional experience*. In the so-called "mystery religions"
of New Testament times, which were as popular as some cults today,
there were emotional orgies in which people worked themselves up to
a fever pitch.

A third way of trying to know God was the Jewish way, which is
the Christian way, too. This way said that intimate knowledge of God
comes from *revelation* from God Himself more than by people's intellectual speculation or having exotic emotional experiences; it does,
however, embrace warmth and love.

But none of these ways necessarily results in *goodness*, and John's
letter assures us that anyone who says "I know God" and doesn't keep
His commandments is a liar. Our sacred author courageously reminds
one and all that because God is holy, His worshipers have an obligation to be holy too. We don't neglect intellectual effort and emotional
experience, but true union with God must prove itself by issuing forth
in moral action. On the other hand, it's not true that the Christian life
means almost solely the living out of moral precepts.

Christian life is bigger than that, and today's readings show us
how it really goes. Christian faith is first and foremost a response of
belief to the person of the risen Christ, as in today's Gospel. This belief embraces the realization that Jesus has won salvation for us by the
sacrifice of the cross, as in Peter's sermon. And, as the letter of John
reminds us, Jesus remains our advocate when we encounter the harsh
reality of sin in our lives. Then, in our pilgrimage of faith the action of
the Holy Spirit in our lives calls for a never-ending conversion of our
innermost selves. We can help the process by keeping always the fresh-
ness of the joy and wonder of the first Easter.

FOURTH SUNDAY OF EASTER
Ac 4:8-12   1 Jn 3:1f.   Jn 10:11-18

Developing Christian Identity through Opposition
Imitation of Christ and Peter in the Joy of the Resurrection;
Following the Good Shepherd; Being God's Children

Many words have similar meanings but a world of difference in over-tones and images. Take, for example, the words "cemetery" and "grave-yard." "Cemetery" signifies simply a burial ground; "graveyard" con-notes in addition a place for ghosts and goblins and all kinds of fright-ful things. Or the words "maternity" and "motherhood." Maternity means simply that a woman has been pregnant. She may then wear maternity dresses; no one ever sees "motherhood" dresses. Motherhood is ongoing, and means not just the generative act but also a woman's close, caring, and loving relationship with her children.

Or consider the word-images from a child's list of "My Loveli-est Things, People Not Counted." Among them were the scrunch of dry leaves as you walk through them; the feel of clean clothes; the cold of ice cream; cool wind on a hot day; climbing up and looking back; and babies smiling. Or a woman's list of the most delicious scents: mint sauce, newly split wood, ripe apples, tea just opened, coffee just ground, a dairy farm, a circus, flowers. Or a man's list of connotations from a loaf of bread: seed flung into brown earth, rains that refresh the sprout-ing grain, golden seed heads, winds that bend them in successive waves across a field, men harvesting, mothers baking homey loaves on Sat-urday morning, and hungry boys and girls filing into the kitchen to ask for some.

The images of today's biblical message are two. Both demand our detailed attention. First, St. John tells us in his letter that we're children of God. All human beings can, of course, call themselves in some way children of God: whether believer or non-believer, bad or good. But we who are baptized are children of God in a more intimate and loving sense. If we who try to be good Christians want to be God's children in the sense that God intended, we begin with the realization that we're brothers and sisters of one another through the fatherhood of God and the elder brotherhood of Jesus Christ.

That dignity means that we have duties. The unity of all people, for example, is possible only by our being children together under the fatherhood of God. If we seek a unity of black people and white and yellow and red, of rich and poor, of employers and employees, and of nation and nation, all of that can come in a meaningful and lasting way only if we, God's children, recognize God's fatherhood.

Today's second highly expressive picture is from St. John's Gospel, and is one of the most beautiful images in the Bible: Jesus as the Good Shepherd. Visualizations of shepherds and sheep are relatively unfamiliar to today's city cultures. City people's knowledge of *shepherds* is probably limited to stained glass windows with lambs as white as new-fallen snow, or the shepherd's staff carried by bishops at official ceremonies, which would scarcely frighten even the most timid wolf or mountain lion away from the sheep. Children's knowledge of *sheep* is probably limited to the tune of "Mary Had a Little Lamb." None of it is tainted by sweat, mud clinging to wool, or sheep manure.

Even the image of "good" in the phrase "Good Shepherd" has more than one meaning. The Greek language in which St. John tells us that story has two words for good. One is *agathos*, which simply means "morally good." The second — the word John used here — is *kalos*; this adds to the idea of moral goodness a physical beauty. Jesus as Good Shepherd contains the notion of one who is both noble and lovely. At one and the same time he's a strong leader and a gentle companion — strong enough to give his life for our wretched human race, with a gentleness that mustn't be over-emphasized to the point of sentimentality.

The contrasts between good and bad shepherds in the agricultural country in which Our Lord told that story go back hundreds of years before him to prophets like Ezekiel, from whom the imagery came. Ezekiel had reminded the king-shepherds of Israel in his time that they had harshly and brutally fattened themselves instead of their sheep, fed off the sheep's milk, worn their wool, but hadn't strengthened the weak, healed the sick, bound up the injured, brought back the strayed, or sought the lost (Ezk 34:1-6). But there were always also concerned shepherds whose sheep knew them and who knew their sheep. Though "to know" for us emphasizes intellectual content, its biblical usage emphasizes love and care. *The* good shepherd who loves and cares for his sheep is, of course, Jesus.

Within John's differentiation between good and bad shepherds are descriptions that provide vivid contrasts: thieves and bandits over and against the gatekeeper, the voices of strangers versus the voice of the shepherd, the uncaring hired hand versus the loving shepherd who will lay down his life. This last is a new dimension in scriptural descriptions of shepherds.

One of the most significant aspects of this story is what Jesus says in the last verses of today's Gospel. He indicates that he doesn't just *surrender* his life for his sheep: He *lays it down*. Out of love, he gives us his life *willingly* — and he said at the Last Supper that no one has greater love than to lay down one's life for one's friends. He did this not when we were redeemed and had aspects of lovability, but when we weren't redeemed or lovable. Of that kind of love, a wise man (Teilhard de Chardin) once said: "The day will come when, after harnessing space, the winds, the tides and gravitation, we shall harness for God the energies of love. And on that day, for the second time in the history of the world, we shall have discovered fire."

As shown by today's reading from the Acts of the Apostles, Jesus' willingness to lay down his life was communicated to the apostles. It's a sermon on Jesus by St. Peter. Peter was initially a blustering, imprudent, spontaneous, but generous human being, who was willing to make all kinds of promises that he was unable to keep.

This same Peter, after the resurrection and the coming of the Holy Spirit on Pentecost, grew in faith and courage. Just as Jesus' sermon on the Good Shepherd had taken place after a miracle of healing, Peter's sermon followed upon Peter and John's cure of a crippled beggar in Jesus' name. In today's reading this unpretentious fisherman was able to stand up to the wealthiest and most powerful body in the land: the dreaded Sanhedrin. They consisted of the elders of the people, scribes, Pharisees, Sadducees, and representatives of the priestly families. Although Caiaphas had had the Sanhedrin removed from the Temple Mount to weaken its power, this group had power over life and death, and had exercised it in handing Jesus over and persuading Pilate to execute him by the barbaric cruelty of crucifixion. Peter hadn't forgotten that.

To the Sanhedrin, the preaching of Peter and the other apostles was doubly serious: The Sanhedrin considered the apostles heretics and potential disturbers of the peace. Being disturbers of the peace was as serious as being heretics: Palestine was flammable, and the apostles could cause a popular uprising, which would bring about Rome's intervention and the potential loss of the Sanhedrin's prestige. In the face of that powerful opposition, Peter — and the other apostles — showed not only courage, but greatness. They had grown into men of principle: Their one overriding thought was that God must come first. And they had a clear idea of their duty: to be witnesses for Christ.

So Peter now stood before the Sanhedrin, as Jesus had done, more like their judge than their victim. The Sanhedrin thought that Jesus' death had proven that he couldn't be the Messiah because he had died and their tradition taught that the Messiah couldn't die or be defeated. Peter's message was essentially the same as today's Gospel and Responsorial Psalm: the stone which the builders — the Sanhedrin and other leaders — had rejected had become the cornerstone of a whole new edifice of salvation.

Today's two images, of our being children of God and of Jesus as the Good Shepherd, picturesquely teach us God's love and care. They also suggest some corresponding attributes which the followers of Jesus should have: compassion, insight, care, fidelity, recognition, and love. As sheep of the noble shepherd, we should follow him trustingly, all the way. As having been made children of God in a special sense through our baptism, we should recognize our new dignity by growing, as did Peter and the apostles, into being willing to lay down our lives — meaning, in our case, to empty ourselves — in order to cultivate a meaningful, loving, personal relationship with Jesus.

FIFTH SUNDAY OF EASTER
Ac 9:26-31   1 Jn 3:18-24   Jn 15:1-8

Interior Life and Growth
Our Dependence of God and People; The Church as a Community;
The Church Is Alive with the Life of Christ

The art of the motion picture has made the world familiar with the director's command, "Lights... Camera... Action!" This seems to strike a responsive chord in the psyche of United States citizens. From the time that our ancestors colonized the United States, cleared the forests, moved West, built shelters, and started industries, we've especially loved action.

But action of itself may go nowhere meaningful. It needs direction. Before our frontier people did what they did, they had to think out purposes and goals. We can't have action for action's sake, or we'll be going around in nonproductive circles. Suppose you wanted to arrive at a specific location in central Chicago. A street map of the city would be a great help to you in reaching your destination. But suppose that through a printing error your map labeled "Chicago" was actually a map of Detroit. Can you imagine the frustration, the ineffectiveness of trying to reach your destination?

Even when we watch the growth of our children, if all we see is quantitative physical growth, we're cheating ourselves and them of an emphasis on the most important kind of growth: the spiritual. Pascal said that the trouble with people of the Western world is that they don't know how to be content in an empty room.

To describe spiritual growth, in today's Gospel Our Lord uses a figure that was familiar to the Jews — the figure of the vine and the branches. Over and over the Jewish Scriptures pictured Israel as the vineyard of God, the Jews as branches of God's vine. The coins of the Maccabees had the symbol of the vine, and the Temple had a great golden vine carved into the front of its Holy Place. Jesus speaks of himself as the *true* vine — bearing sweet grapes — with us as his branches. We receive our spiritual life from our connection with him. He gives us the injunction to live on in him. That's good advice, because of ourselves we're as spiritually worthless as the cut-off branch of a vine, which is just about the most worthless of all wood.

It's especially good advice for those who've been successful in their actions: Some experts say that for every hundred people who can handle adversity, there's only one who can handle success. Lest we become proud, to bear abundant fruit we need pruning and trimming to be cut down to size. Only the humble can bear fruit in Christ. Jesus' secret was his contact with God; ours is contact with God through Jesus. This means dependence. We're dependent upon God for everything, right up to life itself.

Some people don't like to admit dependency. But we're dependent on many things as well as on God. The average person might awaken in a bed built on a pattern which originated in the Near East, to a clock, a medieval European invention. He slips into soft moccasins invented by American Indians. He showers with soap invented by the ancient Gauls, and dries himself on a Turkish towel. Returning to the bedroom, he dons garments derived from the clothing of nomads of the Asiatic steppes and in ancient Egypt.

At his breakfast table, he has pottery invented in China; his knife is made of an alloy first produced in southern India; his fork is a medieval Italian invention, his spoon a derivative of a Roman original. His food originated in discoveries from all over the world. He reads the news of the day imprinted in characters invented by the ancient Semites by a process invented in Germany upon a material invented in China. Some time during the day he may thank a Hebrew God in an Indo-European language that he's one-hundred-percent American.

Even some people who acknowledge their dependence on other people sometimes don't sustain a sense of dependence on God. That's one of the reasons why our world is in the mess that it's in. To sustain a sense of dependence on God — that is, to be true branches — requires work. Branches have to be pruned back and cared for, and the soil has to be prepared. If our spiritual life is to bear fruit, we have to work at enriching our souls by reading, thinking, praying, good conversation, and the like, and bringing glory to God. There's no higher or more ultimate purpose to life than that.

Only after cultivating our interior life and growth is proper action possible. What is proper action? Sometimes it may seem like inaction: As Milton said in his Sonnet on his Blindness, "They also serve who only stand and wait." People are wont to ask how much a person has *done*. They say little about the *virtue* he's cultivated: how poor in spirit he or she is, how patient, how devout.

Today's reading from St. John's first letter tells us more. In today's last verses, John speaks of two actions which are very pleasing in God's sight. One is the contemplative part of it: that we believe in Jesus Christ and all that he stands for. The second is the active part: that we love one another as Jesus loved — that is, with a love that's completely generous, real, and active. We're to love in deed and in truth, and not merely talk about it. It's not simply hatred which is opposed to the law of love, but also indifference. This means loving our neighbor in God — under His fatherhood — and taking care of our neighbor's needs. That means we're to spread love everywhere we go.

A college professor had his sociology class go into the Baltimore slums to get case histories of 200 young boys. They were asked to write an evaluation of each boy's future. In every case, the students wrote, "He doesn't have a chance." Twenty-five years later another sociology professor came across the earlier study. He had his students follow up on the project to see what had happened to these boys. With the exception of 20 boys who had moved away or died, the students learned that 176 of the remaining 180 had achieved more than ordinary success as lawyers, doctors, and businessmen.

The astounded professor decided to pursue the matter further. Fortunately, all the men were in the area, and he was able to ask each, "How do you account for your success?" In each case the reply came with feeling, "There was a teacher."

The teacher was still alive, so he sought her out and asked the old but still alert lady what magic formula she had used. Her eyes sparkled and her lips broke into a gentle smile. "It's really very simple," she said. "I loved those boys."

Today's reading from the Acts of the Apostles provides another example of a good combination of contemplation and action. It was a scene that must have been full of strong human emotions. It introduces us to St. Barnabas, whose job was to receive St. Paul in Jerusalem — Paul who had been Saul, the fiery persecutor of Christians, understandably not trusted either by the group he had persecuted, despite his conversion, or by his former coreligionists. Barnabas' interior life had grown sufficiently, however, that he believed the best of others and never held people's past against them. So he received Paul. After Barnabas' courage and commitment, when the brethren learned that the Hellenists were out to kill Paul they escorted him from Jerusalem to Caesarea, a considerable distance, and at some inconvenience to themselves saw him off to Tarsus.

After his conversion, Paul had grown, silently, slowly, and unnoticed — like a branch of the true vine, as it was with Barnabas and as it is with us. Paul's attachment to the vine was sincere, and therefore his growth was real. So he was able to use the same fiery nature he had had before, but now to preach the Gospel boldly and give witness to Jesus. That Paul found it necessary to return to Jerusalem shows the importance of legitimately depending on the Christian community. Christian living is never solely an independent individual venture.

An independent individual venture? Think of it! We're proud of the progress our time has seemed to make over the past. But are we essentially different from a Cro-Magnon person, who lived in the Pleistocene era some 30,000 years before the dawn of civilization? The truth is that a Cro-Magnon reared today would be virtually indistinguishable physically and mentally from the rest of us. If we were the last persons on the planet, would we be able to make electricity? Stripped naked, could we make cloth? Left alone to record civilization, could we re-invent a piece of paper?

We're products of the most advanced society in the history of the planet. And yet we don't have the basic knowledge or skills that kept primitive people from extinction. Let's recognize our dependence on others — friends, community, parish — but especially on God, and the importance of our interior life and growth. It's only after we've acknowledged our dependence and figured out where we want to go that we can wind up going in the right direction. Only the director who has something purposive in mind can call "Lights... Camera... Action!"

SIXTH SUNDAY OF EASTER
Ac 10:25f., 34f., 44-48   1 Jn 4:7-10   Jn 15:9-17

Expressing the Love We Celebrate
Practicing the Faith We Profess; Joy, an Offspring of Love;
Famous Last Words; The New Commandment and Bond of Love;
God Is Love!; Love One Another

Last words often shed light into lives. Thus, the last words of General Robert E. Lee were appropriate to his life. He said, "Let the tent be struck!" More enlightening, and often humorous, are epitaphs. A be-liever once designed an epitaph to a non-believing friend that read, "Here Lies an Atheist: All Dressed Up and No Place to Go." Provid-ing even more insight are epitaphs people write for themselves. Rob-ert Frost once wrote:

> I would have written of me on my stone:
> I had a lover's quarrel with the world.

St. John's Gospel devotes over four of its twenty-one chapters to the last words of Jesus. Like other last words, they reflect the life and personality of the speaker. Jesus' farewell discourse is patterned upon that of the great Jewish leader Moses. Unlike most other last words, those of Moses and Jesus look to the future. Moses's last words stressed the importance of the commandments, and Jesus' last words alluded to his new commandment: love.

Today's Gospel passage follows right after and develops last Sunday's Gospel on the vine and the branches. It gives the way in which the branches can receive life from the vine and in which the branches can remain alive, grow, and be fruitful: that is, to remain in Jesus' love (v. 10). This we can do by keeping his commandments, just as he has kept his Father's commandments. The result of following his advice will be joy (v. 11). That, too, is new: It's *his* unique joy that will come our way, more fulfilling than any other and with a new completeness.

Jesus' unique command is that we love one another as he has loved us (v. 12). He knew he had to remind us of this, because sometimes we act as though we're made for competition rather than love. Jesus has given us the example of a love greater than any other: He laid down his life for us (v. 13). He calls all of us for whom he died *friends* (v. 14). Many people who kept on the straight and narrow through terrible temptations and were asked about how they did it, answered, "I had a friend." "How did you overcome alcoholism?" "I had a friend." "How did you stand losing your job?" "I had a friend." "How did you survive your loss?" "I had a friend." It's been said that even in paradise it's not good to be alone.

"Don't bug me! Hug me!" says the bumper sticker. One man who believes this strongly went around giving hugs to all sorts of people. Challenged to come to a home for the disabled, he hugged people who were terminally ill, severely retarded, or quadriplegic. Finally, he came to the last person, Leonard, who was wearing a big white bib, on which he was drooling. Overcoming his initial reluctance, the man took a deep breath, leaned down, and gave Leonard a hug. All of a sudden Leonard began to squeal, "Eeehh! Eeeeehh!" Some of the other patients in the room began to clang things together. The man turned to the staff — physicians, nurses, orderlies — for some sort of explanation, only to find that every one of them was crying. To his inquiry, "What's going on?" the head nurse said, "This is the first time in 23 years we've ever seen Leonard smile."

The relationship of love, intimacy, and trust involved in friendship enabled Jesus to commission the apostles to witness to him to the ends of the earth. Today's reading from the Acts of the Apostles records a giant step in the fulfillment of that command and of Jesus' command to love. The story of the centurion Cornelius isn't just another conversion story. It's the conclusion of one of the first dilemmas facing the early Church: whether a pagan could become a Christian without first accepting Judaism.

The first Christians were, after all, all Jewish. Jesus himself had been brought up in the Jewish religion, and the earliest believers, the apostles included, were converts from Judaism. The Jewish understanding was that God gave His privileges to them alone, and other nations were outside that pale. No Jew would, for example, have a Gentile as a house guest, or be the house guest of a Gentile. The prejudices of our time are no less strong: whites against blacks, blacks against whites, Christians against Jews, and others down the line.

Despite that background, St. Peter entered the house of Cornelius (v. 25). A man who was devoted to God and gave alms to the poor, to the Jews Cornelius was nevertheless a pagan Gentile. Peter saw in a vision that it was God's will that the Gospel, despite its Jewish origin, now be spread to everyone, of whatever nationality or culture — a realization that changed history. Cornelius met Peter, fell on his knees at his feet, and bowed low — an approach not without possible superstition, because in those times these actions could imply that the person honored was either a god or an angel.

Peter, duly embarrassed, helped Cornelius to his feet and reminded him that he, Peter, was only a man himself (v. 26). Peter then became the first to accept a non-Jew for baptism — a revolutionary step in the life of the Church, for it was an acknowledgment that blood, ethnic origin, being one of the so-called "beautiful people," or other extrinsic traits, mean nothing.

Thereupon Peter proceeded to give his last great discourse in Acts, of which today's reading contains only the introduction (vv. 34f.). The result of Peter's message was that the Holy Spirit, the moving force behind all of the Acts of the Apostles, took over (v. 44). The Jewish Christians were surprised (v. 45), the audience spoke in tongues (v. 46), and many were baptized (v. 47). Baptism in water is the sign which marks entry into the Christian community, but it points to another equally profound baptism — baptism in the Spirit, which all true Christians receive as a gift of God when they're open to His word. So the new Gentile Christians asked Peter to stay for a few days (v. 48), because they wanted more instruction. Duties to membership in the Church don't end, but only begin, with joining: We must be constantly learning.

Jesus' injunction to love and the apostles' inspiration to bring Jesus to the whole world didn't end in that age. The First Letter of John tells Christians of all times and places that the heart of Christianity isn't knowing inner secrets, or understanding science and technology. That doesn't seem to have contributed to a better world. No, the essence of Christianity is love's self-forgetfulness and total dedication. If we spent as much time and energy trying to love as we spend on technology, the world would be a much better place. John tells us that love has its origin in God (v. 7). In fact, the person without love doesn't know God (v. 8). Paradoxically, it's only by knowing God that we can truly love, and it's only by loving that we can come to know God (or anyone else).

Then John makes one of the greatest statements about God in the whole Bible: "God is love." This is the one and only place that this amazing statement is made in the whole of the New Testament. That statement, though not a complete definition of God, is a beautiful description of Him with relation to human beings. It answers many questions.

It explains creation: Why did God create our world, many aspects of which we've caused to wind up in a mess? If we found the complete answer to the question of why it is that we and the universe exist, it would be the ultimate triumph — for then we would know the mind of God. But we do have insights into an answer.

It's because God is love.

It helps us to understand free will: God who gave us this most precious faculty doesn't take it away, even when we use it against Him.

God is love.

It gives an appreciation of divine providence: Had God been only intelligence or law and order, He would have created the world and left it to its own laws and devices.

But God is love.

It helps understand redemption: Had God been only justice, He might have left the human race in its sin.

But God is love.

And it puts into perspective the world beyond the grave: Had God been simply creator with a lesser love, He might have left people to die and remain dead forever.

But God is love!

The chief way God revealed His love to us, though, is not by having brought about creation, or giving us free will, or establishing His providence over us, or accomplishing our redemption, or providing a world beyond the grave — but by sending His only Son into the world (v. 9). And He did that in order that through His Son we might have life. His coming made more possible a differentiation between full life and mere existence. All our love-life originates with Him. He has given His love freely. His sending His Son was an act of mercy and forgiveness, shown finally through His Son's death (v. 10).

God is love!

Because God is love, love should characterize God's human family. God's love is the why and the how of our love for one another. It's love that gives wings to our freedom. To enrich the lives of our relatives and friends as well as our own, we as children of the Father must express His kind of love: a love that is serving, seeking the welfare of others, and being a channel of God's grace in the world. To express our love isn't something that should wait for our tombstone. It's our mission in life, an action which should take the initiative toward all others. Let's ask God to help us to express in our lives the love we celebrate.

SOLEMNITY OF THE ASCENSION
Ac 1:1-11   Eph 1:17-23   Mk 16:15-20

Mission Accomplished
The Signs of Jesus' Followers; Christ Beyond Our Sight;
Making God's Kingdom a Reality; Preparing for Heaven;
Religion: Pie in the Sky When You Die?

We in the United States call an instrument that carries someone or something upward an elevator. In some countries, the word for elevator is similar to the word we use to celebrate today's feast: In French, for

Note: This homily is mostly on Ephesians. For mostly Matthew on the Ascension, see
      Cycle A; for an amalgam of readings including Luke 24, Cycle C.

example, the word is *l'ascenseur* and in Italian *l'ascensore*. All suggest an upward movement that's gradual and steady, like a balloon rising. That's the connotation of Jesus' ascension. This took place after he had been with his disciples after his resurrection, teaching the final things that had to be taught and doing the things that had to be done before he left earth in his bodily form.

St. Mark gives the essence of it in today's Gospel by writing that the Lord Jesus was taken up into heaven and took his seat at the right hand of God (v. 19). This doesn't mean simply that the risen Lord had not, until then, gone to the Father. Nor does it mean that Jesus was taken up into heaven elevator-like. We must realize that heaven is at the bottom level (nadir) quite as much as at the top (zenith). The movement isn't from the ground up into the clouds, but from the human place to the divine place.

In human words Jesus is said to be at God's right hand as a figurative expression to indicate a divine place that reveals Jesus' status as Christ (Messiah) and Lord. He's seated rather than kneeling or standing at the right hand of the Father because sitting was then considered a position of power and authority. These expressions symbolize Jesus' close relationship to God and his role as God's agent. That's truly "Gospel," or "Good News." It's "news," because it represents something that is completely unheard-of: The disaster of death has been turned into the triumph of life. It's "good," because it concerns not only Jesus, but all those who hear it: They, too, are destined for life.

All together this "Good News" is cosmic: Jesus' life, death, resurrection, and ascension affect not only human beings, but the whole universe. And through his ascension Jesus ceases to be present in his Church in one way in order to be present in another — a way that's more profound and intimate. He's with us when we gather, two or three, in his name. He's with us in the proclamation of his word and in the sharing of bread and wine. He's with us in saving those who approach the heavenly Father through him.

Today's section of the letter to the Ephesians is a prayer that its readers receive full spiritual understanding of this and other mysteries. As he approaches his subject, the author (perhaps St. Paul, perhaps another who knew the development of Paul's theology) prays for a church he loves.

The church at Ephesus was surprisingly like the Church in many parts of the world today: possessed of prosperity, skepticism, hardness,

deprivation, and self-indulgence. Ephesus was the capital of the Roman province of Asia. Croesus, the rich king of the Lydians, had ruled
there, and so did Cyrus of the Persians and then Alexander the Great.
It had been a major Greek settlement with a temple to Artemis, or Diana,
four times larger than the Parthenon in Athens — one of the seven
wonders of the ancient world.

Many museums have images of Diana (Artemis), but Ephesus
was her headquarters, and the museum there shows her as the goddess
with the confounding attribute of row on row of multiple breasts. Obviously connected to fertility, this particular goddess was the ruler of
everything and the mother goddess, despite the fact that one of Diana's
chief attributes was her permanent virginity.

Her cult spread as far as Marseilles, and over the centuries she
hasn't lost her power to fascinate. From the Renaissance on, artists have
depicted her: Raphael painted her in the Vatican, Cellini put her on the
base of his Perseus, Hogarth made a merry picture of putti drawing her
statue, and Tiepolo tucked a representation of her into one of his pictures.

At least by the first century A.D., travelers who journeyed to
Ephesus could buy little silver goddesses and little silver replicas of
her temple. St. Paul nearly ruined this trade, and it almost cost him his
life. Living and preaching in Ephesus for a time, he insisted that there
were no gods made by human hands. This message convinced so many
people that the business of a silversmith named Demetrius, who spe-
cialized in images for pilgrims, began to fall off. So Demetrius called
a meeting of skilled artisans and craftsmen and created an uproar; they
spent two whole hours in the outdoor theater yelling, "Great is Artemis
of the Ephesians!" Paul had to leave town.

A New Yorker walking through the streets of Ephesus today (less
than an hour south of Izmir in Turkey), past its remnants of libraries,
temples, brothels, and public privies, past its theaters and heroic statues, has no trouble relating to its lapsed pride and grandeur. Obviously,
if you could have made it there you could have made it anywhere. Next
to Ephesus almost every place else was Podunk.

(So what happened? Where did all the Ephesians go? Ephesus
wasn't destroyed by earthquake or devastated by epidemic. It turned
out that the Menderes River, on whose port Ephesus depended for its
commerce, cut itself a new channel, leaving the city's port high and
dry. Cut off from the sea, the population gradually left.)

Paul prays first for what we often forget these days: a spirit of wisdom and discernment to know God clearly (v. 17). Wisdom is more than mere factual material, superficial data-basing, information, or intellectual knowledge: It's insight into eternal truths. A gift implanted in the deepest core of our being, wisdom is a revelation of a God in love with his creation; it's what enables us to have a deep personal appreciation of God's love of humanity.

Those qualities will help us to know Jesus clearly. To "know" doesn't mean just a conceptual knowledge of facts, like the facts of Jesus' life. It's an experience of God's great love in Christ for people. It can be shown visibly in a true brotherhood of people divided by social and racial barriers. To know in this way is essential: A friendship which doesn't grow over the years vanishes over the years. This enlightenment of our vision enables us also to come to realize the hope that belongs to his call and the wealth of his glorious heritage (v. 18).

Our age is a time of pessimism and despair. Look, for example, at that group in society that's always supposed to be hopeful: youth. They have so many depressing possibilities for their future hanging over them which, without specific attention to Jesus as their "great hope," can justify pessimism. If the Christian message is true, our worldview should be optimistic. If the Christian message is false, what are we doing in church?

To have this wisdom will provide, for those who believe, a knowledge of the surpassing greatness of Jesus' power (v. 19), which can overcome humanly impossible obstacles. Thus Jesus' resurrection and ascension overcame the sins that put him to death (v. 20). The resurrection and ascension and glorification of Jesus, taken as one great continuous act of the Father, is, to Paul, the supreme proof of the power of God. That power brought into stark relief the contrasts between the despair and darkness before that great event and the hope and light after it.

When he was visibly present on earth, Jesus was limited by time and space. By his ascension, Jesus is no longer limited to the dimensions of earth. Jesus' enthronement signifies that Jesus in his humanity has now reached a position of equality and association with the Father where all God's power can act through him. All of this accomplishes also a continued action shared by the people who make up the Church, united to its head. All God's power is made available to people in Christ. The heavenly realm and all its power have been brought to earth for the believer.

That Jesus ascended far above every principality, authority, power, and dominion (v. 21) may not be as meaningful to us as it was to the people at Ephesus, who believed in many grades of angels, some good and some bad, having control over human destiny. The author's point is that Christ is over all powers. The Father has, in fact, put all things beneath Jesus' feet (v. 22). As the first Adam had the glory of being ruler over creation, Christ, the new Adam, has a glory that extends much beyond that.

In Christ as head of the Church can be found the solution to the disunity of the world. It was to make one family out of people that Christ died. The Church is his mystical body. As with the human body, the head without the body or the body without the head isn't complete. Both constitute an organic unity. Christ has chosen the Church as his instrument for us. The Church is the fullness of Jesus (v. 23): Just as Jesus is the fullness of the Father, so the Church is the fullness of Jesus. Everything that makes God God abides in Christ Jesus! And everything that makes Jesus Jesus abides in the Church!

So in no way does the Feast of the Ascension suggest that "God's in His heaven and all's right with the world." Nor do any other clichès fit: "Out of sight, out of mind," for example, or "Absence makes the heart grow fonder." Jesus isn't out of sight or out of mind, and it's not his absence but his profound presence that makes our hearts grow fonder.

Nor is the "three stories" theological geography true, in which heaven is "up," hell is "down," and we're at present in between. The scene of the ascension doesn't mean that Jesus "went up," but that the Lord has been taken into the Father's glory. Why the picture of "up" and "down"? Well, we humans have always given greater dignity to "up" than "down." Even in modern motion picture technique, the "good guys" are photographed from below, looking up, and the "bad guys" from up, looking down.

Jesus' ascension doesn't mean that he has departed from us. He has gone from our sight in order that he may more perfectly come to us. Jesus' ascension is to show us who we are, where we're going, and what we must do now. Both heaven and hell are all around us, and God's plan is that Jesus fill "all things in every way." God's plan for the world will, however, be brought about only bit by bit, and is in the hands of the Church. That means you and me. Because of Jesus' Passover — his death, resurrection, and ascension — we can no longer look at ourselves as mere earthlings: We must realize our heavenly dignity and destiny.

It's significant that today's Gospel is the conclusion of the Gospel according to Mark and our First Reading is the beginning of the Acts of the Apostles. The end of Jesus' public life on earth is the beginning of the life of the Church: you and me. He had lived and died in an area less than 150 miles long, yet has come to be known throughout the world because his life was a life of service. We, too, have to realize that the only form of witness that most people will initially accept today is service. If we who believe in Jesus gave ourselves in service, the world would have been Christian a long time ago.

Our commemoration of Jesus' ascension is a call to active service in spreading the Good News, to sustained effort without discouragement or depression. St. John Chrysostom said, "There is nothing colder than a Christian who does not care for the salvation of others." And prayer will help us to fill our role in the world with insight, wisdom, enlightenment, and all the other gifts which Paul prayed for on behalf of the Ephesians.

As we think about today's liturgy, let's ask two important questions of ourselves. One is, "Am I doing anything to make God's kingdom a reality in places that I reach, like my home, my parish, my workplace?" The other is, "Does the quality of my service give me grounds to hope to get to heaven?" Let's pray with the Church that we may follow where Jesus has led and find our hope in his glory.

SEVENTH SUNDAY OF EASTER
Ac 1:15-17, 20   1 Jn 4:11-16   Jn 17:11-19

Unity
Apostleship; The Way; Continuity of Christian Faith;
Truth; Life Goes On

Organizations that want to send people out to represent them give candidates for the job substantial training: lectures, panel discussions, seminars, videotapes, simulations, exercises. It's important for the organizations to be able to stand behind the people who sell their vacuum cleaners, household brushes, perfumes, and soaps. Countries do the same with their diplomats, so that the diplomats abroad won't misrepresent, either intentionally or unintentionally, what their country stands for. The Christian religion is similar: Its representatives are on a "mission," which means "to be sent," and its personnel are "apostles," which means "those who have been sent." Everyone who is baptized into Jesus and believes in him is an apostle — one sent, a salesperson, a representative, a diplomat.

Today's Gospel, which is from Jesus' farewell discourse, presents part of his sublime priestly prayer, in which he consecrates all who will carry on his work. His prayer parallels the Lord's Prayer. In addressing God, "Father" is the title in both, and both put a strong emphasis on the priority of God's will.

Jesus uses four key ideas. The first is *protection* (vv. 11f.): Jesus had been with the apostles, and he would remain forever, and he will defend us when the going in the world gets rough. The second concept is *the world*. On this, Jesus is paradoxical. On the one hand, the world is the object of God's love — so much so that Jesus was to give his life for it as the Lamb who would take away its sins. On the other hand, the world is a kind of anti-God, a Satan which is opposed to everything that Jesus' missioners represent. We who sincerely try to discover and live up to our role as apostles continue to be concerned over *involvement* in the world.

That has two extremes. One is to become so involved in the world that we accept its values. The other is to flee from the world — a position that overemphasizes the evil of the world and forgets God's love for it. This position mistakenly thinks that Christianity is somehow a way to save one's own soul without regard for the cares and problems of the world. Jesus' prayer was not that his disciples be taken out of this world, but that they work within the world and find victory. Jesus' training of his apostles shows that Christian apostleship means not to withdraw from life, but to become better equipped for life; not a release from problems, but a way to solve problems; not an easy peace, but a triumphant warfare; and not an avoidance of troubles, but facing and conquering them.

A third key concept for those who go into the world representing Jesus is joy — *Jesus' joy* — an aspect we frequently forget. Even those who are suffering have an instinctive awareness of their need for a *joyful* message, and the message of Jesus is in the final analysis the only real, lasting, deep joy that the world can know.

Lastly (v. 19), Jesus speaks of a very important aspect of life — *truth*. He speaks of his emissaries as being consecrated in truth. Consecration implies intentionally participating with the divine. We can be dedicated to anything: a task, a cause, a nation. But we can be consecrated only to God. Consecration requires that we trust more in grace than in our personal capabilities. It calls for a giving of ourselves to a power greater than our own.

Taken all together, it's hard to imagine a more forthright statement than this Last Supper prayer of Jesus. Based on the experience of the Church, St. John wrote it at the end of the first century — when there was a need for unity in the Church, for preaching, for teaching truth, for realizing the identity of the churches with each other and with Jesus' total Church, and for the comprehension that Jesus really sent the Church and empowered it to continue doing what he had done. But because being an apostle of God-in-Christ to the world is much more demanding than being a vacuum-cleaner salesperson or a diplomat, it brings a greater anxiety than is present with the others.

Anxiety was present in the apostles especially in this time of their life which we commemorate today — that time after Jesus' ascension and before the Holy Spirit came upon them in the first Pentecost, which we commemorate next Sunday. They were perhaps disappointed that Jesus was no longer physically present. More than likely, it took a long time for them to encounter the dimension of the new presence of God in them and among them. It probably didn't dawn on them for a long time what their mission was in life and exactly what they should do. Nor did they know what the Church should be. Very likely they didn't expect the Church to last very long: They expected that Jesus would return in glory very soon.

St. John showed this also in today's Second Reading, one of the jewels of the New Testament, our sixth and final selection from his loving letter-sermon. Because John was an old man when he wrote it, he spoke of those things which he considered to be important. He wrote on his favorite theme, *the* virtue that fascinated him most, the virtue which shows that we belong to Jesus: *love*. John applies love in the context of both God and people. With respect to God, he repeats what we saw last Sunday to be the greatest and most inexhaustible statement in Scripture (v. 16): "God is love."

John shows that Jesus is the means by which we know God's love. God's love sent Jesus to become a person with heart — a heart that beat in the womb of his mother, a heart that was moved by the frailty of our human nature, a heart that humanly rejoiced and suffered. His heart welcomed the poor and the sick, accepted Thomas's doubt as well as Peter's enthusiasm, Mary Magdalene's humiliation as well as his mother's humility, Judas's distance as well as John's intimacy.

In the same context of love, John goes from God to people. Our life is to be in imitation of God's. We're to exercise some measure of the same kind of love that God shows. Clement of Alexandria wrote that the real Christian "practices being God." John indicates that it's only by knowing God that we learn to love, and only by loving that we learn to know God. Our Church is always to have the essential characteristic of being a community of love.

Today's portion of St. Luke's Acts of the Apostles complements today's Gospel and indicates the consciousness of love in the Church. Luke tells us that there were in the early Church 120 brothers — the number given by the rabbis for the ideal synagogue. In a Holy Land population of four million, the Church numbered only 120; but it gradually spread to Rome, which represented the entire world. Luke called the 120, "brothers," the first name given to the Church, because they knew by now the bond of deep fraternal communion that exists between Jesus and his members. A name given them in derision was "the followers of the fellow from Nazareth." Later, at Antioch, they would be ridiculed with the name "Christian." Only at the turn of the century would they receive the name "Catholic," or "universal," to distinguish the real, mainstream Church from various splinter groups which had sprung up.

Considering the importance of apostleship and its necessary qualities, it's no wonder that the apostles took great care in selecting Judas's successor. If it seems strange for the early Church to find a successor to an apostle by tossing dice, let's remember that the most important element is the fact that, before throwing the dice, they prayed. (And one in an exalted position would be forever humble if he realized that he'd been chosen by a toss of the dice!) This was, actually, the first case of apostolic succession.

All today's readings present the ideal of unity. In the Gospel, Jesus prays that we may be one even as he and the heavenly Father are one (v. 11). While that model may leave us aghast, it's not an impossible dream, because Jesus sent the Holy Spirit to help accomplish it — an event we will commemorate next Sunday, the Feast of Pentecost. The Acts of the Apostles shows that our Masses and Communions aren't acts of private devotion, but actions of a community that should have an influence on relationships. And John's letters about love are products of the harsh reality that Christians even then were hurting one another.

The overall qualification for unity is love. This is the function of an apostle: not to only know *about* Jesus, but to *know* Jesus. That means not only the Jesus of books, but as we experience him in our lives. To qualify, we must act in *oneness* with God and with one another, even as the persons in God are one. That's not easy. But Christians can *never* — in the early Church or now — make the Age of the Church better unless and until we take our divine election for apostleship seriously. That means an awareness of Jesus' protection of us, the bubbling out of an inner joy, a love for the world, and a constant search for truth. Unless we have at least those four qualities, we're not even good trainees, much less apostles.

·

PENTECOST SUNDAY
Ac 2:1-11   1 Cor 12:3-7, 12f.   Jn 20:19-23
(All A, B, and C)

All Things Made New
The Opportunity for Re-Creation; Witness

Today, the feast of Pentecost, means many things, all of them having to do with the commemoration of God coming to meet the human race. Among the ancient Jews, this was originally a harvest festival, a feast in which God's generous abundance was celebrated with joy and thanksgiving. It became the feast of Shavuot, which in turn was fifty days after that super-eminent feast of Passover that celebrated the Angel of Death passing over the Jewish homes in Egypt during one of the

Note: This homily is mostly on John. Cycle A is on Acts, Cycle C mostly on 1 Corinthians.

plagues. Because it was a day more than a "week of weeks" after Passover, it was also called the "Feast of Weeks." It marked the establishment of the Covenant of God with the Israelites, recalling the moment
when the Israelites came to constitute themselves as a people of God.
By the first century A.D., for the Jews it was the Festival of the Law
given on Mt. Sinai.

Among Christians, its name from the Greek means it is the fiftieth
day after Easter. It's the birthday of the Christian Church. (We could,
of course, say with equal validity that several other days might be called
the Church's "birthday" — for example, the Last Supper, when Jesus
declared that he was sending the apostles forth as he himself had been
sent by the heavenly Father; or when, as St. John says elsewhere, from
Jesus' side on the cross flowed blood and water; or Jesus' resurrection,
which is communicated to us by baptism.) It's the festival celebration
of our New Covenant with God. It's the Feast of the Holy Spirit, to
honor his coming on this day. It's a celebration of our own particular
giftedness: There are varieties of gifts, but the same Spirit who gives
them. And it's the Last Sunday of Easter, signifying that Easter is one
long and glorious time.

In order to convey Pentecost's essential meaning — as an event
connected with Easter — the Church chose as today's Gospel reading
a scene from the first Easter night. Because we're so familiar with the
story, we often miss the strangeness of it. It tells us how the apostles
had locked themselves up out of fear for their lives. That was understandable. It had been a terrible week, in which they'd seen their leader's
triumph in the beginning of the week turn to betrayal, pain, torment,
and death. They'd been absent when he needed them most, they had
all kinds of regrets for which they needed the solace of one another,
and they knew that their leader's fate could easily befall themselves. It
was not unlike some of the times of our lives when everything goes
wrong: the passing away of loved ones, the loss of jobs, terrible loneliness.

And now, despite Jesus' promise in his farewell discourse on Holy
Thursday night that he would come back to them (14:18), nothing seems
to have been further from the mind of the disciples than his reappearance. Yet here he was! Far from berating them for their fear, he wished
them "peace" — but now with a new and deeper meaning than the traditional greeting of "Shalom." In his new meaning, and in the sense
we wish it to one another at Mass, peace emanates from the tranquil

activity of a well-ordered life. In his case, the greeting isn't a wish, but a declaration — as had been the angel's address to Mary: "The Lord *is* with you." Likewise, peace *is* with those who receive the Lord's greeting with good will.

And, wonder of wonders, the apostles' fear changed to joy. This kind of intense joy is one of the fruits of the Holy Spirit, who is now for the first time revealed as a person. It's a joy characteristic of all Jesus' followers, as Jesus had explained at the Last Supper. It's a joy that should be evident in this assembly. Our joyfulness should project the image of the Church as proclaiming the presence and action of the Spirit in our midst.

Then Jesus gave a mission: "As the Father has sent me, so I send you" (v. 21). This was a new kind of mission — a mission to spread the love of God to the world. To all of us who hear the Gospel, that mission is one of Jesus' farewell gifts — along with peace and joy — from Eastertide and Pentecost. It puts meaning into our life — a meaning that is beyond superficial, everyday, ordinary experiences.

In giving this mission, Jesus *breathed* on the apostles. This may seem a strange procedure to us, but from the Jewish Scriptures the apostles were familiar with God doing this. The first creation account (Gn 1) describes God's breath as a wind hovering over the primeval waters. Isaiah portrays the Spirit as a guide directing the Messiah from within. Elijah recognized the presence of the Spirit in a whispering wind.

But of the many dramatic examples of God's breath on the earth, two are especially noteworthy. One is when God created Adam and took this creature formed from dirt and breathed on him, giving him life (Gn 2:7). The other is the mystical experience of Ezekiel being led by the Spirit into a plain in Babylon and having a vision of a field full of the unburied dry bones of thousands who had fallen in battle. The bones had long been lifeless. In one of the most unusual and dramatic scenes in all literature, when Ezekiel prophesied in accordance with the directions of the Spirit, the breath of God — which Ezekiel summoned from the four winds — brought the bones to life, and they stood upright, a vast army (Ezk 37:1-14; Pentecost Vigil Mass).

With Jesus, examples of the Spirit are equally dramatic. He was conceived in his mother's womb by the Spirit. The Spirit had descended on him at his baptism and the Spirit had driven him into the desert to be tested. The Holy Spirit had formed his first disciples into the beginnings of Jesus' Mystical Body. Now Jesus' breathing on the apostles is a sign of a new creation, a new life as the Spirit is breathed into those who are being sent forth. This new life which the Spirit gives the Church at Pentecost is no less wonderful than the new life which God had given the human race when He created us and which the Spirit had given to the nation Israel.

The Spirit plays complementary roles with the Son. Just as the Father needs the Son in order to reveal the Father's love, so the Son and the Spirit need each other in order to reveal the life and the power of the Godhead. Moreover, the resurrection needs Pentecost in order to reveal the power of the Son, and in its turn Pentecost needs to draw its energy from Jesus' death and resurrection.

The Spirit of God continues to breathe over the universe. Through his Spirit, God creates, vivifies, propels people to leadership, and stimulates religious enthusiasm — in short, makes all things new. Signs of the Spirit's presence are such of his gifts as compassion, mercy, forgiveness, reconciliation, and peace — and witness. The Greek word for "witness" is "martyr." Although we're all called to be witnesses to Jesus, only some will be called to shed their blood. All of us are called to witness in other ways. The Mass we're now celebrating, for instance, is a way of witnessing to God. The long and continuous effort to remain faithful to Christ in the details of our daily lives is witness — and can be more demanding, humanly speaking, than the tyrant's sharp sword or quick bullet to the martyr.

The power of Pentecost is in the hands of those who choose to love and forgive and share the peace that is borne from above. As the dried bones in the book of Ezekiel came to life, and the apostles' fear in the Upper Room turned to joy, so the wind and the fire of the Spirit make it possible for ordinary mortals to confess Jesus as Lord before hostile audiences. God's intervention shakes the world.

With our new life won by Jesus' saving death, resurrection, ascension, and gift of the Spirit, we, like the disciples, become truly alive. Some people are so spiritless that, had they been present at the first Pentecost, they would have come to the scene with fire extinguishers. To help make all things new, Jesus has given the Church the authority to forgive sins even as he did — or, better, to transmit the forgiveness that only God can bestow.

We can show our gratitude for these gifts by not hiding them in the attics of our lives, but using them. Today, the Holy Spirit is given in a new way. In the words of today's Solemn Blessing over the People, may "the Father of light [who] enlightened the minds of the disciples by the outpouring of the Holy Spirit... bless you with the gifts of the Spirit"; "May that fire which hovered over the disciples as tongues of flame burn out all evil from your hearts and make them glow with pure light"; and may God "strengthen your faith and fulfill your hope of seeing him face to face."

TRINITY SUNDAY
Dt 4:32-34, 39f.   Rm 8:14-17   Mt 28:16-20

The View at the Top of the Mountain
The Lord Is God; Carry On, in God's Name;
The God Whose Children We Are; Family Responsibility

People argue whether it's better to live on a mountain or in a valley. Most cities are built in valleys because of conveniences like better transportation, milder weather, and easier access. Mountain dwellers point to crisper air, less pollution, and an expansive view. In the Sacred Scriptures, mountains have been important, from the book of Genesis in the Bible's beginning to the book of Revelation at its end. Abraham went to sacrifice his only son Isaac on Mount Moriah. On Mount Sinai, God gave the law to Moses. On Mount Zion, the Temple was built.

In today's Gospel from St. Matthew, it was to a mountain in Galilee that Jesus summoned his apostles after his resurrection (v. 16). One can understand that the disciples doubted (v. 17). A mountain is a good place to dispel doubts and see God. Perhaps one reason why some people don't believe in God is that their vision isn't as large as a mountain view can provide; their resulting concept is so narrow that, if some believers saw God that way, they too mightn't believe.

In Matthew, there are many mountains that contrast with today's. There's the Mountain of Temptation (4:8), the high mountain on which the devil showed Jesus all the kingdoms of the world in their magnificence and promised to give Jesus all these kingdoms if he would recognize Satan's power. On today's mountain in Galilee, Jesus says that all power in heaven and on earth has been given to him (v. 18) and he gives that power to his apostles.

Matthew also has the Mountain of Prayer (14:23), where Jesus went to be with his Father; on today's mountain, Jesus is with the Father and the Holy Spirit. There's the Mountain of Healing (15:29), where the crowds brought their sick; from the present mountain the apostles will go forth to heal as well as to teach. Matthew also has the Mountain of Transfiguration (17:1), where the Father's voice from heaven declared Jesus to be His beloved Son and commanded the disciples to listen to him (17:5); today the risen Son, one with the Father, is making provisions that the whole world may have the chance to listen.

Last is the Mount of Olives (24:3), where the apostles asked Jesus about the end of the world and where Jesus promised that the good news would be proclaimed throughout the world (24:14). Now Jesus' reappearance after his death is ushering in the final age, and he promises his abiding presence until the end (v. 20). Spiritually, this is the loftiest peak on today's mountain: From it the mountain climber can see not only what has passed, but what lies ahead and all around.

Jesus' commission to his apostles is three-fold. The first is to make disciples of all nations (v. 19), a world-wide outreach that gushes from and reflects the overflowing love of the triune God. Jesus' second commission is that the rite of initiation be baptism in the name of the Trinity. Being a true disciple of Jesus involves being plunged into the "name" — or reality — of God as Father, Son, and Holy Spirit. That means participating in and being related to each of the divine persons. It also means leading a way of life based upon Jesus' moral teaching.

Thirdly, Jesus commissions the apostles to teach everything that's in the Gospels (v. 20). This last teaching contrasts with the Mountain of the Sermon (Mt 5:1-8), where Jesus *began* to teach. In a further contrast in Matthew, Jesus' *final* words, that he is with us always (v. 20), joins with Matthew's first chapter on Jesus' birth, in which he shows Jesus as "Emmanuel" — "God with us."

As today's Gospel presents Jesus' last words, today's First Reading presents Moses's last words, which offer a vision of a transcendent God Who goes all the way back to creation and then across history. They too were spoken from a mountain — a mountain of Moab, east of the Jordan, to which Moses had led the Israelites in their long wanderings from Egypt through the desert. From there Moses could see the Promised Land. Tragically, God wouldn't permit him to enter it, because when at God's direction Moses had struck a rock for water once and nothing happened, he had doubted God. When he struck the rock a second time, water gushed forth. But his initial doubt was sufficient for God to punish him by not allowing him to enter the yearned-for Promised Land.

Although many people who suffer complain, Moses with his poignant last words spoke of God's fidelity and love. Other peoples had their own gods, said the chastened Moses, but there's only one true God — the God who is the Creator (v. 32), the God of Revelation (v. 33), the God of Israel (v. 34). God had spoken to them from the heart of fire — fire being a symbol of the powerful, terrifying presence of God — on Mount Sinai. They had come into the very presence of God and survived! Moses's advice to the people for whom he had risked all was to fix in their heart that the Lord is God and there is no other (v. 39), and they must keep his commandments (v. 40). Moses recognized God as not only the one true God, but also a personal God who is in constant dialogue with His people.

Today's reading from St. Paul's major theological treatise, his letter to the Romans, reflects an early Christian recognition that the one God has three persons. Paul's concern in this chapter, one of the most beautiful in the Bible, is the tremendous result of the Christian's relationship to the triune God: We who are baptized, by reason of the presence of the grace of the *Spirit* within, enjoy a new relationship to the *Father*: that of adopted children and heirs through *Christ*. At the Last Supper, Jesus had asked Philip whether, after Jesus' being with them so long, they didn't realize that anyone who has seen him has seen the heavenly Father (Jn 14:9).

While Jesus is God's *natural* son and heir, we're God's children and heirs *through adoption*, this gift of God giving new rights, unearned love, and inherited glory. Thus through the grace of the Holy Spirit we enjoy an intimate relationship with the persons of the Trinity. Therefore, we don't look for God only "up in heaven." One of the areas where we may expect to meet God is in the depths of our being. God told St. Catherine of Siena, "I call the soul 'heaven' because I make heaven wherever I dwell by grace."

Since we're children of God, we should live and act as worthy brothers and sisters of Jesus. For Paul, such people are those who've been following the lead of the Spirit (v. 14). And we didn't receive a *whenever you talk to a young child a question are taking a big chance what that this [handwritten marginalia]*

spirit of slavery (v. 15): We're privileged to call upon God with the same affectionate and intimate term that Jesus used in his moment of supreme earthly confidence in God (Mk 14:36): "Abba," "Dad!"

Today we celebrate the unity of Father, Son, and Spirit. A priest went into a second-grade classroom of the parish school and asked, "Who can tell me what the Blessed Trinity means?" A little girl lisped, "The Blethed Twinity meanth there are thwee perthonth in one God." The priest, taken aback by the lisp, said, "Would you say that again? I don't understand what you said." The little girl answered, "Y'not suppothed to underthtand; it'th a mythtewy."

That's true, but our understanding of the mystery should mature with the rest of our growth. Jesus revealed that God has three persons: one God, but never solitary; one God whose three persons are in constant dialogue with one another; one God whose three persons show that God is love. The beautiful summary of our faith life is the conclusion of each Eucharistic Prayer: "through him [Jesus], with him, in him, in the unity of the Holy Spirit, all glory and honor is Yours, Almighty Father, forever and ever." And we conclude every liturgical prayer to the Father "through Jesus Christ... in the unity of the Holy Spirit."

We are, however, involved not only in liturgical prayer, but also personal prayer. Trinity Sunday doesn't only celebrate who God is in Himself, but what His threefold nature means for human beings. All today's readings show that. In Deuteronomy, Moses reminds the Israelites of God's immense love for them. In his letter to the Romans, Paul teaches that through baptism we have entered into the life of the Trinity, an idea which is echoed in Matthew's Gospel, where the risen Jesus commissions his disciples to introduce all humanity into the life of God through baptism. The essence of our religion, therefore, is a relationship: the relationship of human beings with God. We should continually deepen our relationship with the Father, Son, and Holy Spirit.

Our heavenly Father sometimes seems far away; yet Jesus has made God visible to us. Jesus seems so "long ago"; but the Holy Spirit lives and moves among us now to make us one in Christ. In both heat and cold, on the mountain and at the shore, may we meditate deeply about our triune God and get to know Him better. And may we reflect in our community the love and unity we find there. We came together today in the name of the Trinity, and in the name of the Trinity we shall go forth to love and serve one another.

child will somehow surprise or even shock you or maybe humble you a little bit — [handwritten margin note]

SOLEMNITY OF THE BODY AND BLOOD OF CHRIST

Ex 24:3-8   Heb 9:11-15   Mk 14:12-16, 22-26

The Mass

Reverence for the Eucharist; The Roots of Our Eucharistic
Sacrifice; Our Duty to Share and Nourish; Eucharist,
Sign of Love and Unity; The Meaning of Covenant

Most of us have an innate tendency to look down upon those who are different from us — those who have different colored skin, or those who dress differently, or those who lived in the past. We look down upon the beliefs and practices of primitives who engage in war dances to their gods. We consider alien and inferior the ancient Central American Indians who offered human sacrifice and upon the American Indians who wanted to be united with the courage of their victims by eating their hearts or drinking their blood.

But human nature is essentially the same for all times and places. No matter what historical era people have lived in, no matter what kind of clothes we wear, and no matter how seemingly strange our practices, we all have many things in common. Among them is the fact that one who loves wants to sacrifice for the beloved. This is true of our love for one another: For example, we sacrifice for our children and our spouses and our friends because we love them.

High regard is sometimes true even between strangers. In one seat of a bus that was bumping along a back road in the South sat a wispy old man holding a bunch of fresh flowers. Across the aisle was a young girl whose eyes came back again and again to the man's flowers. When the time came for the old man to get off, he impulsively thrust the flowers into the girl's lap. "I can see you love the flowers," he explained, "and I think my wife would like for you to have them. I'll tell her I gave them to you." The girl accepted the flowers, then watched the old man get off the bus and walk through the gate of a small cemetery.

That kind of love is true between us and God: The only evidence that we love God is the extent to which we're willing to sacrifice for Him. "Sacrifice" means, literally, the making of something holy. In the First Covenant, that of God with the Jews, the sacrifices were symbolic: the ritual victim substituting for the self-offering of the person making the sacrifice. In Jesus' Covenant, at the Last Supper Jesus reveals that the real sacrifice will be his blood.

In today's reading from the Book of Exodus, Moses alludes to what we might consider the grotesque: the kinds of sacrifice the ancient Jews offered and the use of blood. Why the spilling of blood? Possibly because it meant there was no going back. The blood was a sign of the Israelites' *covenant*, a special word the Hebrews borrowed from others, a word used in all three readings today. As their neighbors used the word, it was a pact or contract or treaty or alliance between unequal parties — an emperor and vassal kings, or a king and vassal nobles, or a landowner and his tenants. It was, however, freely entered into, binding perpetually, and sealed in blood.

That was the background of the earliest historical covenant in the Bible: that between God and Abraham. By the time we come to the next historical covenant in the Bible, the blood has taken on a new meaning. Now it's not merely threat-blood; it's sacrificial blood, as described in today's readings from Exodus and the Letter to the Hebrews. Now the covenant is with God and is sealed with a sacrifice, a religious act of worship offered to God alone. The blood — the life — of animals is offered to God. Moses splashed half the blood on the altar (representing God "walking through") and half on the people (representing them "walking through").

As Moses sprinkled the blood on the people, he said, "This is the blood of the covenant which the Lord has made" (v. 8). At the Last Supper, Our Lord modified Moses's words only slightly: "This is my blood of the New Covenant. ..." The Old Covenant was between God and the Hebrews; the New Covenant is between God and Jesus and, through Jesus, between God and us. This New Covenant is sealed with Jesus' death. Through this covenant we enter freely into a commitment with God.

It's a universal practice for all sectors of the human family to make public, official, communal sacrifice as well as personal sacrifices to their gods. Although the methods of some peoples may seem bizarre to others, there's nothing wrong with the principle. Recognizing people's yearning, and answering our need, Jesus made it easy by instituting the sacrifice to God *par excellence*, *the* opportunity to show God we love Him and to give Him our worship: the sacrifice of the Mass. It's a continuation and a summation of all other sacrifices.

When Our Lord celebrated the Last Supper, an excerpt of which is in today's reading from St. Mark, he was continuing something that had been going on as the Jews' way of offering worship and love to God and thanks for their deliverance since they left Egypt: the Passover meal. Mindful of the sacredness of that meal, Jesus was careful to do in correct minute detail what had been prescribed.

What he did in the Upper Room was, first of all, an adaptation of the Passover of the past. So it was in accord with the structure of the ancient Passover ritual still used by Jews today: the Cup of the Kiddush (sanctification), the washing of hands, the breaking of bread, the story of the Deliverance, the second cup of wine (of Haggadah [Explaining]), grace, the eating of the bitter herbs, the eating of the Lamb, the singing of the Hallel (psalms of praise to God), and the prayers of thanksgiving. And Our Lord took the part of the Jewish father who, at all times but especially on this occasion, provided religious instruction for his children. The Mass is modeled upon the Sinai covenant ceremony, the Liturgy of the Word corresponding to the reading of the covenant and the Liturgy of the Eucharist corresponding to the covenantal sacrifice.

This Passover meal was also an anticipation of Jesus' offering of himself and a commemoration for the people of the future. It looked to Jesus' sacrifice when he would give his life to the very last drop of his blood. He spoke of his blood that would connect Passover with the Eucharist for the community and would be the sign of a New Covenant between God and people.

His hearers looked upon blood differently from the way we do. They knew blood to be in some way identified with life. They saw that if people were wounded and seriously bleeding, their life ebbed away. Though they didn't have knowledge of scientific aspects of blood that we have, like the balance between red and white corpuscles, transfusions, and plasma, they were right: Blood *is* identified with life. Jesus used their perspective to indicate that his blood was thereafter to be *the* preëminent sign of the relationship between God and people. All their sacrifices to this point — of goats and sheep and heifers and bulls and doves — would be superseded by what Jesus gave: his blood for the life of the world.

In addition to being an adaptation of the past and an anticipation of the future, what Jesus did at the Passover meal was important for what he was doing now. "This is the blood of the covenant," he said (v. 24). Some people have been known to symbolize the seriousness of their covenants by signing them in blood. Here, God signs this covenant between us and Him, and not in just a few drops of blood, but in His every last drop. When Jesus affirms (v. 25) that he would never again drink wine (the sign of a special festive meal) until he does so in the kingdom of God, he is affirming *ipso facto* that this is the last festive meal of his life in this present world.

One of the most stunning, moving, and joy-bringing sentences of the Letter to the Hebrews is that which speaks of Jesus' blood cleansing our consciences (v. 14). The letter interprets Jesus' death and exaltation in the light of the annual Jewish Day of Expiation, when the High Priest entered the Holy of Holies to expiate the sins of the people, committed over the past year, through the sprinkling of the blood of sacrificed animals. Accordingly, Jesus has entered the heavenly sanctuary, and the sacrifice which he represents is that of himself, the blood his own. He's the mediator of the new, eternal covenant.

All of our readings today demonstrate the fidelity and love of the Lord in His part of the covenant with us. They imply return obligations on our part. The holy sacrifice of the Mass and participation in the Eucharist is our preëminent way of showing our love and our worship of God and our attitude toward one another. We can't possibly think we've fulfilled our obligation of love and worship to God at Mass if all we do is give money. Each time we come to Mass, at the words of consecration *anamnesis* (remembering) takes place: The words of Jesus are repeated and re-enacted. But we must make Jesus' statement our own: We must be willing to enter the agreement by saying, "This is *my* blood," meaning "I give myself entirely to be united with you in doing the heavenly Father's will" and, as the people said in Exodus, "We will do everything that the Lord has told us."

At the end of the Eucharistic Prayer, we affirm all of that by our great "Amen" before the Lord's Prayer. By it, we're saying that we come under the covenant, that we will heed and do all that the Lord has said, that we will have his covenant written in our hearts, that we'll live for him, and that we shall offer *through-*, *with-*, and *in-him* all glory to the Father. Unless that's true, the Eucharist is for us a sham, a contradiction, a lie, a piece of hypocrisy.

Our taking part in the Eucharist requires preparation of both soul and body. For the soul, it means openness of heart, wanting to share with Jesus, coming out of the maelstrom of the week to a time of calm and thanksgiving. God wants us here: warts and all — joy, despair, sickness, pain, troubled conscience, and whatever.

Bodily, it means cleanliness, proper dress, punctuality, a realization of the importance of what we do here, reverence, and courtesy toward others. After all, we believe in the importance of the body, because the fact that the eternal Word of God took human flesh in the person of Jesus of Nazareth is central to our faith. Today's feast celebrates his body, which he identified with bread and wine at his Last Supper, given us as the food of faith. In addition to today's feast, we seem to celebrate the human body endlessly: We cherish sacraments that affirm God's presence in our births and dyings, and our feast days are remembrances of deaths, births, and even conceptions.

Our recitation of the prayers should be as wholehearted as we can make them: We may not be able to be as strongly vocal as a group of young marines, but in no case should our participation be unenthusiastic or meaningless. Integral to participation is receiving Holy Communion. The Eucharist, Jesus' continued presence in the community of faith, is Christianity's most precious possession; all aspects of this breathtaking reality require whatever profound reverence and purity of soul we can muster. And the realization that we all — rich and poor, similar and dissimilar — receive the same Lord should increase our awareness that we're one parish family.

If we put the lessons of today's liturgy into practice, our attitude toward the Eucharist will radiate outward and further the solidarity of our faith community and all people. We'll reach out not only to those in the same pew, but to all in our neighborhood who are lonely or in any other way needy: an elderly friend, teenage seekers, and all pitiable unfortunates.

TENTH SUNDAY IN ORDINARY TIME
Gn 3:9-15   2 Cor 4:13-5:1   Mk 3:20-35

Moral Maturity
Blaming Others; The Conquest of Sin; Whose the Final Victory:
Good or Evil?; Which Way Adulthood?

One of the international case studies used to determine moral growth
and maturity is that of Heinz, whose wife is dying from a rare disease
that can be cured only by an expensive drug. Heinz is too poor to afford the drug, and the question is whether he should steal the drug to
save his wife. The response of ten-year-old Tommy was, "Heinz
shouldn't steal. ... If he steals the drug, he might get put in jail." In
this longitudinal study, the response of Tommy at age thirteen was,
"Heinz should steal the drug. ... He might get sent to jail, but he'd still
have his wife." Tommy's response at age sixteen was, "If I was Heinz,
I would have stolen the drug for my wife. You can't put a price on love.
You can't put a price on life, either."

At age 21, Tommy's response was, "When you get married, you
take a vow to love and cherish your wife. Marriage is not only love,
it's an obligation." And he seems to have grown into an understanding
that, if an owner clutches property for his *luxury* when someone else is
in dire *need* of it, that's not stealing properly speaking.

Everyone's life is full of moral decisions. That includes Jesus.
By the time today's event in St. Mark's Gospel took place, Jesus and
his disciples were so inundated by people that they couldn't even eat
(v. 20). Jesus' relatives, seeing it, said that he was out of his mind (v.
21). So opposition was coming not only from those outside, but even
from his family who were close!

Jesus' moral choices could have given his relatives reasons for
thinking as they did. Before all this, he hadn't only made the decision
to leave home, but also to leave the woodworking business at Nazareth.
That had brought in money every week; now, as a wandering preacher,
he had no place to lay his head. He had also seen it as morally necessary to put himself on a collision course with the leaders of the people.
No one could hope to get away with that over the long run. It would
have been better to stay on their good side. If you wanted to get things

done, people believed then as they believe now: You have to have clout to force the powerful to listen. Besides, this little group that Jesus had started didn't look very impressive: some fishermen, a reformed tax-collector, a nationalist fanatic, and others of like ilk.

So Jesus was turning his back on what makes people tick. Whereas most people want a job and money coming in, Jesus was throwing material security away. Whereas most people play life safe, he was taking a course that involved moral considerations and risk. And, whereas for most people the voice of their neighbors speaks louder than the voice of God and they're concerned to ask, "What will people say?," he cared little for the verdict of society.

Substantiating his relatives' criticism were the scribes who had come from Jerusalem (v. 22), probably in an official capacity to investigate this as yet unknown man from Nazareth. They couldn't deny the reality of his cures, so they claimed that he was possessed — worse, possessed by Beelzebul, a detested demon. The first part of Beelzebul's name is akin to "Baal," which can mean "Lord." The second part can mean "of the Flies," or may refer to excrement. In neither case was the name flattering, and in the latter case it's close to what bawdy people would say today about being full of it. Further, they attributed to Jesus a sort of black magic, whereby he was expelling little demons by the great demon. Words like theirs, once spoken, are bullets let fly.

The calumny of these men of authority was inspired by a cold venom. But their report was important: Although truth has endurance, a lie has speed. And their report was of a kind to turn even people of good will from Jesus. Jesus' answering argument made eminent sense: The power of evil would certainly not allow itself to be divided, because that way lay sure defeat (vv. 24-26). Put another way, said Jesus, anyone wanting to plunder another's house must first tie the owner up (v. 27).

Jesus went on to put good and evil under still another perspective. No matter what evil that people do, and no matter what blasphemies or calumnies they utter — whether against God or other people — God will forgive (v. 28), with one exception. That exception is blasphemy against the Holy Spirit (v. 29). Meaning different things in different places in the New Testament, it always means what is *essentially* evil. Here, it's attributing God's miracles to demonic action. To thus call evil good and good evil is a complete inversion of all moral values. The moral wreck who commits it has no sense of sin. Such a person, conscious of no sin, can't repent; and, unable to love, he can't reach out for forgiveness, nor can he receive forgiveness.

In a refreshing change of pace, Jesus' mother and some of his kin appear on the scene (v. 31). When told they were waiting, Jesus laid down the conditions of true kinship (vv. 33-35). The bond of *spiritual* relationship is more important than that of blood relationship. Because that was a society in which family was all important, it's hard for us to realize the strength of what Jesus was saying. Nevertheless, our observations confirm that the apostles couldn't have been brought together except by a committed spiritual relationship with God: Otherwise Matthew the Jew-defying tax-collector would never have been able to get along with someone like Simon the Jewish Zealot.

Today's reading from the Book of Genesis provides an example of moral immaturity. After Adam and Eve's sin, they began a process of self-righteous rationalization and immature passing the buck. God questioned Adam first because Adam came first in the order of creation. Adam passed the buck to Eve; he even seemed to blame God because of the "woman whom you put here with me" (v. 12). Eve in turn blamed the snake.

In some cultures, snakes are revered. For one thing, they have amazing powers of survival. Because they're close to the earth — which some cultures worship as the goddess Gaia — they're considered to have wisdom. The caduceus, the symbol of medicine, has two snakes intertwined. In many other cultures, they're hated for their silent hostile approach and lethal poison. So from jungle to desert, their powers have with fascinating contradiction made them symbolic of both eternal life and agonizing death. In this instance, Genesis uses the natural characteristics of the snake to symbolize evil. The snake has a central position in the story which, after all, is trying to explain the existence of evil in a world created by an all-good God.

By saying that in the ever-present enmity between good and evil the human race, especially its best representative Jesus, will strike at evil's head and evil will strike only at humankind's heel, the passage gives the first glimmer of hope, though vague, of the victory of the human race. Later revelation will confirm this optimism. Today's Gospel, for example, presented Jesus' conquest of Satan as reversing the curse in Genesis.

In contrast with Adam and Eve's immaturity, today's section of St. Paul's Second Letter to the Corinthians shows Paul's maturity.

Accused of insincerity and selfishness, he doesn't blame anyone else for his possible faults and thus distance himself from God, but rather achieves the highest level of maturity in having a spirit of faith.

Paul's faith tells him that the one who raised the Lord Jesus will raise us also (v. 14). His long-range viewpoint is optimistic: While each day our outer self, our body, is wasting away, our inner self is being renewed (v. 16). He perceives that his suffering ultimately earns a disproportionately great amount of glory: The momentary sufferings of this world, endured for Christ, will prove to be as nothing compared with the glory of the next (v. 17). And he recognizes that the things of this world, which we can see, will pass away; those that are unseen, the things of heaven, last forever (v. 18). It's easy to see why this reading is often used in ministering to the sick.

Some of today's conduct is as immature as anything done by Adam and Eve, the Corinthians, and the Gospel's scribes. Nowadays, blame is more common than harmony, judgment than reconciliation. Church members blame each other — conservatives blame liberals, liberals conservatives, parishioners their priests, priests their parishioners, and so on. Often these actions are simply ways of coping with our own inadequacies by placing them on others.

Maturity means turning the mirrors of our childhood, which concentrated on ourselves, into windows which enable us to see other people. Breaking that down, maturity means many other things. Maturity is the ability to control anger and settle differences without violence. Maturity is patience, the willingness to pass up immediate pleasure in favor of long-term gain. Maturity is perseverance, the ability to stick with a situation in spite of discouraging setbacks. Maturity is the capacity to face unpleasantness, discomfort, and defeat, without collapse. Maturity is the bigness to say "I was wrong," when we were wrong and, when we were right, resisting the satisfaction of saying, "I told you so." Maturity is the ability to make a decision and follow it through. Maturity means avoiding the alibi, keeping one's word, and coming through in a crisis. Maturity is the art of living in peace with what we can't change, the courage to change what we know should be changed, and the wisdom to know the difference.

Moral maturity gives radiance to our person. It's the reason for respect and the grounds for veneration. The more maturity, the greater the person. Like Tommy of our initial example, let's try to grow into moral maturity commensurate with our age.

ELEVENTH SUNDAY IN ORDINARY TIME
Ezk 17:22-24   2 Cor 5:6-10   Mk 4:26-34

How Fulfilled Persons Grow
The Growth of the Christian Life; How Spiritual Life Grows;
Grace and Responsibility; Little Stories, Great Truths; Hope

Every adult generation has important truths that it wants to pass on to
bring about the proper growth of its youth. To attract youth, we use
alluring literary forms. Among them are parables, short fictitious stories, usually homely and simple, that illustrate spiritual truths, usually
a single one, with not every detail being important or true. Mark
Twain's *Adventures of Huckleberry Finn*, for example, through a boy,
Huck, and his friend, Jim, memorably portrays a historical period and
the various classes of people who lived along the Mississippi River.

Jesus told many parables. Some of them might better be termed
"riddles" — which the crowd loved, but whose point the "sophisticated"
Pharisees, humorless, didn't get. To understand New Testament
parables, we have to remember three contexts: the context of the Gospel itself, the context of the Church before the Gospel was written but
after the time of Jesus, and the context of the time when Jesus told them.
We must understand what was going on in the Church when the Gospel writer wrote.

When St. Mark put today's two parables into writing, he had seen
the death of the two great apostles of Rome, Peter and Paul. The expected Parousia — Jesus' expected Second Coming — hadn't arrived,
and people were discouraged. Nero had blamed the burning of Rome
on the Christians, and persecuted and decimated them. Perhaps the few
remaining Christians were wondering why they must continue being
made sport of in the arena by being fed to the lions. It looked as if the
Church was doomed.

Today's two parables provide an insight into Jesus' kingdom on
earth and its growth. Jesus' first parable of the seed (vv. 26-29) on the
surface tells of nature's mysteries of life and growth. The farmer's seed
sprouts, grows, forms leaves, and gets itself ready to produce, with no
one understanding exactly how it happens — aside from helping it along
by watering, fertilizing, weeding, and (as the Galilean farmers listening to Jesus knew) driving away crows.

Take a field of corn, for instance. From a small seed it grows in eight weeks to a plant with over 1,400 square inches of leaf surface — one of the most remarkable feats of growth in the plant kingdom. And in that time the plant establishes a root system which, if laid end to end, would extend a distance of seven miles. In ideal weather the plant often grows as much as four inches a day, giving rise to the legend that you can hear the corn grow.

Jesus' parable of the seed is comparing natural growth with our soul's growth in grace. Nature's growth is often imperceptible; we can see it only by using a time-lapse camera or by returning at intervals. So, too, is the spiritual life. Nature's growth is constant: It takes place night and day, day and night, whether people are awake or asleep. In contrast, human spiritual growth is spasmodic: One day we may take a giant step forward, the next day a baby step backward. Nature's growth is inevitable, human spiritual growth anything but.

There's nothing so powerful as nature's growth: Seeds, borne on the wind far from their source, will grow; sprouts will shoot forth around boulders; tree roots can split concrete sidewalks; weeds push through the cracks in asphalt; lilacs grow in crannied walls. Human spiritual growth, though less visible, is no less powerful: More things are wrought by prayer than this world dreams of. With nature's growth, there's a consummation, a crop; at harvest time, the produce is separated from the weeds. In the spiritual life, harvest time is a term for judgment. The main lesson is that, although we don't always perceive God's action and sometimes think He has abandoned us, He never ceases to act.

Jesus gave his equally brief, simple, and homey parable of the mustard seed, which he called the smallest of all the seeds of the earth (v. 31). It really isn't the smallest, but was proverbially so in Palestine, and Jesus accommodated himself to his audience. But that isn't the point: As with the first parable, this one also contains several points. One begins with the observation that the grown bush has large branches, so that birds can dwell in its shade (v. 32). A common First Testament way to speak of a great empire was to describe it as a full and leafy tree that reached far out, with its tributary nations finding shelter in it like birds. Despite its insignificant beginnings, Christ's kingdom has grown tremendously and will continue to grow. It too reaches far out, giving shelter to all races and nations of people. Truly, the "kingdom of God" in the Gospel's two parables is the rule of God in our lives and the way God works among us.

Another point of the stories is that we should never be daunted by small beginnings. As with the little mustard seed that eventually grows into a large bush, we need patience and participation. We sometimes feel that our little bit will make no difference. But it does — in voting, in speaking out, in a small kindness, in a friendly smile, in putting together a large enterprise — and every little bit can contribute to huge results.

The prophet Ezekiel, too, used stories to teach. A remarkable prophet who lived during the Babylonian Captivity in the sixth century B.C., he expressed hopes for his people. Today's story is an allegory, which is the expression, through symbolic fictional figures and actions analogous to real-life situations, of truths about human existence. One way in which it differs from a parable is that even its details apply to the truth or generalization that it's trying to put across.

An example in secular literature is John Bunyan's *Pilgrim's Progress*, a seventeenth-century vision of the good man's pilgrimage through life, and at one time second only to the Bible in popularity. A First Testament allegory is the Song of Songs, which uses the love between bride and groom to illustrate the love between God and His people.

Today's passage from Ezekiel is a foretaste of the parable of the mustard seed. Ezekiel told his fellow Jewish captives — weak in power, insignificant in condition, and small in number — that some day this twig of a nation would become, through the Lord's power, a huge and noble cedar. In Ezekiel, as in Jesus' parables, God shows His love for the tiny, the unnoticed, and the most vulnerable — all of which He makes into the great, the remarkable, and the strong.

St. Paul's Second Letter to the Corinthians adds another aspect to God's way of dealing with the world: the demand for human responsibility at the same time as having hope. Today's passage is, like last Sunday's excerpt, from Paul's defense of himself against the false accusation that he was insincere. Paul wrote with strong emotions and, most likely, frequent tears. For all Paul's yearning for his problems to be over, he didn't despise this life (v. 6). He didn't look for the solution to his problems in the extinction of self like some Eastern religions do, or in the freeing of a disembodied spirit through death as in the Greek religions around him. He did, however, yearn for God's final judgment that today's Gospel speaks of in connection with the harvest. His message was one of *confidence* and *hope*.

That whole way of thinking — confidence and hope in the midst of pain and suffering — can be accomplished only by growth in *faith*. Between his conversion on the Damascus Road and the day of his death, Paul walked by faith (v. 7) and so would rather have been home in heaven with the Lord (v. 8). Today, in contrast, it sometimes seems that everybody wants to go to heaven, yet nobody wants to die! A pastor, at the end of a lesson to little children on being good, asked, "Where do you want to go?" The little voices shouted out "Heaven!" The pastor then asked, "And what must you be to get to heaven?" Without hesitation, the loud chorus yelled, "Dead!" But as St. Theresa said, all the way to heaven is heaven.

The time and patience with which fulfilled persons grow can be illustrated by the building of the modern city. That had to await eight primary inventions that came into common use during the 17-year period from 1876 to 1893. Until that time buildings were limited structurally to five or six floors in height. In 1890 the Chicago School of Architects became the first to use steel structural systems independent of a building's walls, creating a new form — the *skyscraper*. Second, throughout history, for moving up and down in buildings people used stairways. The development by Elisha Graves Otis of the safety latch for *elevators* made vertical movement in skyscrapers practical by 1889.

Thirdly, for *electricity* to become part of a city several other primary inventions were needed, such as power generators, distribution methods, and the electric light invented by Thomas Edison in 1880. The electric light allowed buildings to be designed with deeper interior spaces and permitted them to be used around the clock. Fourth, for heating it would have been difficult to bring wood or coal to all the stoves and fireplaces of a high building; *central heating* grew slowly in the latter 19th century.

Fifth, in the 1880's *unpolluted water* was supplied from central reservoirs in pipes below ground, finally making the village pump obsolete; and the delivery pressure made possible the flushing toilet. With the addition of sewer systems to carry away wastes, the typhoid epidemics which had scourged the large cities of Europe for more than 100 years were largely eliminated. Sixth was the invention of the *telephone* by Alexander Graham Bell in 1876. Seventh came the *automobile*. And eighth, the *subway*, first installed in London in 1890, made mass urban transit feasible and affordable.

While we live, we're to be aware of the mystery of growth. This mystery is within us as well as all around us. For us, it applies particularly to our growth as persons, which is the greatest perfection of all. Each of today's readings indicates that our growth comes from God, but we're responsible for working it out. God reveals His power with those who are in human eyes the weak, the insignificant, and the poor. That may be us. We, walking by faith, should be the *channels* of God's power in a world where there are so many people who are exiles, refugees, persecuted, despised, outcast, homeless, hungry, and sick. The critical issues in whether we achieve fullness of life are receptivity in faith, openness to God's action within us, confidence, and prayer.

TWELFTH SUNDAY IN ORDINARY TIME
Jb 38:1, 8-11   2 Cor 5:14-17   Mk 4:35-41

Patience and Peace in Personal Storms
Christ's Saving Presence in the World; Victory over Suffering,
Evil, and Death; Is God Asleep?; Who Can God Be?

Of all the forces around us, one of the most awesome is the sea. If you've done nothing more than swim in the ocean, you've felt its power. If you've ridden its deeps in a ship, you've come to respect it even more. The most awesome, however, is the sea in a storm. If you've had to go out unprotected in a gale, your awe changed to sheer terror as you struggled against the might of high and forceful waves.

To many ancients who had to battle the seas in tiny ships, the water showed the power and victory of God's creation. Sometimes, when they saw how wind and sea conspired together for the destruction of everything in their way, they identified the raging sea with the forces of evil. Israel's faith was influenced by these beliefs. For Israel, only their true God could "rule over the surging of the sea" (Ps 89:10) and "be more powerful than the roar of many waters" (Ps 93:4).

That's part of what today's First Reading is about. It's from the key section of the Book of Job, which book Alfred Lord Tennyson called "the greatest poem of ancient and modern times." Job was a tormented and rebellious man who raged against the human condition and demanded that God justify His ways to people. In a very long book, only two chapters at the beginning portray a patient Job, and he's rewarded for that patience in a few lines at the end. In between there's a very impatient Job — indeed, a Job who rails against the God who seems to have allowed him to suffer even though he's innocent. In today's passage, God speaks to Job out of a storm (v. 1) — a storm which, like others, revealed God's power and creative grandeur.

God's speech sweeps away all the irrelevant entanglements of the Deuteronomic argument that the good prosper and the wicked suffer in this life, which seem to be accepted by both Job and his friends. God puts Job's problem in a new perspective and opens up a vista in which, although still without an answer, it ceases to require an answer. Throughout God's long speech, of which we have here only a few lines, He doesn't make any positive propositions: He only puts to Job — majestically, patiently, ironically — a series of further questions that lead to God as the Creator and Master of the universe and who, therefore, has a wisdom and justice that transcend those of humans.

God, pretending to believe that Job knows what he, Job, is talking about, cross-examines him on what Job knows about God's activity in the universe. God's questions cover the most familiar phenomena of nature. If Job can't answer, how can he and God debate, and how can God explain to Job the deeper mysteries of His providence over people? Everywhere there are marvels, and everywhere also mystery.

Today's section deals only with God's actions with that tumultuous and threatening element, the sea. Through it, God reminds Job that he, Job, is just a creature, and only God is the Creator. God alone formed the earth and the seas, and He alone can calm the winds and waves of storms. He pictures the sea more as a troublesome infant, in need of a loving parent to keep it calm, to clothe it in clouds and swaddling bands and feed it, and thus stop its movement and its cries. He has set limits to his child, telling it where it can and cannot go. Job's imagery tends toward a picture of God as mother. And that's fitting. Although God transcends the human distinction between the sexes, God's parental tenderness can be expressed by the image of motherhood as well as fatherhood (*Catechism of the Catholic Church*, 239).

It's easy to see why Mark, Luke, and John all told the story of Jesus in the storm on the lake: It's a revelation that Jesus was truly God. There was nothing abnormal about the storm rising. Storms on the lake of Galilee, then as now, come up suddenly. The surface of the lake is 682 feet below sea level, and the mountains which surround it on almost all sides are between 1,000 and 2,000 feet above it. The air near the water therefore becomes warmer than that on the mountains a few miles away. When this warm air begins to rise rapidly, the cool air, rushing down from the mountains, causes sudden violent storms. This happens especially toward evening, when today's event took place (v. 35).

To the disciples, who earned their livelihood from fishing in this lake and knew its temperament, this storm must have been especially violent: Waves were breaking over the boat so violently that it was filling up (v. 37). Today's Responsorial Psalm echoes the storm theme. Sailors — even the most macho — who are at the mercy of the elements in a fierce storm at sea may well become instantly religious.

Mark's telling us that Jesus was asleep (v. 38) through it all is not just a description of a person resting: It's a theological statement. Just as in creation God had brought calm and order out of primordial chaos, here Jesus, who is equal to God, rests in Him. The disciples, however, didn't understand this. Like all of us in trouble, they cried for help. In their anxiety, they lost their respect a little: They asked, "Don't you care that we're perishing?" (v. 38).

Surprisingly, at the same time they called him "teacher." Jesus — like a teacher — reveals God to us. In this episode, Jesus' teaching is remarkably clear. He is indeed the one who does the things of God. His command to the wind and the sea — "Quiet! Be still!" (v. 39) — are words we would use today to a barking dog. They're the words Jesus had used to rebuke the "unclean spirit" who had possessed the demoniac in the synagogue at Capernaum, indicating that here the raging sea was identified with the forces of evil. The words suggest that God alone can exercise control over the forces of chaos. Jesus' concluding words ask the apostles why they were so terrified and why they were lacking in faith (v. 40).

In the silence after Jesus' rebuke, there descended a great awe (v. 41), not unlike that of the ancients facing the mysteries of the sea. Dramatically, this awe came upon all — those in the other boats which were with him (v. 36) as well as those in his own. Even kings couldn't do what he did, and the disciples' final question about who this could be (v. 41) needed reflection — and still does.

St. Paul's whole life consisted in one storm after another, most for the sake of Christ, and many with the people of Corinth. The occasion for his writing today's excerpt was that the Christians of Corinth were forsaking him, forging impossible loyalties with his opponents, and calling him names. Further, they were claiming mystical experiences — ecstasies — which they valued more than anything else. In their view, Paul was inferior to these ecstasies, because he never said anything about his having had mystical experiences himself, nor had he performed miracles.

In today's excerpt, Paul reminds everyone that, through all the storms of life, it's the love of Christ that counts. There's no doubt about the love coming from Christ's side of the equation. It remains for everyone to return that love in the ways Paul here enumerates: by being convinced about what Christ has done (v. 14), by living not for oneself but for others (v. 15), and by seeing all things in the new light of faith (v. 16). In that way people can be, in a favorite Pauline expression, "in Christ" (v. 17).

The three readings of today have several things in common. For one, there are absolute truths: that God can do all things, that Jesus is God, and that all of us go through storms in life. Shakespeare's use of the tempest for King Lear is an image of what life is for all of us, especially when we're not aware of Jesus' presence. Another lesson is victory over suffering and death. The Book of Job shows that the only one who has power over suffering is God. Paul applies it to our being "in Christ," which makes us "a new creation." That's not just an intellectual doctrine of faith, but a reflection of Paul's lived experience. It means that since Christ has died for us, we should be willing unselfishly to die to ourselves and live for him; it means that, just as Job ended up seeing God and all creation in a new light, so the experience of being in Christ leads us to see everything anew.

And the Gospel story of the storm is true not only in a literal sense wherein it happened once upon a time in Galilee, but in a symbolic sense as well. The great theologian St. Juliana of Norwich's most famous words are, "All shall be well, and all shall be well, and all manner of things shall be well." This is no pie in the sky; she heard the words in her visions of Jesus, on her sickbed at the age of thirty. Jesus told her, "You will not be overcome." She was very specific as she described her vision: "He did *not* say, 'You will never have a rough passage, you will never be over-strained, you will never feel uncomfortable,' but he *did* say, 'You will never be overcome.'"

Life presents all kinds of storms: disease, natural disasters, epidemics, and famines; and human anger, hatred, prejudice, injustice, betrayal, and selfishness. For Christians, acceptance of Jesus isn't a guarantee that we'll sail on trouble-free waters. To the contrary, Jesus invites us to travel on *unchartered* waters and to make for unfamiliar shores — and all this as darkness falls. The risk of faith demands a radical trust that, whatever our particular storms, Jesus is present; being conscious of his presence will give us a calm peace in all the storms of our life.

THIRTEENTH SUNDAY IN ORDINARY TIME
Ws 1:13-15;2:23f.   2 Cor 8:7, 9, 13-15   Mk 5: 21-43 [or 5:21-24, 35-43]

To Life!
Quality of Life; Life's Goal; The Mystery of Evil;
Faith and Trust; Life in Christ; True Healing

Henry Thoreau said that the mass of people live lives of quiet desperation. In support of that theory a study some time ago showed that people generally would — or think they would — order their lives differently if they could begin all over again. For instance, nearly one-third of all Americans would follow different occupations. Almost another third would seek more education, and about 15 percent would try to save more money. About 3.6 percent said they would develop their social lives more assiduously. Only 15.1 percent of the people — just more than one person in six — professed to be completely satisfied with life. Some people's lives are overshadowed by a fear of death.

Today's two Gospel stories, especially rich and touching, have in common attitudes to life and death. Both reveal the nature of a life beyond the mundane: a world of faith and salvation. All these — true life, faith, and salvation — are supremely positive realities. Life is the most precious of all human values.

Jairus, as an official of the synagogue (v. 22), had to be a big man to forget his prejudices against Jesus the outsider, big enough to swallow his pride to seek Jesus' help, and big enough to abandon his dignity to fall at Jesus' feet. Perhaps what motivated this good man to be so big right now was the tragedy that his daughter's illness would prevent her living into full womanhood. His daughter was now twelve years old (v. 42); at the age of twelve years and a day, she would be considered a woman. In his distress, Jairus asked Jesus to lay his hands on her. If that seemed to be telling Jesus how to perform the cure he was asking for, it was only because he had seen Jesus heal the sick that way, and so he thought it necessary.

It was while they were on their way to Jairus's daughter through a large crowd (v. 24) that a woman who'd been hemorrhaging vaginally for twelve years (v. 26) appeared. Her pathological bleeding rendered her legally unclean; its duration had also probably prevented marriage and motherhood. At the slightest suspicion that she suffered from this complaint the people would have driven her away mercilessly for exposing them to defilement. The physicians' remedies were prescriptions like eating a grain of barley found in the dung of a white mule, but they had no real cures and, as St. Mark tells us, they had taken all the money she had (v. 26).

The humiliated and embarrassed woman, unable to mention her difficulty, and fearful of being detected, came up behind him in the crowd for a cure (v. 27). Whereas Jesus' other miracles were done by his word or touch, here it's poignantly the woman who touched him (v. 28). Her touch didn't bother Jesus. He was able to break through some of the taboos of his time and, hopefully, will break through other taboos against women that still plague society today.

Her conduct, like that of Jairus, is a model of approaching Jesus in faith. It worked: She was cured of her infirmity (v. 29). But Jesus was immediately aware that power had gone out of him (v. 30). Jesus' healings, far from being an almost magical power that operated with no effort on his part, cost him. That's the way all worthwhile human endeavor works. People produce nothing great in life if they do no more than act with mere technical correctness. Actors, musicians, ministers, and all others who work with people must put themselves out if they're to truly affect others.

Up to now, in the midst of the tumult only the woman and Jesus knew what had taken place. Now the woman, with the turn of events making her tremble with fear, fell down before him and told him the whole truth (v. 33). What a relief! Now everything was out, and she deeply felt that Jesus understood! He let her know that it was her faith, not some magic or her furtive touch, that won her cure (v. 34).

No sooner had he finished with this grateful woman than people from Jairus's house arrived to tell Jairus with brutal directness that his daughter was dead (v. 35). At the news, Jairus's fear was as strong as that which had caused the woman's trembling. Jesus counseled Jairus not to be afraid and just have faith (v. 36). At Jairus's house, though, everyone had already begun their mourning customs of wailing, crying loudly (v. 38), and flute-playing — noises so that all might know that physical death, and its complete separation and desolation, had struck. Just as the messengers' despair had contrasted with Jairus's hope, now the mourners' unrestrained distress contrasted with Jesus' calm serenity.

When Jesus arrived at the scene, against the evidence he brashly said that the child wasn't dead but asleep (v. 39). We don't know whether Jesus meant this literally or theologically (that death is only a sleep). In either case, Jesus left the girl's condition unclear, so that he could more easily prevent the witnesses from speaking of the event as an unmistakable showing of his power to raise the dead. Perhaps he needn't have bothered, because at his words they ridiculed him (v. 40). Popular applause is never permanent.

That didn't bother Jesus: He put them all out. In a moving scene enacted before only the child's parents and Jesus' companions Peter, James, and John in the sick room, Jesus took the girl's hand and told her, in one of the few New Testament phrases in Aramaic, the language the Lord spoke, to get up (v. 41). (Perhaps the reason for the language is that Mark is quoting an eye-witness source, St. Peter.) The family and the three apostles were utterly astounded when she did (v. 42).

In today's portion of the Book of Wisdom, the author also speaks of life and death. He interprets the beginning of the Book of Genesis to arrive at the conclusion that God didn't make death (v. 13). God is the author of life, and He wants our lives to be imperishable. God created all things good, and made people in His own image and likeness; this means that we've been made for eternity.

Death is the work of the devil and people who choose his way. The book's author speaks not of physical death, but of that of which physical death is a sign: spiritual death, or the alienation from God caused by sin. True life is more than mere biological life; it's a fullness of existence which comes from intimacy with God. People are to live full lives — truly *full*, truly *alive* — by applying wisdom to moral conduct.

With regard to mourning and physical death, modern life has come to give them the same unmentionability that sex had in Victorian times. This suppression goes against the experience of the human race. Mourning is one of the traditional "rites of passage" through which people can pass over the loss of their dead and return to normal living. African-American funeral parades, Irish wakes, Jewish sitting *shivah*, and other customs like black arm bands, each in its own way fulfills this function. Psychologically, our attempts to hide death may result in various degrees of depression, alcohol, and callousness.

Some even go so far as to say that it's good to die. Testimony to that comes from the growing numbers of people who have "died" (that is, their heartbeat and breathing stopped) and then been revived. Survivors of these "near-death experiences" typically say that they felt themselves rushing through dark space, saw their lives pass before their eyes, and then entered a realm of light where they euphorically encountered deceased relatives or friends. Some find their flirtation with death so blissful, so intensely filled with joy, love, and peace, that they get a bit grumpy about returning to life. "Why did you bring me back, Doctor?" one complained. "It was so beautiful!"

What intrigues people about near-death experiences is more the tantalizing possibility that those who have them have caught sight of heaven. But what appears more likely is the physiological basis of the near-death experience: the fact that the human nervous system responds to threatening situations by releasing a deluge of chemicals into the bloodstream. These include polypeptides which, when activated, result in reduced sensitivity to pain and a sense of euphoria.

But the near-death experience leaves us with a greater riddle: Why is it that a human being's encounter with death is often attended not by grief and despair but by a sense of illumination and ecstasy? The most obvious message of the near-death reports — that death is nontraumatic — isn't news. Scientists have been saying as much for years. Certainly a *cause* of death can be disagreeable — it's no fun to have cancer, heart disease, or multiple sclerosis — but physicians who regularly tend to the dying agree that death in itself is not all that unpleasant.

To help us live — really *live* — St. Paul today encourages the people of the big, bustling, commercially rich city of Corinth to be as caring for others as Jesus was. They were to contribute generously to help the church of Jerusalem which, because of persecutions, was experiencing hardship. He said that to give us life, Jesus became poor (v. 9). Being equal to the Father, Jesus was rich, but he took on a human nature, thus becoming a part of our poor world of weakness and death, so that all who believe in him might receive his kind of riches. That surpasses all earthly riches in the same way that the life of salvation surpasses a life of quiet desperation. Paul's advice, if followed, would transform the world: that is, if those who have an excess were to give to the less fortunate, so that those who have little have no lack.

Life is precious. We may not understand why a twelve-year-old girl dies or why a woman is afflicted for many years with an awkward disease. That's in God's hands. Apart from miracles, God doesn't make exceptions to the laws of gravity or inertia or the confluence of physical vector forces; these are the laws that He has put into nature which enable the human mind to discern order in the universe and improve the world. And we must have faith to see beyond our present problems, troubles, and suffering to allow the Lord to be the master of our lives.

When life is in our hands, we should plead for it like Jairus, try to live it to the full like the woman with the hemorrhage, hang on to it like Paul — and define it correctly like the Book of Wisdom. The woman cured of the hemorrhage would die, and the little girl whom Jesus brought back from death would die again. But because of Jesus' action their chances for eternal and unending life were hopefully enhanced. We should do our utmost to better life's quality for everyone, including the unborn, and to trust in the Lord of Life. It's fitting that we join in the time-honored Jewish toast: *L'Chaim!* To Life!

FOURTEENTH SUNDAY IN ORDINARY TIME
Ezk 2:2-5   2 Cor 12:7-10   Mk 6:1-6

The Difference between Good and Evil
The Dignity of Persons; Reality vs. Appearances; Mistaking
Evil for Good — and Vice Versa; How Handle Weakness?;
Perseverance in Times of Discouragement

One of the most difficult jobs in the world is to tell the difference between good and evil. What is the face of evil? Count Dracula, a suck-
ing vampire with the close-up ugly face of a bat? Frankenstein, a man-
made monster who, when left to himself, will destroy and hurt? Some
unknown horror run amuck? The product of nightmares or of the imagination of a motion-picture director? If evil looked like any of those, it
would never attract anyone.

No, real evil is clean, brushed, scrubbed, shiny, and smelling of
the best perfume. He seems solicitous, asking, "How may I help you?"
He uses the correct spoon at dinner, knows the right wines, and is suave
and urbane. He laughs in elegant parties, cries at Mozart, and has a piece
of enough corporate structures to support him. Most dangerous, his
inner thoughts and desires are wicked, but his smile and pleasing appearance lead even the careful into his trap.

And, as Alexander Pope's famous lines (*Essay on Man*) attest,
we grow accustomed to the face of evil. He wrote:

> Vice is a monster of so frightful mien,
> As to be hated needs but to be seen;
> Yet seen too oft, familiar with her face,
> We first endure, then pity, then embrace.

It's fitting that "evil" is most of the word "devil," because evil
always has something to do with the father of lies. It's also fitting that
"evil" is "live" spelt backwards, because evil always involves spiritual death or murder.

It's not their sins *per se* that characterize evil people — everyone falls on occasion — but rather it's the persistence and consistency
of their sins. This is because the central defect of evil isn't the sin but
the refusal to acknowledge it. Evil people are to be pitied, not hated,

because their superficial equanimity masks depths of sheer terror known
to few. We don't become partners to evil by accident. As adults, we're
not forced by fate to become trapped by an evil power; we set the trap
ourselves.

When Jesus came to Nazareth in the scene in this morning's
Gospel, those at the synagogue had to make a choice between good
and evil. They made the wrong choice: They rejected goodness. Their
rejection of him was not a product of personality clash, temperamen-
tal differences, or issues related to immaturity and behavior, but followed from Jesus' faith and commitment. It was easier for them — as
it is for us — to do nothing than to do something, easier to be negative
than positive, easier to be destructive than creative — easier, in short,
to confuse good with evil. The anonymous student poet put it well:

> I will do more than belong — I will participate.
> I will do more than care — I will help.
> I will do more than believe — I will practice.
> I will do more than be fair — I will be kind.
> I will do more than forgive — I will love.
> I will do more than earn — I will enrich.
> I will do more than teach — I will serve.
> I will do more than live — I will grow.
> I will do more than be friendly — I will be a friend.

Jesus' being rejected was also due to the growing opposition from
the authorities. His first preaching at the synagogue in Nazareth had
aroused the townspeople to the point of their wanting to kill him by
throwing him from the hill on which their town was built. After that
he moved his mother to live at Capernaum for safety, and he worked
out of there instead of Nazareth. It took a great deal of courage for him
now to return to Nazareth, but he loved his home-town neighbors.

They, however, thought him not worthy of a hearing, for two
reasons. First, he was merely a worker. He worked with his hands in
wood, and stone, and metal. He fixed doors and windows, built houses,
and made plows. Some of them, like some of us, thought that people
who work with their hands are incapable of any level of intellectual
capacity which could command their respect.

The second reason for their rejection of Jesus was that they were
so close to him. They called him the son of Mary, whom they knew.

Inasmuch as customary usage referred to one's lineage in terms of the father, they probably intended their phrase as an insult, a way of calling him illegitimate. It's also possible that no insult was intended, but that Joseph had died.

He was also related to many of the townspeople. The word translated as "brother" may mean extended family in the sense of cousins or other remote relatives. Two of the names listed here — James and Joses — are elsewhere described by St. Mark's Gospel (15:40) as sons of a different Mary. Mark tells us that the people's lack of faith so distressed Jesus that he could work no miracle there — not that he *chose* to work no miracle there, but because of their hardness he *couldn't* work any miracles there.

Ezekiel, the prophet of today's First Reading, also suffered rejection. He lived before, during, and after the exile of the Hebrews in Babylon — some time between 593 and 571 B.C. One of those who were carried off into captivity in Babylon by Nebuchadnezzar, he's the only prophet ever called to be a prophet outside of the Holy Land. Before his time his people were mostly known as Hebrews; after him they were known as Jews, for Judea, the name of their southern kingdom.

In the first part of his book, from which today's excerpt comes, Ezekiel tries to call his people to repentance; even God recognizes the futility of the job. It's frustrating to be called to be God's spokesman and to realize that people won't listen. It's the same at any time for good people of God whose society rejects God's message.

Because of the people's sins, Ezekiel predicted the destruction of Jerusalem and the further devastation of their country. His preaching forced the people to choose between faith and politics — between a creative God-respecting pull and a destructive God-rejecting one. Seeing mighty Jerusalem as inviolable, the hard and obstinate people didn't believe him and continued to wallow in their sins. In 587, when King Nebuchadnezzar destroyed Jerusalem and Ezekiel was vindicated — too late — Ezekiel changed his message to a promise of salvation through a New Covenant with the Lord.

Ezekiel saw enough evil in people to warrant giving up trying to help them. His temptation would have been to magnify the faults of others and to minimize their goodness. But he says here, as well as many times elsewhere, that God's Spirit entered into him to strengthen him to speak in God's behalf. The Spirit addressed Ezekiel as "Son of Man," a phrase Ezekiel used over 90 times to contrast people, all of whom are essentially transitory, weak, changing mortal flesh, with God, Who is essentially unchanging, strong, immortal spirit. Despite the evil that people sometimes do, the temptation for some — in our own time, too — is to give the human race a position far above what it deserves. We have to see the dignity of persons in its proper perspective — making persons neither too little nor too great.

Not only must we be careful to discern the differences between good and evil in *others*: We must be equally careful with *ourselves*. In today's Second Reading, St. Paul gives us the example. Paul tells of the "thorn in the flesh" with which he was afflicted. Many have speculated as to what this might have been: persecution at the hands of his own people, temptation of some kind, his physical appearance, an affliction like epilepsy, a disease like malaria, some psychosomatic illness, or Paul's sufferings undergone specifically for Jesus — such as abandonment by former friends, Christians suspicious of a converted persecutor, beatings, imprisonment, betrayal, and shipwreck.

Paul's letters have many metaphors involving sports. It's doubtful that he would root for the Yankees or the Cubs or the Red Sox, though: Of all the aspects of sports that the early Christians could have condemned, such as nudity, it was professionalism that they deplored. While they might have favored such one-on-one sports as tennis, they might have seen rooting for the Washington Redskins over the Dallas Cowboys — not many of whom come from Washington or Dallas — as analogous to rooting for GM over Ford or General Electric over Westinghouse. Perhaps he would favor soccer, in which the players truly come from the place they represent, if it keeps professionalism out.

But Paul admired strength and deplored weakness. Yet God taught Paul that what some considered weakness can mean strength, and that Paul's affliction was not an evil but a benefit. It kept him humble. Even more, it gave God an opportunity to show His strength through Paul's weakness.

We may find it difficult to discern what's good for our lives. Everyone has a thorn. It may be a physical disability, a complex, a potential for neurotic behavior. That isn't necessarily all evil. If God doesn't take away our thorn, He will give us the strength to bear it. One thing is sure: We're called to be God's prophets. The Good News must be preached to the end of time, even to those who are unwilling to listen.

In the Responsorial Psalm a few moments ago, we said, "Our eyes are fixed on the Lord." That's the bottom line of what differentiates good from evil. Let's pray for goodness: that God will make us as courageous as Ezekiel to speak His word to our world, that we may be as able as Paul to find strength in our weakness, and that we may follow "the way" of Jesus in order to share God's word with others, even when our audience is unwilling to listen.

FIFTEENTH SUNDAY IN ORDINARY TIME
Am 7:12-15   Eph 1:3-14 or 1:3-10   Mk 6:7-13

A Cosmic Plan for Life's Meaning
Mission Impossible?; The Gospel as the Light of Truth; Cosmic Figures

One of the reasons given for modern youth's use of drugs and alcohol, their rates of crime, accidents, suicide, and other problems, is that youth perceive life as a mindless meaninglessness. According to the theologian Paul Tillich, the word "God" translates as the depth of our life, the source of our being, and our ultimate concern: what we take seriously without any reservation. So our search for meaning connects with our search for God.

Little of youth's exposure — in school, in the media, or among their peers — prepares them to seek life's meaning. They see nothing worth dying for. And if you have nothing to die for, you have nothing to live for. As a result, when youth think of the future, they think of how they're going to make a living instead of how they're going to live their life.

The author of the "Queen of the Epistles," Ephesians, which we read today and for the next six Sundays, tries to suggest meaning — affirmative, positive, beautiful meaning — to life. The beginning of the letter, one of the most profound passages in the New Testament (parallel to Col 1:15-20 and comparable to the prologue of St. John's Gospel), contains what isn't popular today: lyricism and praise. Praise is the form of prayer which recognizes most immediately that God is God. It lauds God for His own sake and gives Him glory, quite beyond

what He does, but simply because He is. By praise, the Holy Spirit is
joined to our spirits to bear witness that we're children of God (*Catechism of the Catholic Church* 2639).

For unfathomable reasons, God has chosen us for blessings which
are otherwise found only in heaven. What God has given, we can't
achieve on our own. We *can* arrive at knowledge, acquire skills, reach
positions of power, and amass wealth on our own — but by ourselves
we *can't* come to every spiritual blessing in the heavens (v. 3) which
God freely gives to us in Christ. Why did God choose to give us so
many spiritual blessings? The letter (v. 4) gives three reasons.

The first reason is that God wants us to be *holy*. That means to
be set apart, to be different from the ordinary. People's calling to be
holy isn't to take them *out* of the world, but to make them different
within the world. Christians should be sufficiently different from other
people to be recognizable as Christians in how they transact business,
in the way they converse, and in everything else they do.

The second reason for God giving us so many blessings that provide meaning to life is that His cosmic plan has made it possible for us
to be *blameless*, or *without blemish*. In the Jewish sacrifices, to be
worthy of being offered to God an animal had to be certified by inspection to be unblemished. Christians, too, must be certifiable — not
as being only *respectable*, but as people who by their *perfection* are
worthy of God. Christians aren't to meet only human standards, but
those of God. They do this especially by living in His love.

That brings us to the letter's third reason for God giving us so
many spiritual blessings: to fill us with His kind of *love*. Many who
fail to see meaning in life dwell pessimistically upon the evil in the
world and in people. They gloss over an equally important part of the
divine plan: We've been *redeemed*. Part of God's deliverance consists
in the forgiveness of sin, that haunting deterrent to holiness, blamelessness, and love — a situation from which we ourselves are powerless to set ourselves free.

Many scholars opine, though, that to show God's love Jesus
would have come among us even if the human race had never sinned.
The implications of that are staggering. Without believing that, it's no
wonder that some of the world's most sensitive minds wind up frustrated over their feeling of utter inadequacy and sheer powerlessness.

God's cosmic plan calls for us to develop a virtue which we don't
think about sufficiently any more: *wisdom* (v. 9). This is the quest of

searching minds for depths of insight and understanding and a long view of God's cosmic plan. If properly handled, wisdom can be a source of oneness for people in all our personal and social tensions.

If, however, we think that our efforts for meaning in life are going to be easy or show immediate results, we will be disappointed. The oldest writing prophet, Amos, reminds us of that. He lived in the eighth century B.C., a contemporary of Isaiah, Micah, and Hosea. It was a time of great prosperity in Israel, unfortunately accompanied by falling social and religious standards characterized by widespread corruption. A good psychologist by nature, he began his message by condemning the crimes of the entire circle of Israel's neighbors. As long as he stuck to criticizing others, the crowd applauded loudly. But then Amos condemned the crimes of Israel, and that didn't go over well at all. People want to feel good, to be thanked, to be appreciated, to be told how good they are — and they don't want to be told that they're sinners.

Called the "Prophet of Social Justice" because he spoke out against the social ills of his day, Amos had three things going against him. First, his message of social justice was unpopular among the high-living wealthy who were the ones benefiting most from the extraordinary economic expansion at the time. Second, Amos was a Southern dirt-farmer from Judah now in the royal shrine at Bethel, one of the sophisticated Northern territory of Israel's most prominent sanctuaries. And lastly, Amos, poor himself, spoke aloud of his insight that the evils around him stemmed from greed.

The reactions against Amos were no different than they are today in those places where there's a gap between rich and poor, or where words of prophecy come from people who have no official standing. The powerful priest Amaziah — a time-serving professional chiefly interested in his fees — attacked Amos bitterly and told him to leave and never show his face there again. Amos's humble answer was that he was no professional prophet; he was a man involved in the livestock and fruit trade who prophesied only because God commanded him to.

The contrast between the two men was between acceptance and rejection, faithfulness and unfaithfulness, arrogance and humility. So Amos was expelled from Israel; but today, while we well remember the prophet Amos, we have a difficult time even pronouncing the name of the priest Amaziah, and a hard time remembering that the name of the king against whom Amos railed was Jeroboam II.

Jesus took steps to provide the world with what the letter to the Ephesians and the Book of Amos were talking about: meaning to life, hope to a fragmented world, and cosmos (unity, order) out of chaos. (It's amusing that the word "cosmetics," which comes from "cosmos," has the same meaning: to bring order out of chaos.) As Amos had been sent to preach social justice and Paul to preach repentance to pagans as well as Jews, both in the face of rejection, so Jesus sent the twelve apostles.

Jesus sent them forth two by two to do a job that wasn't like parents dealing with their small children who want to help paint the living room: Parents might give their children a little brush and assign them to work on a small corner, intending to cover it later with their big brush. No, this is a job that's incumbent on all of us through the entire history of the world: to bring the Good News to all who will listen. They were to go forth in such utter simplicity, complete trust, and phenomenal generosity that they weren't to take much more with them than the clothes on their backs, and they were always to give of themselves. They weren't to demand anything in return, but had the right to rely upon hospitality.

Jesus' rules were probably prudent practices that he himself lived by. Neither he nor his followers were to have the trappings of the usual itinerant preacher. At that time, wandering preachers each had his own bag of tricks or enticements to people. Not unlike the medicine show barkers of our country's frontier days, although these preachers may have had a few good thoughts, their primary purpose was to make money.

Not creating any message of their own, the apostles were to present Jesus' own meaning to life: conversion of heart, a total and radical reorientation. Disturbing to those whose way of life was just a dawdling toward death, this meant a vigorous turning around of one's whole value system — away from self and in the direction of intense service in behalf of God and others.

Life has the potential of being chock full of meaning. Actualizing that potential can unlock the vast untapped resources for good in all of us. No steam or gas drives anything until it's confined; no life ever grows great until it's focused, dedicated, disciplined. Everyone who takes seriously God's word in today's portion of the letter to the Ephesians, the example of Amos, and the transaction between Jesus and his apostles will have plenty to think about in discerning life's meaning. Then it's incumbent upon us, as with Amos, and the author of the letter to the Ephesians, and Jesus and his first apostles, to make life's meaning known.

SIXTEENTH SUNDAY IN ORDINARY TIME
Jr 23:1-6   Eph 2:13-18   Mk 6:30-34

Leadership and Followership
The Authority of Service; The Lord Is my Shepherd;
Vocation; Smugness; The Compassion of Jesus

Someone once said that a leader is a person "who knows the way, goes the way, and shows the way." It's also said that management is efficiency in climbing the ladder of success; leadership determines whether the ladder is leaning against the right wall.

Yet the idea of a leader varies from time to time and place to place. On the American frontier, it was a two-fisted gun-slinging defender of the wronged. In the business world, it's a person — man or woman — making crisp decisions, single-handedly setting far-ranging policies, in command of many subordinates. In the military, it's a person who can get others to follow through thick and thin.

Various types of leadership are shown in major sports. In baseball, where each player is fundamentally on his own, the manager is literally below ground, watching the field action from the dugout. In football, whose top-down leadership has to be in tight control, the coach is in a sense high above the team, since he has spotters sitting in the stands to help him call formations. In basketball, which is flow, process, spontaneity, real team play, voluntary cooperation, and chemistry, the coach positions himself right next to the action and communicates with his players as they move up and down the court.

Today's Gospel picture gives joy to anyone who considers the measure of leadership to be popularity: People were coming to Jesus in great numbers, and he and his apostles had no opportunity even to eat (v. 31). For Jesus, however, a religious leader's life is a series of goings from the presence of people to the presence of God and back again. But he knew that there are dangers in each of the alternatives. One can spend too much time in the activities of people and thus gradually lose the vision of God. And one can go to God to escape the companionship of people. The *good* religious leader knows the middle way: being refreshed by God to have something to offer to people, and loving people enough to help them with their lives.

Jesus, seeing that it was time to get away from people and go to God, extended an invitation to his apostles to come away by themselves to an out-of-the-way place for a while. In truth, the press of the crowds wasn't the *whole* reason for getting away: Herod's recent murder of John the Baptist affected Jesus deeply. The place Jesus and his apostles headed for was four miles across the Lake of Galilee by boat and ten miles around the top of the lake on foot. People saw Jesus and his apostles leaving by boat (v. 33) and spread the word, so that thousands hurried to the place on foot, arriving ahead of them.

Beating Jesus there wasn't hard to do, especially if there were a dead calm and oppressive heat which made rowing exhausting or if the boat faced a strong head wind. As they disembarked Jesus saw the vast crowd (v. 34). A sham leader would have been annoyed: His private space had been invaded, his much-needed rest denied, his special time spoiled. But Jesus' heart was moved with pity for the people, because they were like sheep without a shepherd.

His words recall the metaphor early on in the Jewish Scriptures of the shepherd being the many kings, priests, and prophets; they protected, provided for, led, and guided their people. The image indicates that the authority of such leaders isn't to be equated with power, or with the ability to impose their will on the people they govern. The shepherd's role is one of service. He must set directions, enable a community to function smoothly, and try to create conditions that will enable people to live with dignity.

Equally importantly, the ancient Hebrews applied the metaphor of the shepherd also to God. Some religions believe in a God who is a creator, who merely makes the world and people and sets things in motion. One of the distinctive understandings of the Jewish and Christian Scriptures is that God, who created us in love, continues to reach out to us and to care for us as does a shepherd with his sheep.

So it was with the tender-hearted Jeremiah in today's First Reading. Already in his time — the troubled times before the Babylonian Captivity — the Holy Land's rocky and hilly terrain was more suited to sheep grazing than agriculture. Sheep were not often killed for a meal, but were raised primarily for milk and for wool: milk for drinking and cheese, wool for clothing and blankets and tents. Shepherd and sheep were very close, the shepherd giving his sheep names as we give our pet animals — names to which the sheep would respond.

The other side of shepherding is the place of the sheep. They're among the dumbest of animals, often needing help even in giving birth. They require the constant care of a dedicated and long-suffering shepherd. The shepherd had to provide all their needs: He led them to good pastures and to water, rescued them from dangers, searched for them if they got lost, and protected them from predatory animals. For this he had his rod, staff, and slingshot; the last was like David's in the Goliath incident; with the slingshot he was very accurate, for his life and the life of his sheep depended on his skills. It's not very flattering for the people of God to be thought of as sheep. Some of them — a small percentage — direct their lives into unsolvable problems to be bailed out of, thinking to do so without God.

The kings of Jeremiah's time, the last of Judah, weren't good leaders, being either weak or cruel. Jeremiah begins today's passage by asserting woe to shepherds who mislead (v. 1). With the current King Zedekiah, the long line of kings who succeeded David was coming to an end. The vacillating Zedekiah, heedless of Jeremiah's advice, would be taken captive by King Nebuchadnezzar in the final moments of Judah's history. But, like a flower growing out of a dung hill, in the midst of despair sprang hope. Jeremiah predicted that God would raise up in David's line a future king of justice and honesty (v. 5). The Church's response in today's liturgy is the Responsorial Psalm, the "Good Shepherd" Psalm (23).

That Jesus fulfilled the eternal plan of God is a major thought of the letter to the Ephesians. Today's passage refers specifically to that part of God's plan to bring together Gentiles (those "who once were far off") and Jews (those "who have become near" [v. 13]) and to make a new, universal Church, all united under the leadership of the Good Shepherd, Christ.

That the letter would extend God's compassion to those outside Israel was a real surprise. When the letter was written, some time after the middle of the first century A.D., the Jews hated the Gentiles. The division between them was rigid. The Jew was circumcised as a sign of his covenant with God, the Gentile not. The Gentiles had no hope of a Messiah, the Jews had; so for the Jew, history was always linear, going somewhere, optimistic, while for the Gentile history was cyclic, going in circles, therefore pessimistic. Jews considered themselves a *holy* people, therefore separate from others, the Gentiles not. The head of Gentile peoples might be a king, tyrant, oligarch, senate, or council; the Jews considered their head to be God. The Jews had a covenant with God, the Gentiles not.

Part of the barriers separating Jew from Gentile was psychological. The Mosaic Law for the Jewish people made social intercourse with Gentiles impossible. No Jew could enter a Gentile's home, for fear of contamination from idols. And the rigorous Jewish dietary regulations made any contact with Gentiles at meals a source of anxiety. On the Gentile side, some admired Jewish purity of morals while others responded with scorn.

The barrier was also physical. The Temple in Jerusalem consisted of a series of courts, as would be present at the palace of a king (which was in part how they saw their God). Farthest out was the Court of the Gentiles, then came the Court of the Women, followed by the Court of the Israelites, and finally, adjacent to the Holy Place and the innermost Holy of Holies, the Court of the Priests. Each court was raised a bit above the previous one, making a good line of sight from one to the other difficult. Between the Court of the Gentiles and the rest of the Temple was a partitioning wall, on which were signs prohibiting any non-Jew from going further under pain of death.

The rest of the ancient world, too, was full of barriers. For the most sophisticated people of the time — the Greeks — everything non-Greek was barbarian. We get our word "barbarian" from the fact that the Greeks looked down upon all other languages than their own, claiming they sounded like "bah, bah." For the Greeks, it didn't matter that other civilized people existed. Naturally, the "barbarians" reciprocated the hatred.

Do you think all of that strange? Think of our own time. We have tariff barriers, divisions of nations, race discrimination, economic disparity, the war of the sexes, and class hatred. Shamefully, even in Christian churches there are divisions between denominations. Within parishes, there can be divisions between "old-timers" and "newcomers," between rich and poor, between one clique and another.

To bring all together, there's no better leader than the self-giving Jesus Christ. Dying on the cross for *all* people, Jesus made it possible to break down the dividing walls of enmity (v. 14) and to create a new people (v. 15). That word "new" has at least two meanings. One is in the order of time. Thus a widget off an assembly line is new, but it's exactly like the thousands of other widgets that came off the assembly line before it. The other meaning of the word "new" is in the order of novelty. This means to bring an item into the world that didn't exist before. That's the sense in which Jesus makes possible a new human race.

No matter what your idea of a good leader, you will see it in Jesus. Those who partake of his leadership are not only clergy in the Church and officials in the State, but also shepherds at such other important levels as parents and teachers. It's they who help develop youths' character, lay the foundations for growth, communicate values by which people live, and foster faith and commitment.

But good leadership, to be effective, also requires followers. Followers of Jesus come in all kinds: those who are faithful, those who stray from the group, those who contribute to crises of authority. More than just a mob or a group, we must form a true community, a part of the Good Shepherd's flock. Those principles of leadership and followership provide the formula for a new human race.

SEVENTEENTH SUNDAY IN ORDINARY TIME
2 K 4:42-44   Eph 4:1-6   Jn 6:1-15

A Hierarchy of Values
Values without God: Possible?; Unity and Fellowship;
Signs of God; God Answers All Our Needs

A story's told about a man who dreaded making up his mind, and with good reason. He once inherited $4 million, but he had to accept it in either Chile or Brazil. He chose Brazil, but it turned out that in Chile he would have received his inheritance in land on which uranium, gold, and silver had just been discovered. In Brazil he had to choose between receiving his inheritance in coffee or nuts. He chose nuts. The bottom fell out of the nut market, and coffee went up 80 cents a pound. He lost everything.

He sold his watch for money to fly home. The ticket-seller made him choose between New York and Los Angeles. He chose Los Angeles just as the New York plane taxied up. It was a brand-new super-duper job with red carpets and chic hostesses. The Los Angeles plane, a trimotor with a sway back, took what seemed like a day to get off the ground. It was filled with crying children and tethered goats.

Over the Andes, one engine fell off. Our man crawled up to the cockpit and said, "I'm the jinx on this plane. Let me out if you want to save your lives." The pilot agreed, but added, "On this airline, anybody who bails out must wear two chutes."

He jumped out of the plane, and spent a minute trying to make up his mind which ripcord to pull. Finally he chose the one on the left. The wire pulled loose. He pulled the other handle. The chute opened, but its shroud lines snapped. In desperation, the poor fellow cried out, "St. Francis, save me!"

A great hand reached down from heaven, seized the fellow by the wrist, and let him dangle in mid-air. Then a gentle but inquisitive voice asked, "St. Francis Xavier or St. Francis of Assisi?"

Many people think that, as they go through life, they're choosing a hierarchy of values which will stand them in good stead when they arrive at a period of crisis. Others say that to choose a hierarchy of values is impossible: Life's constantly changing, and the only way you can tell your values is to live each moment and make your choices on the basis of whatever comes up.

Among those who believe that we can prioritize a set of values are the authors of the Sacred Scriptures. And among the many passages in the Scriptures which catalogue values is today's section of the letter to the Ephesians. It mentions values for the Christian community at Ephesus to cherish — values that should result in unity and charity in the Body of Christ, the primary effects of what today's Gospel is about.

The first value befitting the life worthy of our call is *humility*. Christian humility is a brand-new value that had never existed before. When the ancient Greeks, who achieved the highest level of culture people have ever achieved without God's revelation, spoke of humility, they meant something mean and debasing. Even today, when non-Christians speak of humility, they look down upon it as something soft, weak, and unworthy of a human race that's expected to fight and dominate nature.

Christian humility isn't soft or weak, and it isn't easy. To practice it means to be aware of oneself completely, warts and all. But we can't know where we truly stand unless we hold ourselves up against a measuring-rod. People who consider themselves good golfers can't appraise themselves realistically unless they know how the best pros are playing. Amateur painters can't know how good or bad they are unless they know what the masters have done. And with humility, as with all values, Jesus is the model.

The *gentleness* mentioned in Ephesians as a value means, essentially, *self-control*. It's the mean between being too angry and not angry enough. It means not being angry at the wrong time, and being angry at the right time. Like Jesus, we're not expected to be placid to the point of being phlegmatic, not rising to occasions when we witness evil. Like Jesus, we must get angry with hypocrisy and with money-changing at the expense of the poor and powerless. Like Jesus, we must become angry to the point of doing something about the injustices in our world.

The next value mentioned is *patience*. This is a species of *courage*. Of that Shakespeare wrote, "Cowards die many times before their deaths; the valiant never taste of death but once." Patience means imitating God, who if He weren't patient would have destroyed the human race a long time ago. It pertains particularly to our dealings with other people: not taking revenge, suffering fools with as much tolerance as we can muster, and avoiding such mottoes of the world as "Don't get mad, get even!"

What makes it possible to practice these values is a more finely-honed *love*, which is the queen of all values and virtues. Love was important even to the ancient Greeks, who gave it not one word, but at least four. *Eros* was the lowest level for them, a matter of getting and not giving: not only sexually, as in our derivative "erotic," but in other areas as well. *Philia* meant brotherly love, a matter of giving as well as getting: a mutual exchange of conversation as well as other things, and wishing fellow humans well. Then they had *storgé*, which characterized family affection.

At the top of the Greeks' list was a word they didn't use often: *agapé*, which was a total giving, a kind of ecstatic experience in which you go outside yourself — for that's what "ecstatic" means — in your love for another. That's the word that the letter to the Ephesians uses for Christian love.

If we *practice* these values as well as *esteem* them, we can achieve the much-needed but difficult value of unity. Unity for believers is the consequence of one body, one Spirit, one hope, one Lord, one faith, one baptism, one God and Father of all (vv. 4f.). The passage mentions the word "one" seven times, in Jewish thought a perfect number. From faithfulness to all these values will issue forth peace, which many seek, but not all find.

To show the merit of adherence to values despite obstacles, today's First Reading asks us to consider one of the "Elisha Cycle" of stories. In the ninth century B.C., Elisha was the successor of the awesome prophet Elijah. Elijah became a figure whom the Jews connected with the final age, a sign that the greatness of his time would be restored. Thus some bystanders at the foot of Jesus' cross would misunderstand him to be calling Elijah (Mk 15:35), so ominous were the events surrounding Jesus' crucifixion. Jews recall Elijah's memory even today when they put out a cup of wine for him at their Passover meal.

Because Elisha succeeded Elijah, many stories were told of Elisha as well — stories that make the two prophets larger than life. The stories are at times legends, and are narrated to establish the prophets' power and authority as men of God. Today's Elisha story takes place during a time of famine. The story sets the pattern for the Gospels' story of Jesus' multiplication of the loaves and fish. There are similarities between the stories: in both, food is brought to a man of God, a large number of people are fed with a small amount of food, the food used is bread, a servant protests that the task is impossible, yet the people have enough to eat, and there is in fact food left over.

Today's Gospel is from St. John's sixth chapter, parts of which will be read for the next four Sundays. Today's story is one of the few told by all four Gospels. Its words of Jesus' taking the bread, giving thanks, and distributing it reflect the Eucharist. The Eucharist is a special kind of bread: one which we need as much for the nourishment of our spiritual life as we need material bread for our bodily life. Gandhi once said, "To the poor man, God does not appear except in the form of bread and the promise of work." The Eucharist renews the deepest springs of our humanity through bread broken and eaten for the life of the world.

The Eucharist makes us companions — literally "bread-sharers," from the Latin *cum* and *panis*. And the miracle of the bread shows God's abundance, in which we recall the abundant wine at Cana, the abundant water which Jesus promised the Samaritan woman at the well, and the abundance of the Spirit which would be poured out. God's generosity is a recurring theme throughout the Bible.

The Gospel story presents for our consideration three people. There is, first of all, Philip, who lived in the region in which Jesus faced this crowd of thousands. When Jesus asked Philip what to do about feeding the crowd, all Philip could see were the difficulties: A half year's wages wouldn't buy enough food for each of them to have a little bit (v. 7). Like some of us, he seemed reluctant to get involved in a problem that looked too big to solve.

Andrew knew the logistics, too, but his attitude was a bit more optimistic, pointing to a boy there who had five barley loaves and two fish (v. 9). Barley was the cheapest kind of bread there was: the bread of the poor. Fish at that time before refrigeration wouldn't last long, and to preserve them one had to pickle or dry them not too long after catching them. It's hard to tell what Andrew had in mind in bringing forward the loaves and fish, but he had faith in Jesus and felt it worthwhile to take a chance.

Then there was the boy. Did he, like other boys, run as fast as he could for no reason but to feel the hard ground under his feet? Walk along kicking rocks and dragging a stick, amazed by the buds on the trees? Push damp hair from his hot face, cheeks streaked from dirty hands that built roads, lakes, and towns in lumpy gravel? Stomp through puddles in light rain until his pants and shoes were soaked? See no difference between reality and make-believe, seeing with his heart instead of his head? Did he remind Jesus of his own boyhood?

In any case, this boy had either to eat his fish himself, bring them home, or sell them among the crowd. He had the innocence, trust, and openness which were among the qualities that Jesus admired in children. He came forth as bidden and, as far as he knew, if he gave up his food he wouldn't be getting anything back. But he gave his bread and his fish — which, aside from the clothes on his back, were all he had.

Let's pray that the poet's (T.V.N., *Loaves and Fishes*) observation of the boy after the multiplication of the loaves and fish might be true of us:

> Then perhaps the lad said proudly,
> "Jesus took my little lot,
> Blessed and broke my loaves and fishes,
> See what everybody's got!"
> Lord, I haven't much to give you,
> But I'll give you all I've got.
> You could make it work a wonder,
> Bless and use my little lot.

EIGHTEENTH SUNDAY IN ORDINARY TIME
Ex 16:2-4, 12-15   Eph 4:17, 20-24   Jn 6:24-35

God in the Image of People, or Vice Versa?
The Goodness of God; The Spiritual over the Material; Get the Spirit!

A man in the Bible Belt owned a remarkable horse which he had trained
to go only if the rider said, "Praise the Lord," and would stop only if
he said, "Amen." The man decided to sell the horse, but when he explained the horse's peculiarities to a prospective buyer, the buyer said,
"That's ridiculous. I've been raising horses all my life. I'll make him
go *my* way." So he jumped on the horse and kicked him until he started
to run. The horse ran faster and faster. Worried, the buyer reined back
and yelled, "Whoa!" But the horse wouldn't stop. Suddenly the man
realized they were galloping toward the edge of a cliff. Desperately he
yelled, "Oh, all right, *Amen!*" The horse screeched to a halt just in time.
Peering down over the edge of the cliff, the man wiped the perspira-
tion from his brow. "Whew," he said, "Praise the Lord!"

As we think of God do we, like the buyer of the horse, try to make
Him in the image of ourselves or do we truly understand that we're
made in the image of God? If we're not God-man, then we're man-
god; what word comes first is important.

In today's passage from the Book of Exodus, for example, we
see the Jews rejecting the God who is; at that point they — like many
people of all times — would rather have had a god of their own making. During the years in the desert, when the Jews were coming to the
Promised Land and God was giving many signs of His special providence, they complained of being hungry. So God directed them to
manna, a natural food that was perhaps the gum of a tree, or the hon-
eydew excretion of insects that live on a common desert shrub, the tama-
risk.

Because manna resembled white corn, it was later described as
the bread of angels. God told them they were to collect enough manna
each day to satisfy their hunger for that day, and the day before the
Sabbath they were permitted to collect twice as much in order that they
could devote the Sabbath to God. As today's Responsorial Psalm says,
"The Lord gave them bread from heaven."

Many of the people, more self-centered than God-centered, went out to gather manna on the Sabbath. And many complained that the manna was monotonous; they wanted it to taste differently from one day to the next. So God provided quail, exhausted after their long migration from Europe and easily caught. This didn't satisfy them, either. Frequently they even languished for the pots in which they cooked meat in Egypt, even though their enslaved condition there had made them very unhappy. Complaints about the way God acts come down to our own times. Having a god in our own image is more comfortable than having ourselves in God's image, and makes a god easier to handle.

So it was in Our Lord's time, too. When he multiplied the few loaves and fish into enough for more than five thousand people, the enthusiastic people wanted to make a king of this god in their image. Next day, when the people finally caught up with him as he fled from them into Capernaum, their petty chit-chat caused them to ask him how he got there (v. 25). Jesus, realizing that life was too short for banter like that, ignored the question. He told them, in effect (v. 26), "You people are unable to think of your souls for thinking of your stomachs." He added (v. 27), in our terms, that junk food can never satisfy spiritual hunger, and advised them to go for food that remains into eternity.

As for material food, in their time the luxurious meals of Roman society were matters of legend. There were feasts of peacock's brains and nightingales' tongues; there were emetics between courses so people could vomit and eat more; there were meals costing thousands of dollars. But some people had a deep hunger that none of this could satisfy. And we still hunger for things beyond food: for forgiveness, for reconciliation, for kindness, for restoration in relationships, for justice, for joy in place of bitterness and cynicism, for peace, for unity — in short, for taking away the emptiness of our lives.

Indeed, up to this point Jesus may have been accommodating himself to the crowd by speaking of food and bread metaphorically. They understood Jesus to be telling them to keep the Torah. Even today we speak of earning bread, meaning money. We speak of meals as "breaking bread together" even when we may not be eating bread. We speak of catching crumbs which fall from a master, meaning that we're getting only a little of the wisdom that a good teacher has.

In like manner, the Pharisaical Jews believed that their bread was the Torah. Although to us the Torah is simply the first five books of the Bible, in Pharisaical theology the Torah is the ultimate Word of God, His eternal self-revelation, the place where one would find life. For them, from all eternity God manifested Himself in His Word, the Torah. From all eternity, the Torah was the model of creation which was to come. All things were created by God for the Torah, to fit in with the Torah, and to find life through the Torah. The entire universe has as its model, purpose, goal, and cause, the Holy Torah. Even for Jews in our day, the Torah scrolls must be on parchment, may be copied only by an ordained Scribe, are veiled with velvet brocade, topped with gold and silver crowns, and kept in the ark of the synagogue.

The Pharisees believed the eternal Torah to have been delivered in the realm of time (about 1290 B.C.) to Moses on Mount Sinai. The Pharisees distinguished 613 precepts in the written Torah, with additions in the oral Torah that were handed down authentically from Moses by the Scribes. These teachings were really their "bread of life."

So they asked (v. 28) what they should do to perform the works of God that are in the Torah — in other words, "How can you make it easier for us to keep the hundreds of laws of the Torah?" His answer (v. 29) was that, in contrast with all the "works" of the Torah, there's only one real "work" of God: to have faith in God *as He is*, not as *they would have Him be*. And Jesus was showing Him as He is. But even though the crowd had miraculously received a free and satisfying meal the day before, they still wanted God to come to them on *their* terms. Despite the fact that God was speaking to them in ways that they should have understood, they wanted God's signs to be accommodated to *them* (v. 30).

They cited (v. 31) the part of today's First Reading (part of the Torah) that referred to the manna that Moses had given as a sign of God's approval — but conveniently made no mention of their ancestors' dissatisfaction with it. Jesus knew what some modern psychologists have discovered: Finding our *real* needs, and not just our *perceived* ones, isn't easy. And tricks weren't his style. Truth was. So he answered (v. 32) that it wasn't Moses who gave the manna: It was God. And the bread of God gives life to the world (v. 33).

Then Jesus said startlingly (v. 35) that he himself is the bread of life. Although Jesus would soon talk of the Eucharist, here he was accommodating himself to the meaning of the crowd — namely, that "bread" is "doing the works of God." Jesus was clearly stating that he is replacing the Torah. He, not the Torah, is the way of eternal life.

Unless we fill ourselves with him, we're not just empty and hungry: We're spiritually dead. We are what we eat. If we pursue only junk food like fame, prestige, wealth, or power, we shall die of malnutrition.

One consequence of accepting God as He is is a new satisfaction in our life. For our *self*, this means a new spirit — one that comes from outside ourselves for a change. It's like the spirit of the black woman, born without arms, who fought to have custody of her baby. The judge made it a condition that before he would even listen to her case she would have to prove that she could take care of her infant. There in open court she changed her baby's diaper, holding the pins in her teeth and using her feet in place of the hands she didn't have. She won her case: The judge observed that he had never seen a more attentive, tender, and loving mother, and remarked upon the spirit of the woman.

Not only ourselves, but our *world* needs this kind of new spirit. Today's reading from the letter to the Ephesians observes that Jesus is our bread of life! In a Christ-less world, this letter recorded terrible things: man's heart made like stone and at the mercy of all whims and desires. Today's paganism is no less vicious than the paganism when this letter was written.

The perception in the letter to the Ephesians that the world is so turned in upon itself as not to be able to see God is, sadly, still true. As a matter of fact, many material problems are caused in part by spiritual ones. Hunger in today's world, for example, isn't caused by our planet lacking the physical resources to provide food; it's because we haven't the spirit to distribute our material resources properly. If today a family of ten were today's world, and were sitting around a table for Thanksgiving dinner, the mother and the father would each get a plate piled high with huge helpings of turkey, potatoes, vegetables, and cranberry sauce; they would eat all they want and throw away their leftovers. Three children would each get a small slice of turkey, a dab of cranberry, a spoon of potatoes and a tiny portion of vegetables. The remaining five children would each get an empty plate with only a few scraps.

This scene actually represents the whole human family today. The mother and father are the 800 million affluent North Americans, Western Europeans, Australians, and Japanese. The three partly-fed children represent the 1,800,000,000 people from Latin America, North and South Africa, Eastern Europe, the Persian Gulf, and East Asia. The five scrawny children represent the three billion hopelessly poor children, women, and men from the rest of Africa, Pakistan, India, and China. Half of the people of the world go to bed hungry every night and one-third actually die of hunger. By the end of today, 60,000 more people will die of hunger. Bad as these things are, the unrecognized hunger for God is even worse.

Let's each of us do our part to change ourselves and to turn the world around. Let's begin by not trying to make God into an image that we preconceive: We're made in God's image, not He in ours. Our real hunger won't be satisfied by the dryness, emptiness, and alienation of our greedy and materialistic society, which T.S. Eliot called the Wasteland. In short, let's do what the letter to the Ephesians preached: put on the new self, created in God's way (v. 24). Let's not drive the horse of our life *our* way, but the way *God* has instructed.

NINETEENTH SUNDAY IN ORDINARY TIME
1 K 19:4-18   Eph 4:30-5:2   Jn 6:41-51

Magnanimity
What Is Life and Living?; Who Are the "Greats" of this World?

If you had to choose between a life that would be relatively flat but guaranteed to last a long time, or a short life that was interesting, full of challenge, imagination, creativity, and opportunities for personal growth — which would you choose? Despite Yogi Berra's advice that "when you come to a fork in the road, take it," let's assume here that you *must* choose.

The ancient Greeks without hesitation chose the shorter life. They took every opportunity to praise heroes like Achilles, for whom life was short but glorious in battle. The Greeks had a word for this kind of person, as they did for just about everything else: They called such a person a *megalopsychos*. That word is translated into Latin as *magnanimitas*, from which we get our infrequently-used but beautiful English word "magnanimity." There's no exact translation for it, but it means something like "largeness of soul," one who's "great-minded."

It means overcoming one's narrowness and defects. Just as water shares the good and bad qualities of the beds through which it runs, people share those of their lineage, locality, condition, occupation, and times in which they live. It's a triumph to correct such limitations and acquire magnanimity.

In still other terms, Oliver Wendell Holmes said people are comprised of one-story intellects, two-story intellects, and three-story intellects with skylights. All fact collectors who have no aim beyond their data are one-story people. Two-story people compare, reason, and generalize, using the labors of the fact collectors as well as their own. Three-story people idealize, imagine, predict; their best illumination comes from above, through the skylight. Three-story great-mindedness is the way Jesus told us we must love God.

When Jesus spoke of himself as the "bread of life" in St. John's Gospel of last Sunday and again today, he meant it in the sense of the food that sustains faith: his *teaching*. Only at the end of today's section, and in the next two Sundays' conclusion of this important sixth chapter of St. John's Gospel, does he refer to his bread of life as being the Eucharist.

There's a theory that, on the Sabbaths near Passover, the readings in the synagogues of Jesus' day were taken from the early chapters of the Book of Genesis. Because Jesus is now speaking in a synagogue near Passover time, he may have alluded to those Scripture readings. There are, in fact, some parallels between those readings and Jesus' homily today. Genesis says, for example, that we shall not eat of the fruit of the tree in the middle of the Garden of Eden, lest we die (3:3). Jesus tells us that he's giving the bread from heaven for people to eat and never die (v. 50). Genesis talks of God driving us out of the garden lest we try to live forever (3:22); Jesus says that anyone who eats of the Eucharist will live forever (v. 51).

The leaders were so small-minded that they wanted to grab him — a butterfly in a fine net. Even when they couldn't catch him in his words or deeds, their response was what we see in the Gospel today. How can he claim to come down from heaven? Doesn't he come from an insignificant village? Isn't he the son of people we know? How can any ideas so large come from a carpenter's son?

Unlike some of the leaders of our Lord's time and some of our own, instead of just *hearing* others we must be able to *listen* to them and *learn*. There are many reasons why we listen: frustration, for example, or lack of choice. But this doesn't necessarily mean that we're sensitive enough to truly hear. When we listen to God, we should really want to *hear*. And this takes a certain personal largeness.

Today's portion of the letter to the Ephesians gives us a picture of authentic largeness of spirit. Such magnanimity reflects the God with whom it communes. Many Christians in the first centuries were admired for a kind of love that was the opposite of their society. Today, some Christians rather mirror society than differ from it.

The letter to the Ephesians speaks of our call to greatness by reason of our being sealed with the Holy Spirit in baptism, a powerful image. People often mark their property with a seal. In those days, the seal was often from a special signet ring. The letter, cognizant of the smallness to which human nature can sink, warns against being so small as to live consumed by bitterness — a long-standing resentment that harbors grudges and keeps warm all of those negative thoughts and feelings that we're sometimes tempted to have about other people. Today's newspapers will have their fair share of examples of such small-minded people.

The letter also speaks of passion and anger as bringing about smallness of person. There's a long-lasting type of anger through which we can't see because of our anger's blindness. And there's the short-fused anger of blind rage. The latter is like igniting straw into fire — very easy to do, short-lasting, and not very deep — but while it rages it can do great damage. Those kinds of small person look upon anger as being great fun: To lick your wounds, to smack your lips over grievances long past, to savor to the last toothsome morsel both the pain you're given and the pain you're giving back — in many ways small persons see this as a feast fit for a king. What they don't see is the chief drawback: what you're wolfing down is yourself; the skeleton at the feast is yours.

Further characterizing small persons is shouting, reviling, and the use of harsh words. It takes spiritually generous persons to be always considerate even of the words they use, in order not to unnecessarily offend. The letter's final description of the small person contains the element of malice, as in slander. It may be petty, but it's continuing, and this is precisely what makes a person too small to measure up to his calling to be a follower of Christ.

Then the letter uses words to describe a spiritually generous person. For example, to be continually kind, even in the face of the omissions of others, takes outgoingness. As you go through life, you may be sorry that you spoke, sorry you stayed or went, sorry you won or lost, sorry you spent so much. But you'll never be sorry you were kind. Ephesians mentions another characteristic of the large heart: the beautiful idea of "compassion." The word "compassion" is from the Latin, meaning "to feel with": To feel with the pains and the joys of others is characteristic of the large person.

That also involves sensitivity and tact. A story is told of two brothers, Herbert and James, who lived with their mother and a cat named Edgar. James was particularly attached to the cat, and when he had to leave town for several days, he left Herbert meticulous instructions about the pet's care. At the end of his first day away, James telephoned his brother. "How's Edgar?" he asked. "Edgar's dead," Herbert answered.

There was a pause. Then James said: "Herbert, you're insensitive. You know how close I was to Edgar; you should've broken the news to me slowly. When I asked about Edgar tonight, you should've said, 'Edgar's on the roof, but I've called the fire department to get him down.' And tomorrow when I called, you could've said the firemen were having trouble getting Edgar down, but you were hopeful they'd succeed. Then when I called the third time, you could've told me that the firemen had done their best, but unfortunately Edgar had fallen off the roof and was at the veterinarian's. Then when I called the last time, you could've said that although everything possible had been done for Edgar, he'd died. That's the way a *sensitive* man would've told me about Edgar. And, oh, before I forget," James added, "how's mother?" "Uh," said a chastened and confused Herbert, pausing for a moment, "she's on the roof."

At least as significant as compassionate sensitivity is forgiveness — not the kind that only erases a debt, but the kind that imitates the forgiveness of Jesus and is reminiscent of those most beautiful words: "Father, forgive them, for they know not what they do." Finally, Ephesians mentions the highest standard of all: We must be imitators of God. No one but a large person can possibly aspire to that.

Anyone who tries to imitate the largeness of God must take into account Elijah the prophet, a major hero in the history of Israel. He's especially attractive because, despite his achievements, he remained a human being. Elijah had just defeated the priests of Baal in a great contest. He had thought that all Israel would turn back to the Lord. Instead, the people, fickle as always, abandoned him. He's tired, sick, discouraged, depressed, afraid, and tempted to despair of God's promises. Now he's on the run from the wicked Queen Jezebel, who's put a price on his head. He flirted with the idea of abandoning his mission and running away. He prayed for death as the better alternative to what he was facing. But, in the words of today's Responsorial Psalm, because of his faithfulness he would "taste and see the goodness of the Lord."

Like Elijah, let's not be discouraged by our weaknesses and defeats, like him pick ourselves up when we fall, and like him resolve again and again to be equal in size to the greatness of our destiny. To that kind of greatness God called the Ephesians, too, and to it He calls us. If we search our lives, we may find stupidities of bowing to defeat that aren't worthy of us: people who've failed in love and give in to not loving because of fear of further rejection; people who've lost their jobs and are afraid to ask for work; mothers whose children almost drowned who won't permit them to go into the water to learn to swim.

The people of Israel on their long trip to the Promised Land, for the first time seeing manna — the word to which Jesus referred today — asked, "What is this?" The crowds following Jesus asked, "What is this?" Elijah in his wilderness experience asked, "What is this?" We in the wilderness of our lives ask, "What is this?" Each of us must answer for ourselves that question as well as the question with which we began: Can we best develop the magnanimity that's expected of us by a long phlegmatic life or by a short life of attempts at heroism?

SOLEMNITY OF THE ASSUMPTION OF MARY
Rv 11:19; 12:1-6, 10   1 Cor 15:20-25   Lk 1:39-56

Significance of the Blessed Mother's Assumption to Our Lives
Need for Proper Perspectives on the Body;
Ideal Combination between Contemplation and Action

Did you ever wonder as you were looking at huge skyscrapers, or going by glass-enclosed buildings, or passing through planned neighbor-

Note: For other approaches to the Assumption, see Cycles A and C.

hoods, what significance your religion has to any of this modernity and futurology? Aren't some of the symbols of our religion ancient, and inapplicable to current life? People who are religious have the reputation of being traditionalists in behalf of the past rather than modernists in favor of the present or the future. For example, the earliest mention of the fork was in the eleventh century, when the wife of a Venetian doge shunned a single-bladed knife in favor of a tined instrument. St. Peter Damian of Ostia was appalled at this rejection of tradition, as he wrote in an essay entitled, "Of the Venetian Doge's wife, whose body, after her excessive delicacy, entirely rotted away." Religious people so often seem to be the last by whom the new is tried.

So when we say that Jesus' Blessed Mother was taken, body and soul, into heaven because of her purity and because of her connection with Jesus, is that some kind of traditionalism that has no significance to modern life? Is it important to what we do when we shop for groceries or work at the office or clean our house or take care of our children or entertain?

Today's joyful section of St. Paul's letter to the Corinthians, as well as the Gospel, suggests answers to these questions. St. Paul presented two Jewish ideas which were fulfilled in Mary. These ideas are old but also ever new. The first is the idea of the first fruits. The Jews were an agricultural people and every year as their harvest began to come in they were bound by their religious law to take the first fruits of their harvest to the Temple and offer them to God. The Jews treasured the idea, because for them it symbolized the coming of a harvest, the means of remaining alive for the next year. Paul applied the idea to the human race.

Christ himself was the first fruit of the salvation of the entire race, as today's section of the Book of Revelation says. Although the woman mentioned is — in the literal sense — probably the Church, the Church has long used it in an accommodated sense to apply to Mary, whom the Church also calls the Ark of the Covenant, the Chosen of God, and the Mother of the Church. And just as Jesus' resurrection was a sign of the harvest of people to come, so Mary, by her assumption, which was really a celebration of her resurrection, signifies the fact that the human race can be brought into this actuality.

The second Jewish idea that Paul presents is the very close solidarity of the human race, a concept taken from the Book of Genesis (3:1-19). The ancient Jews believed that the human race is so closely one that every single human being can't help but be affected by what the first human being had done: what they called Original Sin. For us, just as Adam represented evil, so the second Adam, Jesus, represents good. And just as Adam because of his sin brought death into the world, Jesus the second Adam brought life into the world, and brought a new power to liberate people. Paul's conclusion from both of these ideas was that just as God had given His Son to redeem our sorry human race, He will receive back a world redeemed.

Today the Church adds to this passage of Paul the suggestion that this process began with Mary. Mary's assumption is another pledge and guarantee of our own resurrection and return to our Heavenly Father. It's also a reminder that we will be saved body and soul. This is a reaffirmation of the greatness of the human body.

The body is a system, as the essayist Joseph Addison said, put together in "so wonderful a manner as to make it *a proper engine for the soul*." There are many wonders of the human body that we often take for granted. One is the extraordinary scope of our *memory*, another the *brain*. More than 100,000 chemical reactions occur in the brain each second, requiring huge amounts of energy. In fact, the brain in intense concentration can burn as many calories as muscles during exercise.

Another is the *nose*. Besides the marvelous phenomenon of smell, the nose's nasal mucus is the first line of defense against the millions of bacteria that constantly try to invade the body. Pollen grains can trigger a sneeze that can eject particles at speeds exceeding 100 miles per hour. Still another is the *eyes*. In addition to the wonderful marvel of sight, with every blink the eyes are bathed with a bacteria-fighting fluid secreted by the lacrimal glands. Our tears are wonders in themselves.

There's also *skin*. One square inch of human skin contains approximately 19 million cells, 625 sweat glands, 65 hairs, 19 feet of blood vessels, 19,000 sensory cells, and about 20 million microscopic animals. Or consider the *stomach*. Stomach acid is one of the most powerful corrosives; it can even dissolve razor blades. In fact, to avoid digesting itself, the stomach must produce a new lining every three days.

Applied to women, Mary's assumption and all the data it brings to mind mean there should be no exploitation of their body. The assumption reveals Mary as fulfilling what women have the greatest dignity to fulfill: She gave life. More, she was *Jesus'* mother. Her body, because of that privilege, was sacred — so sacred that we celebrate its having been assumed into heaven.

Today's celebration has other implications for our time. Mary went with haste the 85 miles from Nazareth down to Ain Karim in a very difficult time of the year, through great personal sacrifice, to be of help to her cousin Elizabeth who in her old age was pregnant with John the Baptist. She was a woman of action — a woman who wanted to do good things — but she was also, as Luke's whole passage reveals, prayerfully reflective, and a woman of deep feeling and strong conviction.

Elizabeth referred to her as blessed. But God revealed in her life the paradox contained in blessedness: not only a beautiful crown of stars but also a sword of suffering. Many have said that the sword to Mary was to watch her child die; the timing of child and parent death usually happens the other way around. Others say her sword was to be an unwed mother, and still others that the sword was seeing her son rejected by his people. Many scholars say her sword was having to discriminate over the question of God — that even Mary had to learn to put God's claims first.

And so it has been with all of God's blessed from the beginning to the present, and ever shall be. As someone said, "Jesus came not to make life easy, but to make people great."

In Mary's beautiful prayer, which has come to be called her *Magnificat*, she brings together a chain of texts from the Jewish Scriptures, which from her get new significance. In it she also reveals her loveliness — not a soft, mushy loveliness, but a loveliness that contains revolutions.

Yes, she speaks of revolutions: not one, but several. These are of God, not people, but the revolutions must begin with each one's own person. One side of the revolution is moral. Mary says, for example, that God has brought low the arrogant of mind and heart (v. 51). People who believe in Jesus and compare themselves with him can't remain proud. People who really know Jesus and really know themselves and put the two together become humble and want to try to bring about change.

A story is told by O. Henry of a young man who grew up in a little town in the United States. At school he sat next to a girl who was lovely and innocent, and in a youthful way he fell in love with her. But, as life would have it, when he grew up he moved to the city; there he couldn't make a go of it and degenerated into a petty thief and pickpocket. One day as he ran from his pursuers after stealing a handbag from an old lady, he saw his childhood love walking toward him, still lovely, still in the full bloom of innocence.

As he looked at her, he realized what he had become. After the chase was over, he leaned against a lamp post and said, "O God, if only I could die!" This is the way it is with us when we compare ourselves with Jesus and Mary. We want a moral revolution that will bring about people who are like them. That moral revolution has only begun, and the human race in all its history since Jesus and Mary still has a long way to go to reach anything like their goodness.

Mary says also that God has thrown down the rulers from their thrones, but lifted up the lowly (v. 52). This is a *social* revolution. Inasmuch as Jesus would identify himself with the poor, the naked, the jailed, the sick, and the otherwise outcast (Mt 25), the Christian does the same. We call no person worthless for whom Jesus died.

Mary also said that God has filled the hungry with good things, and has sent the rich away empty (v. 53). This is the *economic* revolution intended by her son. Much of society is out for all it can get. A truly Christian society, in contrast, is one in which no person dares have too much while others have too little. All have a role in building a society, said Pope John Paul II, "in which none are so poor that they have nothing to give and none are so rich that they have nothing to receive."

So Mary's assumption *is* as deeply relevant to our time and place as skyscrapers, glass-enclosed buildings, and planned neighborhoods. As Mary's assumption is the first fruit of the redemptive love of Jesus, we too are supposed to be part of that harvest. Because of Jesus, humanity is destined for glorification; because of Mary, humanity is shown to be already involved in the fullest realization of its potential.

There's also in today's celebration a reaffirmation to our world of the much-needed lesson of the dignity of the human body: Jesus touches the *whole* human being. We, like Mary, have a body, not only a soul, that's sacred. We must regard it as such. We, like Mary, mustn't allow it to be used in any kind of degenerate way. And we, like Mary, must have faith — not a faith that shilly-shallys, but a faith that's meaningful, a faith that leads to commitment.

Twentieth Sunday in Ordinary Time
Pr 9:1-6   Eph 5:15-20   Jn 6:51-58

You've Got to Fill a Person with Something
Should We Suffer Fools Gladly?; Live in the Light;
Being a Sophomore; The Eucharist

For the attempt to train people in the way they should go, there are various theories. One, the "nurture" theory, says that every human being is born as a blank slate. It's one's outside environment that writes on that slate; hence it's important to provide as rich an environment as possible — like gadgetry in schools — to make learning rich and full. Another theory, the "nature" theory, the direct contradictory of that, says that human beings are born with all their essential qualities, and that environment adds only relatively unimportant details. Both these theories, however, recognize that people need something to fill a void.

Among the possibilities for filling the void of the spirit is the search for wisdom, which is frequently encapsulated in proverbs. These pithy, unforgettable phrases seem to sum up timeless wisdom. But do they? Some of them are simply untrue. "Spare the rod and spoil the child," says the proverb: But research has shown conclusively that the "rod" produces children who are more aggressive than their peers. "Familiarity breeds contempt" — but familiarity is usually more likely to breed liking than contempt: "To know me is to love me." Many proverbs come in contradictory opposing pairs. "Look before you leap," but "he who hesitates is lost." "You're never too old to learn," but "you can't teach an old dog new tricks." "Birds of a feather flock together," but "opposites attract."

Some formulations are humorous common sense attributed to various people, like baseball figure Yogi Berra, rustic Will Rogers, or Sam Goldwyn. To one or the other of them are attributed such sayings as "It's *dèjà vu* all over again" and "I don't want to make the wrong mistake." At a State dinner, one of them is supposed to have said, "How could you get a conversation started in there? Everybody was talking too much."

A teacher who passed out the first part of well-known proverbs to first-graders, asking them to complete each of them, got the follow-

ing answers: "Don't cross your bridge before *you pay the toll.*" "Laugh
and the world laughs with you. Cry and *you have to blow your nose.*"
"If at first you don't succeed, *get new batteries.*" "When the blind lead
the blind *get out of their way.*"

The Bible's Book of Proverbs was a search for wisdom which
was written over a span of 500 years, long before the coming of Christ.
A collection somewhat like our *Bartlett's Familiar Quotations,* it tries
to provide words to live by. Today's reading is a small portion of a
larger diptych in which Wisdom and Folly each invite guests to their
respective banquets. Wisdom — personified here as elsewhere in Jewish
Wisdom Literature as a woman — serves festive foods of meat and
wine, Folly mere bread and water. It takes Wisdom a longer time to
prepare her meal and it takes her guests longer to digest her food.

There are many theories about what the seven pillars of wisdom
are. The number "seven" probably represents the number of perfection, and the house built on the pillars signifies the learning which gives
mastery of life. In order that people may have life to the full, Lady
Wisdom invites into her splendid house those who seek understanding. These are the humble of heart: People who think they know everything can scarcely want anything more — even wisdom.

Today's passage from the letter to the Ephesians, too, presents a
contrast between fools and wise people (v. 15) — between an intelligent, thoughtful way of life based on the Spirit of God and a thought-
less way of life based upon dulling the senses. In all generations, which
are no different from the times of the Book of Proverbs, the "fools"
lead superficial lives of self-seeking, looking for immediate rather than
long-term satisfaction. The Bible associates "fool" with "atheist," in
the realization that many people live like practical atheists.

Whereas the first part of this reading (vv. 15-17) reflects on how
the individual should live wisely in this world, the second part (vv. 18-
20) is directed to the Holy Spirit in the life of the community. The happiness of the Christians of the time made them sing together psalms,
hymns, and spiritual songs. The Psalms both nourished and expressed
the prayer of the People of God gathered during the great feasts. Their
prayer recalled the events of the past, yet extends into the future, even
to the end of history. Prayed by Jesus and fulfilled in him, the Psalms
remain essential to the prayer of the Church (*Catechism of the Catholic Church,* 2586).

The readings from St. John's sixth chapter that we've read on the

past three Sundays deal with Jesus' teaching as being the bread of life
that replaced the Torah. Today, the same chapter reaches its climax in
the motif of Jesus as the bread of life in the Eucharist. Here, he gives
us heavenly food that enables us to share a relationship with the divinity. Here one not only eats food prepared by God, but the food is God.
That idea was objectionable to some of Jesus' Jewish listeners as having the appearance of cannibalistic grotesqueness. For one thing, drinking blood was forbidden by Jewish law. Then, too, the phrase "eating
someone's flesh" was for them an idiomatic expression meaning slan-
dering another person. It was not unlike our saying, "Taxes are eating
me alive."

But the people of the ancient Holy Land believed, like many
outside the "scientific" age, that blood contains life. They believed that
by drinking it you could enhance your life. Jesus was talking to this
type of people. They were brought up with ancient blood sacrifices.
Through this they dreamed of identity with others — and with their
god, which was a union they looked upon as being closer than any
earthly one. This was enhanced by the Middle East idea that sharing a
meal with someone establishes or solidifies a relationship.

In his Gospel, John was, as usual, trying to give the inner meaning of Jesus' words — after about 70 years of thinking about them!
His clear and blunt words in this passage refer to the Eucharist. Three
times here Jesus referred to the importance of eating his flesh and drinking his blood. There could be no misunderstanding. That his audience
understood Jesus to mean exactly what his words say is shown by their
reaction: "How can he give us his flesh to eat?"

Although in our culture this reading is at first sight difficult, we
must remember that the world is larger than any one culture. Here, Jesus
is describing the Eucharist as the place where God and people meet
and unite. And he identifies himself with the "Son of Man" who in the
Book of Daniel embodies the salvation of Israel. Jesus is the new embodiment of salvation: a man, who lives with the glory of God; a mediator in whom heaven and earth meet.

Jesus' Real Presence in the Eucharist has always been a difficulty.
It's contrary to our *senses*, to our *science*, and to our *experience*. Our
senses indicate that what looks like bread *is* bread, and what looks like
wine *is* wine. Our *science* discovers the texture, shape, and composi-
tion of material things; there's no way that we can look at a Host under a microscope and find a tiny Jesus. Our *experience* shows us that

we know reality by what we sense: There's nothing in the mind which was not somehow first in the senses.

Nevertheless, appearances are one thing, reality another. Jesus is truly present in the Eucharist — and that not with a presence that's physical, or moral, or spiritual, but *sacramental*. The reality of the bread has truly become the reality of Jesus' glorified body; the reality of the wine has become the reality of Jesus' blood. Since Jesus can't be divided, wherever his body is there also is his soul, divinity, and blood; wherever his blood is, there also is his soul, divinity, and body.

As he proceeded, Jesus made his teaching constantly stronger: "If you do not eat the flesh of the Son of Man and drink his blood, you have no life in you." And further along, "My flesh is real food, and my blood real drink." Jesus was giving us a share in the life that the Father shares with the Son — a true communion with the real person of the risen Lord. The people of the early Church understood this. The Eucharist made a difference in their lives: It made it possible for them to bear each day.

Remembering that, as with the depths of a diamond, a person's interior is many times more important than the surface, let's develop into wise people today. There are people who are all façade, like a house left unfinished when the funds run out; they may have the entrance of a palace but the inner rooms of a shanty.

Within that context, let's develop a respect and awe for the Eucharist that's reminiscent of the early Church. For sacred events like the Holy Sacrifice of the Mass, let's arrive on time and leave only when everything's over, be physically and spiritually clean, dressed properly, careful and attentive when holding out our hand or putting forth our tongue to receive Holy Communion, and not in any way routine or sloppy. After all, if we're going in the direction we should go, our spirit will be filled more and more with wisdom.

Twenty-First Sunday in Ordinary Time
Jos 24:1f., 15-17, 18   Eph 5:21-32   Jn 6:60-69

Whom Do You Serve?
Personal Growth; Loyalty; Life of the Spirit; Faith;
Christian Marriage; Crisis Times; Belief in the Eucharist

It's always a pleasure to watch the growth of something good. One of the reasons for the pleasure of the Spring and Summer is that you can see the growth of nature: seeds coming into plant, plants coming into flower, and flowers coming into fruit. It's also a pleasure to watch the growth of children. This is especially true if you don't see them for some time and can experience more growth than you can see within the space of a day or a week. In time, you may be able to verify a comparison that's been made between raising a child and building a skyscraper. If the first few stories are out of line, no one will notice. But when the building is 18 or 20 stories high, everyone will see that it tilts. Today's liturgy points to the most important kind of proper growth — the spiritual.

The incident in today's Gospel — the last of our current readings from St. John's account of Jesus' sermon on the bread of life — is one of the signs of the great growth of St. Peter. Our Lord had just finished teaching one of the most difficult but central doctrines of his Church: the Eucharist. Despite all the wonders the crowd had witnessed in Jesus, now they observed that this saying was so difficult that no one could be expected to accept it (v. 60). The hard saying was, at base, that Jesus was God's Word who must be believed; here it was also that he demanded that people eat his flesh and drink his blood if they were to have real life.

If Jesus hadn't meant the Eucharist to be his flesh and blood, he would have called them back; he could have told them, "Wait — I was using a metaphor. Let me explain!" Instead, he made his teaching even stronger. He amplified it by speaking of the contrast between flesh and spirit: between the natural and the supernatural. What's merely natural can't alone attain to anything that's on God's level, the level of the spirit (v. 63). No one can come to the Father except that the Father draw him (v. 65) — that is, through grace, which is supernatural. And people must cooperate with grace by taking the plunge of faith — by believing in Jesus as the ultimate word of the Father.

The crowd may have been perfectly willing to accept Jesus as a fine teacher or as a brilliant and spell-binding rabbi, but they still saw him as the son of Joseph and Mary — not the Son of God. These views were held even by some of his disciples — those whom the Gospels looked upon as not merely followers, but who had accepted the discipline of the master and were often of the master's household.

Rather than compromise the central doctrine of the Eucharist, Jesus turned to his twelve, those who had been closest to him, and asked if they too would like to leave. This suspenseful moment of decision, well into his ministry, was a time of real need on Our Lord's part. At Caesarea Philippi, Peter had come through with his great confession of Jesus' divinity. Would he come through again? The volatile Peter could go either way. Peter's poignant decision was to ask where else they could go, because Jesus was the Messiah, the Son of God (vv. 68f.).

Behind Peter's declaration of faith were the twelve apostles, just as behind Joshua's situation of choice in today's First Reading were the Twelve Tribes of Israel at the ancient shrine of Schechem. Joshua had succeeded Moses in the Israelites' painful journey out of slavery. Arrived in the Promised Land, the Israelites renewed their covenant with God and re-established their identity as God's people. Joshua and the Twelve Tribes of Israel, like Peter and the apostles later, heard God revealing Himself in the darkness of their journey, and saw the dawn light of a new freedom. Joshua and his people stood up and were counted; despite past failings, they grew; they demonstrated Israel's sense of total dedication and loyalty to Yahweh. They would serve Him and Him alone.

Today's passage from the letter to the Ephesians — if not written by St. Paul himself, then written by a follower faithful to his ideas — is tied in with the theme of the other readings. It teaches that the Church's submission to Jesus is to one who gives himself intimately and completely in behalf of the fullness of life. It's our duty to be joined with the two in both Word and Sacrament.

The passage shows also that early Christian ideas grew, especially with regard to that vital symbol of our union with Jesus: marriage. About nine years before this, in his first letter to the Corinthians (Ch. 7), Paul had written what for us seem strange ideas about marriage. He said at that time that one should marry only to avoid fornication;

that although it was all right for a widow to marry again, it would be much better if she didn't; that it's better for everybody to remain single because when people marry they're much more involved in pleasing one another than in pleasing the Lord.

Little did Paul's letter to the Corinthians or the author of Ephesians know the obtuseness of the male of the species. A story's told of a wife who was moody, fitful, and nervous. Her husband wound up taking her to a psychiatrist. The psychiatrist asked the wife some questions about her state of unhappiness, reflected on the answers, then threw his arms around her and gave her an ardent kiss. After that the lady was gay and sparkling. "You see?" said the psychiatrist. "That's all your wife needs. I suggest that she receive the same treatment every Tuesday, Thursday, and Saturday." "If you say so," said the husband. "But there's one hitch. I can bring her in on Tuesdays and Thursdays, but on Saturdays I play golf."

Paul had written his letter to the Corinthians in expectation of an immediate parousia — the Second Coming of Jesus. If Jesus were to come again immediately, institutions like marriage were naturally to take second place. Now, nine years later in Ephesians, the doctrine on marriage had grown. Marriage came to be understood as the most precious relationship in life, a parallel of the relationship between Christ and his Church.

Some readers, seeing the first verses of this passage, are turned off. Paul says that wives should be subordinate to their husbands as to the Lord, for the husband is head of his wife just as Christ is head of the Church (vv. 22f.). Reading that, some feminists sneer that, if Paul weren't a saint, he'd be open to the charge of being a male chauvinist.

What's frequently forgotten is that this passage doesn't pertain to power or control — it pertains to love, where the wife can claim the chief place. The subordination doesn't deny or take away the liberty which fully belongs to the woman both in view of her dignity as a human being and in view of her most noble office as wife, mother, and companion. So it doesn't bid her to obey her husband if not in harmony with reason, nor does it imply that the wife should be put on a level with minors. She's definitely not to submit to violence in any form: physical, sexual, psychological, or verbal.

The first part of this section speaks to wives about their duty and the second part to husbands of their duty. The duties of loving loyalty are difficult for both men and women. In a discussion on how men are truly the weaker sex, but have a strong ego, a long-married woman advised young wives, "Just lean on your husband on one side and prop him up on the other." The letter to the Ephesians insists upon certain facets of love that we frequently forget are innovations of Christianity. It insists, for example, that husbands should love their wives as Christ loved his Church. Jesus loved his Church so much that he gave up his life for it. A husband, by implication, should be willing to give his life for his wife.

Finally, Christian marriage always takes place in the Lord. It takes three to marry: Some say a man and a woman and an anxious mother of a prospective bride, but the real three are the husband, the wife, and God. In the time of Jesus, woman's lot was pitiful. For the Jews, a wife couldn't divorce her husband for any reason other than serious matters like apostasy from the Jewish faith, contracting leprosy, or conducting a repulsive trade like taking care of pigs; a man could divorce his wife by simply writing "You are hereby divorced," for any reason or none.

Among the Greeks, whose culture dominated that time, conditions were even worse. Prostitution was a way of life. The training of women excluded pleasure in marriage. The husband, if he wanted either companionship or pleasure, was expected to go outside his home. As one of the Greek writers put it, the word "wife" was a title of dignity, not of pleasure. For the Romans, whose armies had conquered that world, the situation was worst of all: Marriage and the family were in shambles. Women were counting the years not chronologically but by the names of their husbands, and many women in the course of their lifetime had between twenty and twenty-five husbands. Husbands did the same. Our new paganism hasn't matched that — yet.

We too are called to growth. Like Peter, let's learn that Christianity is a personal response of loyalty to Jesus Christ, our faith a plunge of commitment to him as Word and as Sacrament. Let's remember the letter to the Ephesians as we try to grow in love. And let's answer Joshua's question: "Whom will you serve?"

TWENTY-SECOND SUNDAY IN ORDINARY TIME
Dt 4:1f., 6-8 Jm 1:17-21f., 27 Mk 7:1-8, 14f., 21f.

True Religion
Re-examining our Practice of Christianity; Pride; Hypocrisy;
Our Kind of God; Do-ers of the Word vs. Hearers

The chief issues of our age are religious: They're about ultimates —
for example, what, if anything, is the meaning of life. But many people
are engaged in kinds of religion which are mere ego massage that increases their self-concept. So it's important that we try to find out the
nature of true religion and its application to our lives.

Today's Gospel is a face-off on ideas of true religion. The Pharisees called their customs and traditions as being the sole criteria for
judging true religion. The Pharisees got their name from the Hebrew
parisim — those who were separate from the rest of the people because
they were allegedly abiding by "true religion." Some good people in
the New Testament were Pharisees: among them St. Paul, Nicodemus,
and Joseph of Arimathea.

The Pharisees' customs and traditions began in written form way
back with what the Jews call the Torah — what we call the first five
books of the Bible. They believed that the Torah was God's ultimate,
eternal, unchangeable Word. Delivered to Moses in the order of time,
it pre-existed that event almost from eternity. Right up to today, the
Torah scrolls can't be printed; they must be written by hand on vellum
by a special person. They're kept in the Holy Ark in the Synagogue,
veiled in rich velvet brocade inscribed in gold or silver. The Jews' reverence for the scrolls is comparable with Catholic reverence for the
Blessed Sacrament.

The Book of Deuteronomy, a section of which we read in today's
first reading, is a part of the Torah and prescribes part of that reverence. A law book, Deuteronomy presents a vision of the Mosaic law
as part of the relationship of love and faithfulness between God and
His people. The book's idea is that, if you observe the commandments
carefully, there will be immediate rewards; correspondingly, for disobeying there will be immediate punishment. The ancient Jews thought
that, as the artist's calling is perfected through the discipline of his

specialty, God's gift of life could be fulfilled and kept true and pure through the discipline of the law.

It's always tempting to confuse human codes of law with God's law. Human laws provide, at best, only a part of God's law. The codes of law in Scripture were written for specific people and in specific circumstances. They provide basics, but form only a part of God's law: God's law is wider, deeper, longer, and higher than any code of laws written for human guidance. Law codes in the Bible serve three effective functions: They show in microcosm God's word; they provide guidelines to God's people; and they drive God's people to realize their need of God's grace.

Between the fifth and fourth centuries before Christ, there arose a group of people called Scribes, legal experts who had a passion for definition. They tried to cut the laws into little bits and pieces and spell them out in the finest details. By the time of Jesus, these details had become oral traditions which, along with the 613 written precepts, the Pharisees treasured. The Jews in first-century Palestine had evolved a law code which by its very complexity was impossible to maintain. Jesus condemned those who followed the letter of the law and lost sight of God's word as law.

The Pharisees' great insight was to insist that God's presence was to be experienced not only in the Temple, but in everyone's everyday life and business. Since God is the All-Holy, one needs to be holy to meet that everyday presence. Jesus shared this insight, saying that he hadn't come to destroy the Law but to fulfill it. For the Pharisees, holiness included ritual cleanliness. Their laudable intention was to extend the laws of ritual purity from priests to all Israelites, who were considered a "priestly people." Their difficulty was that this often had the effect of producing a very legalistic type of religion.

The washing of hands before eating, for example — a matter of religious ritual — involved all kinds of minute rules: how much water was to be used, how many fingers were to be washed at various times during the meal, and how far to the elbow was to be washed. There were taboos against unclean cups, jugs, kettles, and many other items (v. 4). This made it difficult to arrive at the heart of true religion. On today's occasion — and others as well — the Pharisees criticized Jesus and his apostles for not abiding by the prescriptions of the Law. Hilaire Belloc, a British author, once said that "an Englishman is one who thinks he's being religious, whereas really he's only being uncomfortable." That's Phariseeism.

Human interpretation of written law is often faulty. As Charles Dickens' Mr. Bumble said in this respect, "the law is a ass — a idiot" (*Oliver Twist*). Jesus for his part criticized the Pharisaic interpretation of true religion for two main reasons. The first was hypocrisy. Now, there's a sense in which hypocrisy can be useful. The human gift for not saying everything one thinks can be a lubricant that keeps us from constantly committing mayhem on every street corner, from braining the woman who sneaks ahead of us in the supermarket line, and from jamming a ballpoint pen through the boss's cold heart.

But we usually use the name of hypocrisy only for its nastier incarnations — such as some of the Pharisees who went to great lengths to have people think them holy when their "holiness" was only outward show. When Dante in his *Divine Comedy* put hypocrites in hell, he had them wear a gold mask because the false face they presented to the public was golden. But as time wore on the gold of the mask became heavier and heavier, which was precisely what caused their hell.

People who believe in religion in only a legal sense are in the end bound to be hypocrites in the bad sense: They believe that, if they carry out correct external practices, they're good persons, no matter what their hearts and thoughts are like. A story's told of a Moslem who, while pursuing a man with an upraised knife to kill him, heard the muezzin's call to prayer from the minaret. He stopped, extended his prayer-rug, said his prescribed prayers — and then arose and continued his original pursuit. Unfortunately, changing what has to be changed, the same could be observed of some Christians.

We church-goers are frequently called hypocrites by those who don't go to church. Instead of going to church, they'd rather listen to Handel's beautiful *Messiah*, or Johann Sebastian Bach's inspiring *Jesu Joy of Man's Desiring*, or Richard Strauss's instructive tone poem, *Death and Resurrection*. They believe these to be sufficiently uplifting, and they perceive that there's a difference between what we church-goers say and what we do. It's true that we who go to church aren't perfect. But church-goers are for the most part at least trying, aware of our failings, and mindful of our need for God's help.

The second reason why Jesus condemned the Pharisees was that their definition of true religion depended upon rules that were in many areas made by people rather than by God. True religion must ultimately come from listening to and accepting the voice of God.

Then Jesus presented one of the most revolutionary passages in the New Testament: He flew in the face of a dearly-held tenet of the Jewish religion — the rules and practices of kosher, a long list of unclean animals which couldn't be used for food, and of rules about cooking. He said (v. 15) that the real defilement of people always comes from within, never from without. So there was nothing wrong with the Gentiles eating pork.

Everybody there knew that Jews had suffered and died for the opposite position. Just about two hundred years before Jesus, the Second Book of Maccabees (Ch. 7) recorded the story of a widow whose seven sons, with their mother's encouragement, refused to eat pork. They were killed horribly — by having their tongue cut out, their extremities chopped off, being fried alive, being scalped — all before the eyes of their mother. They're heroes among the Jews, who still celebrate them on the Feast of Hanukkah.

Jesus wasn't saying anything appreciably different from what other rabbis had said. In fact, it was the prophet Isaiah whom Jesus was quoting when he said that the Pharisees paid God only lip service because their heart was far from Him, and their reverence for God was empty because they taught as dogmas what were mere human precepts. But the cumulative effect of his teaching of the "spirit" of the Torah, and his saying that *all* people were called to be children of God, alienated him from official Judaism.

Phariseeism isn't dead. It finds a fertile field in government and business bureaucracy, where people put red tape before supplicants. They may say that they're only doing what they have to do, yet take a strange satisfaction when their duty hurts others, annoys others, inconveniences others. It's also still a part of many who call themselves religious, in all denominations. Religiously-disposed people are frequently inclined toward keeping to tradition. To uphold human tradition can be attractive, because to try to catch the awesome reality of God in the small nets of our mind can be an insecure, mysterious, and occasionally uncomfortable effort. It's far easier to use traditions as fig leaves hiding our nakedness before God. But Jesus condemned the Pharisees for setting aside God's commandments in order to uphold human tradition (v. 9).

In looking upon true religion, today's reading from the letter of St. James (the first of five Sunday readings), the great apostle of Christian action in the world, gives good advice. First, we ought to welcome the Gospel with a truly teachable spirit: humble enough to learn, able

to face the truth even when it hurts, not blinded by prejudice, and sufficiently self-controlled to accept discipline. Secondly, says James, we
should *practice* true religion. He wants our faith to be not merely an
abstract assent but a practical application in human living. James's
"orphans and widows" (v. 27) are his shorthand for all the oppressed
for whom our religion calls us to care.

The Responsorial Psalm antiphon sums up today's liturgy in saying that whoever does justice will live in the presence of the Lord. The
laws of true religion are overwhelming in their implications, and we
can't replace them with lip-service or empty ritual. In this age when
the chief questions of the world are religious, it's important to believe
in and practice *true* religion.

TWENTY-THIRD SUNDAY IN ORDINARY TIME
Is 35:4-7   Jm 2:1-5   Mk 7:31-37

What Is the Real Poverty Level?
Seeing God in People; Who are the Rich, the Poor?; Favoritism

Coming to the aid of the poor has problems. Does saying "No" to pan-
handlers necessarily mean that you're cruel? Is it true that, since all
good things come from God, one never really gives; one only gives
back? Is it true that the more handouts you give, the more hands are
out? What is the poverty level, anyhow — the level below which an
individual or a family requires assistance? Thanks to our Judeo-Christian heritage, our culture has become sensitive to questions like these.
While today's liturgy doesn't provide exact answers in these matters,
it does provide some guidelines.

St. Mark's Gospel tells us that Jesus had entered the territory of
the Gentiles, whom the Jews looked down upon. According to Mark,
Jesus traveled from Tyre by way of Sidon to the Sea of Galilee, into
the district of the Decapolis (v. 31). That zig-zag is about as round-
about as going from New York to London via Berlin and Madrid. Jesus
could have had at least two reasons for going this way. For one thing,
Galilee, under the control of Herod, was becoming increasingly dan-

gerous for Jesus and his followers, and this route took them out of Herod's jurisdiction. For another thing, since this journey was of lengthy duration — perhaps as much as eight months — Jesus was taking his disciples out of the public eye to prepare them to continue his ministry after his death.

The people brought a man who was both deaf and had a speech impediment (v. 32) and begged Jesus to cure him. Jesus began by taking him off by himself away from the crowd (v. 33), consonant with Mark's idea of the Messianic secret, whereby Jesus wanted to keep his Messiahship quiet until the proper time.

Then Jesus conformed to the actions of healers of the time: He was, after all, in pagan territory. He did what many of us might find repulsive: He touched the man's tongue with his own spittle, because the people thought that spittle had a curative quality — as even now when a child puts an injured finger into its mouth. But whereas the people considered such actions effective in themselves, for Jesus they had a sacramental purpose — that is to say, they brought about what they symbolized, and were effective by Jesus' power through his relation to his heavenly Father.

That's why he looked up to heaven (v. 34) — not as a prayer this time, but because he wanted to show that it was from God that help was to come. He groaned — a sign of his deep emotion over the man's condition: Jesus' way of dealing with people was always compassionate; for Jesus, this man was a *person* and not just a *case*. Then he cried, "*Ephphatha!*": "Be opened!" Why does Mark, who wrote in Greek, record Jesus' native Aramaic in this Greek-speaking region? He preserved other Aramaic expressions, too: *Talitha koum, Qorban,* and *Eloi, Eloi, lama sabachthani.* Perhaps Mark records it that way as a subtle reminder that the Messiah is given to the world through Israel.

The marvelous result was that the man could hear and was able to speak without impediment (v. 35). We can only imagine the effect on the man. When television recently showed a 25-year-old deaf woman who, thanks to an electronic implant, was hearing for the first time (a symphony), she cried, she laughed, she threw her hands in the air at the marvel, she jumped up and down with excitement to the extent that her attached wires would allow, she was intent on hearing every sound, and she looked gratefully and tearfully at her benefactors.

Jesus ordered them not to tell anyone (v. 36): not out of humility or perversity, but because he wanted people to follow him not only as a wonder-worker, but — much greater — as the Messiah. But with their false notions of Messiah they weren't ready for that yet. There were other reasons, too. For example, Jesus was now in non-Jewish territory, and if he stirred up the non-Jews as a hero figure he would be in deep trouble with the ever-vigilant authorities. Besides, the Messiah had to be proclaimed from Israel, and not from Gentile territory. Lastly, Mark was probably writing his Gospel right after Nero's persecution of Christians, and it was necessary, while not denying one's faith, to keep quiet about it.

Nowhere is the amazement of the crowds expressed more strongly (v. 37). Their testimony that he had done all things well alluded — probably unconsciously — to God when He looked at all His creation and called it good (Gn 1:31). The implication was that Jesus was bringing about a new creation. The people's final observation, that he makes the deaf hear and the mute speak, was an allusion to the prophet Isaiah in today's First Reading.

Indeed, today's passage from Isaiah can be regarded as a commentary on today's Gospel. Actually, this portion belongs to "Deutero-Isaiah," a part written toward the end of the sixth-century Babylonian captivity, which was long after the great eighth-century prophet. The vision, dreamed in the midst of disaster, provided a joyful picture of confidence that a new deliverance similar to the Exodus would happen. In highly poetic language that would color the hopes of the Jewish people long after, Isaiah described the future return of Israel from captivity. The promise came to be applied to the age when the Messiah would appear.

At the time, with the Jewish nation in exile, the faithful among them saw how necessary it was to rely upon God. Their understanding was that poverty rarely meant material disadvantage alone. Poverty of material possessions usually meant in addition poverty of spirit, and also disability. Poverty, like illness, was deemed to be a judgment from God. In their history, the great ages of Solomon and David had been marked by prosperity and comfort; but at the Exile the whole nation was plunged into poverty and hunger and sickness. They came to see that the true poverty of the people was their separation from God. A whole theology arose around poverty of the heart and the poor, the *anawim*. The poor trusted in God rather than in their own power or efforts, and they needed Him desperately.

The New Testament, too, highlights the preëminence of the poor.

When Mary visited Elizabeth, she declared that God has "lifted up the lowly" (Lk 1:52). When Jesus preached in the synagogue at Nazareth, he commented from Isaiah to the effect that God had anointed him to bring glad tidings to the poor (Lk 4:18). When John the Baptist sent a delegation to ask whether Jesus was God's chosen one, part of his answer was that the poor have the good news proclaimed to them (Mt 11:5). When Jesus spoke his beatitudes in the Sermon on the Mount, the first he declared blest were the poor (Lk 6:20). In fact, an essential part of the "good news" was that people who mattered to no one else mattered to God.

When the Gospel began, it won wide acceptance with the poor. As the Church grew, and many wealthy were attracted as well as the poor, that brought inevitable conflicts. The temptation to make a fuss over the upper classes was very real, much like the chairman of a corporation today being bowed to. And there must have been awkwardness, as when a master came to church and found himself seated next to his slave. But there should be no class distinctions in church, of all places; Christians are ashamed of those historical times and places where class distinctions were present.

It's that problem which St. James addresses in today's portion of his letter. His specific problem is favoritism: pandering to people for reasons extraneous to their inner worth — because they're rich, for example, or influential, or popular. There can, of course, be inverted snobbery — pandering to the desires of the mob rather than to the upper crust. The Jewish Scriptures had warned about deference going in any direction, even toward the poor (Lv 19:15; Si 35:12). It was a fault of which even Jesus' enemies couldn't accuse him: Indeed, his enemies as well as his friends often referred to his lack of partiality (Lk 20:21; for Peter on this subject, see Ac 10:34; for Paul, Rm 2:11).

God's attitude must be ours. The world can know that we're Christians only by our love. Today those who are rich in material things but poor in everything else show their material wealth by the same kind of ostentation as in James's day, when they wore rings on every finger. What, indeed, *is* the real poverty level? Could it be that it should be measured by spiritual as well as material standards?

Let's become aware of spiritual as well as material poverty in all people, including ourselves. Like James, let our Christianity be practical and true. Let's remember that in his first sermon Jesus declared that Isaiah's prediction that the blind will see, the deaf hear, and the mute speak was fulfilled in him. But very few blind saw, very few lame walked, very few deaf heard again. To multiply the numbers, Jesus intended that his messianic mission continue in us, his followers. Like Jesus' *"Ephphatha!"*, let our ears be opened! — opened to the full teachings of the Gospel, opened to the poor and the rich, the powerful and the powerless, the humble and the proud. Then let's be open in the way of Christ to the needs of the most desperate, wherever we find them. Let's *care*!

Twenty-Fourth Sunday in Ordinary Time
Is 50:5-9   Jm 2:14-18   Mk 8:27-35

Two Dilemmas
Our Real Work in Life; Faith and Good Works;
Joy and Suffering; Is Suffering Necessary?

A grocer, a banker, and an advertising executive got lost in the woods. Eventually they came to a farmer's house and asked if he could put them up overnight. "Sure," the farmer said. "But I've got room for only two of you in the house. The other one will have to sleep in the barn with the animals, and the smell is pretty bad out there." "I'll sleep in the barn," the banker volunteered.

Half an hour later there was a knock on the farmhouse door, and there stood the banker, gasping, "I can't take the smell." "All right," said the grocer. "I'll sleep in the barn." And off he went. In a while there was another knock on the door. "I've put up with some rank odors from spoiled food," the grocer complained, "but that barn tops them all." "You two sissies," said the advertiser. "*I'll* sleep in the barn." Thirty minutes later came another knock. When they opened the door, there stood all the animals from the barn.

We tell that story not to denigrate advertisers, but to assert that they — seemingly with few scruples — might often differ with Jesus' honest approach. In today's Gospel, they would invert Jesus' order and talk first of how to gain life, and try to submerge talk of the price. The scene took place in Caesarea Philippi, a place of gods. The town had formerly been a center of worship of the god Baal. Philip the tetrarch had put on its hillside a gleaming temple of white marble to the godhead of the Roman Emperor Caesar. It was said to be the birthplace of Pan, the Greek god of nature. Jesus took advantage of the isolation of this pagan territory to say some things of prime importance.

The scene comprised three sub-scenes. The first act consisted of questions, beginning with, "Who do people say that I am?" (v. 27). The focus of the question isn't on an identity crisis on Jesus' part, but on the state of the apostles' faith. Already in St. Mark's Gospel different interest groups — demoniacs, evil spirits, Jewish authorities — had given their opinion as to who Jesus is. The apostles' initial answers reflected the confusion that existed in the minds of the people.

Jesus followed up with a question which has to be answered by every person who takes the Gospel at all seriously: "[W]ho do *you* say that I am?" (v. 29). That question was so important to Mark the evangelist that everything before it in his Gospel implies it, and everything after it explains what it means to be the Messiah (or to be his follower).

Moments of breakthrough in life are hard — moments in which all the presumptions of the past lie broken and we have to turn in a different direction. This was such a moment for St. Peter. He bluntly answered, "You are the Messiah." It was amazing that here of all places he would see in a homeless Galilean worker in wood someone that great. With Peter's answer, Jesus realized that he hadn't completely failed. Peter's profession was the moment the Older Covenant waited for. For the advertiser, so far so good.

In the second sub-scene, Jesus began to depart from advertising techniques: He warned the apostles not to tell anyone about him (v. 30). Why? Because his honesty compelled him first to straighten out their understanding of the word "Messiah." Over the years, Jewish theology had come to various ideas of the Messiah. Their visions grew under the oppression they had suffered under Assyrians, Babylonians, Persians, Greeks, and now the Romans. Pharisaical Judaism focused on the fact that the Messiah was to be a descendant of King David, and therefore a king himself, possessing glory and great power. Qumran Judaism looked for two persons: a priestly Anointed and a kingly Anointed — a Messiah descended from the line of the priest Aaron as well as one from David. Apocalyptic Judaism looked for a Messiah who was an angelic figure. And at least one segment of Judaism — the Sadducees — denied that there would be any Messiah at all.

Modern religious Judaism is a linear descendant of Pharisaism;

other branches of religious Judaism didn't survive. The Pharisees' projected dramatic timetable begins with a world in terrible straits of immorality. Then there will be terrible upheavals in nature such as earthquakes, falling stars, and erupting volcanoes. To bring order out of the chaos and to settle fights will first come Elijah, then the Messiah. All pagans will unite against him, but he will destroy them all, cleanse the Temple, renew Jerusalem, unite Jews from all over the world, and bring about perfect peace and joy forever. Peter meant a Messiah — a Christ — after that description. Mark, writing perhaps thirty-five years after the incident, would have known many believers who found it difficult to move from Peter's view to that of Jesus. Their picture had no room for a cross, which was to Peter and the others simply incomprehensible.

Then and now, it seems there's no situation in life more guaranteed to focus us on God and religion than that of suffering. If suffering comes our way, we ask, "Why did a so-called loving God allow this to happen?" (If, on the other hand, we win first prize in the lottery or get a good-paying job, we're less likely to be puzzled as to why God allowed it!)

So Jesus had to remind them that Messiahship was connected with not just power and joy, but also suffering and death (v. 31). It wasn't that Jesus was to suffer because of any mistakes he made: That's retribution. Nor did he actively seek suffering as if it were a virtue: That's sadism. Like many who suffer, he had led a morally good life, and on that score didn't deserve suffering.

He had hinted at his suffering before, but now that they had an inkling of his identity he spoke of it openly (v. 32). Now Jesus would be on the way to Jerusalem, where he would suffer, die, and — important to remember — rise again. That points to the first of two questions in today's liturgy: the connection between suffering and joy in the life of the Christian. Peter, who all his life shared his contemporaries' idea of the Messiah as conqueror, argued about it with Jesus.

Neither Peter nor his contemporaries had reflected carefully enough on such passages from the Jewish Scriptures as today's selection from Isaiah, which refers in tones of resignation to the Messiah as the "Suffering Servant." This servant is all the people of God, personified in the one who exemplified their best goals and traits: to overcome evil by good, violence by love, war by peace-making.

Jesus was the ideal Israelite: docile before the Father, but determined, firm, and silent in the face of suffering. To Jesus, Peter's idea of taking a crown without a cross was like Jesus' temptations by the devil in the desert. When those temptations were over, the Gospels tell us, the Tempter left him — to await another opportunity. For Jesus to go along with the people's notion of a wonder-working and powerful Messiah, and to try to be that kind of Messiah, was another opportunity for the Tempter! As everyone's temptations are tailor-made for them, this one was tailor-made for Jesus! It came as many temptations do: in the voice of a friend. Jesus rejected Peter's temptation in almost the same strong words he had used with the devil (Mt 4:11).

In the third sub-scene, Jesus approached the center of Christian faith, describing the ascent of the soul to the summit of perfection. That ascent begins from one's resolution to be saved: All people who wish to come after him must deny themselves, take up their cross, and follow him (v. 34). To say no to one's self is for most people a hard proposition. The fact that the ancient world's concept of taking up a cross was the ultimate degradation, a wretched punishment meted out to the most monstrous criminals, made it even less acceptable. The Torah, in fact, had said that God's curse rested upon anyone who was crucified (Dt 21:23). So Jesus was going against all received opinions, and wasn't offering an easy way; but he wasn't asking anyone to do what he wouldn't first do himself.

Then Jesus said what a careful advertiser, trying to set out his ideas in an attractive order, might have put first: All those who wish to save their life will lose it, but all who lose their life for his sake and that of the Gospel will save it (v. 35). History is full of examples of people — especially generous youth — who, by spending their life for others, saved it, and whose death was more useful to the human race than their life. People who think first of their own profit, comfort, or security are losing life every moment of their search, whereas those who forget themselves to spend their lives for Jesus and for those for whom Jesus died are winning life all the time.

Such are pioneers who explore new horizons, women who accept the risk of bearing children, missionaries who don't remain comfortably at home, scientists who spend their lives for others. They find that the way to happiness and fulfillment is to live life to the full rather than have it just fritter away. In the final analysis, the solution to the question of the encounter between suffering and joy is to love greatly, because if we truly love we find joy in sacrificing for the beloved.

Today's reading from St. James presents the second question of today's liturgy: the connection between faith and good works. If our faith is strong, do we need anything else? Or, on the other hand, if we do good things, is any kind of faith necessary at all? James's letter says that faith must include good works or it's dead. His words demonstrate a sensitivity made sharp by everyday injustice, and take on the urgencies of our time. Small-minded faith leads to an uncaring world. Jesus taught that people should live in a way that the world, seeing the goodness of their acts, would give praise to our heavenly Father. And he said that people will be known by their deeds and that true faith will express itself by *doing* the will of God.

The questions of today's liturgy have echoes in our lives. As we try to answer Jesus' question, "Who do *you* say that I am?" our temptation is to look for someone of power: one who claims the earth, rules it with strength, and uses advertising techniques to stay on top. We find it easier to believe in a distant God of power than in the Suffering Servant of Isaiah who cries out in pain on the crosses of the world and suffers in humanity.

No matter what advertisers tell you, the profession of faith and the practice of good works are, like joy and sorrow, not an "either-or" proposition; they're a "both-and" proposition. The well-designed life has both joy and sorrow, thought and action. A life of joy with no sorrow can become like a terrain with all sunshine and no rain: a barren desert. Both suffering and joy, and both faith and good works, are necessary for the life of the good Christian.

Twenty-Fifth Sunday in Ordinary Time
Ws 2:12, 17-24   Jm 3:16-4:3   Mk 9:30-37

Is Being Street-Smart Enough?
Childlikeness; Wisdom; Being Significant;
People with God and People without Him

There's a fable that God gave a group of aspiring students a choice between wisdom and knowledge. If they chose knowledge they would know everything; if they chose wisdom they would know a few things well. The students reflected long and hard. They thought first about knowledge. They thought of the ads they had seen in magazines that said, "Take our courses! Unlock the powers of the universe!" They had read articles promising that the possession of knowledge would give unlimited power. And politicians had been telling them that society was on the threshold of a new knowledge explosion which would make nations more humane and less inclined to war.

But then they reflected upon the adult world's loss of rosy optimism in the power of knowledge. They were puzzled that the Egyptians had once known so much and that over time their knowledge had been lost. The Germans, who originated the Ph.D. degree, had been infatuated with knowledge, and had found something addictive about it. But something was missing: The German university had encouraged the pursuit of knowledge mostly as a means to power and wealth. And they reflected that American universities sell knowledge the way Detroit sells cars, pointing to the possession of knowledge as the solution to all social problems. But always the problems remained.

So, they figured, people may know everything and still be foolish. And so the group then thought of wisdom. It can't be sold. Knowledge and wisdom, far from being one, often have no connection. Knowledge is proud that it knows so much; wisdom is humble that it knows no more. Though the pursuit of wisdom had been a concern of schooling for thousands of years, these modern students hadn't been exposed to it.

So, like true budding academics, they talked and talked, and talked some more. Finally they told God that they chose knowledge. But they cleverly added that, since they were to know everything, they should also know what wise people know. God replied that He could tell them what wise people know, but He couldn't make them wise. For example, God said facetiously, one of the things that wise people know is when to keep quiet when their speech won't improve on silence.

Today's liturgy is about wisdom. The Gospel begins with the important information that Jesus was now leaving the north where he was safe and starting toward Jerusalem and the cross (v. 30). Wanting to leave a group who would be prepared to continue his work when he left, he announced for the second time his coming passion and death. His news wasn't only an announcement; it was also a pathetic appeal for insights connected with wisdom (v. 31).

The disciples, though they heard Jesus all right, didn't understand what he said, particularly the part about rising again (v. 32) — even though, according to Mark, on more than one occasion Jesus very clearly spelled out the manner of his death and resurrection (8:31-33, 9:30-32, and 10:32-34). But they were afraid to question him. It was risky business, asking Jesus a question: You never knew what answers you might receive. They got the general drift that great afflictions were awaiting their master.

Their lack of wisdom when they arrived at their quarters in Capernaum showed even more how far they were from understanding what Jesus was all about. It turned out that they had been arguing about who among them was the greatest (v. 34). Of all things to discuss at this time! What a contrast with wisdom! They were still thinking of Jesus' kingdom as an earthly power, with themselves as its head.

To Jesus, the difference between where he wanted them to be and where they were was heartbreaking. When he asked them what they'd been discussing (v. 33), they fell silent. It was all right while they were arguing about it among themselves, but not before Jesus. They knew at least that much. What they didn't seem to realize was that we should think of everything we do and say in the light of Jesus' presence.

Seeing their need for instruction and the opportunity to give it now, Jesus took the official position of a rabbi teaching his students: He sat down (v. 35). He got right to the point: "If anyone wishes to be first," he said, "he shall be the last of all and the servant of all." Service is the keynote of his true followers — service that is an attitude as well as an action. Even those who volunteer to work for his Church should have the desire to be of service, and should have the competence to do that for which they volunteer — whether that be as priest, deacon, eucharistic minister, lector, altar server, musician, usher, or other.

Then he took a little child (v. 36) and, putting his arms around it, pointed out more wisdom. Note the verbs: He *took* a little child, he *placed* the little child among them, he *embraced* the child, and he spoke (v. 37). Even aside from Jesus, we need children. An ex-convict, recently returned from four years in prison, addressed an assembly of students about not ending up where he had. While much of what he said was predictable — stories of violence, boredom, and loneliness — he made one point that no one expected. He described prison as "a world without children." He spoke of what it was like to go four years without ever seeing a child, or anything belonging to a child. He never saw a toy. He never heard a little girl's squeals of delight or a little boy's laughter.

What does Jesus see in the child that the adult lacks? Certainly not childish charm: That would be a lyricism. Innocence? The Bible is much too realistic to call a child innocent: The Bible knows human nature. The small child already contains all the ingredients of wrongdoing — mainly dormant, to be sure, though often astonishingly awake and active. The "innocent child" is often an invention of those grown-ups eager to stake a sentimental claim to the vanished purity of their own childhood.

What Jesus sees in the child is the exact opposite of the chief negative characteristics of maturity. Grown-ups seek security, and in the process can become sly and hard. They're often afraid, and fear abases. Children, on the other hand, live in a world of *unruffled trust*. Adults see everything with an eye to its usefulness, thereby rendering everything unfree. The child *meets reality as it is, with simple acceptance*.

To the adult there's much unnaturalness. This, that, and the other natural reaction "is simply not done." The child says what it thinks — often to the embarrassment of adults — and it shows what it feels. Hence it's considered ill-mannered. In children's attitude toward life lies their *humility*. Their consciousness brims mostly with people. Thus their world is dominated by what really counts. Two wings raise children up from the earth: *simplicity of eye and heart*, which welcomes all that's new and great and salutary, and *purity*. To understand all that is proper wisdom.

So is today's reading from the Book of Wisdom. Written at Alexandria in Egypt about a hundred years before Christ, the Book of Wisdom wisely understands that without a belief in God true goodness isn't possible. Many indeed try to be good out of ideals that have no connection with God, but their principles wind up in violence and hate.

Today's passage describes wicked people as plotting against the just man (v. 12), because his life and words are a reproach to them (vv. 12-16) and the wicked determine to test the just man's claims (vv. 17-20). Things haven't changed. Virtuous people continue to be a hated provocation to people of vice. In our ruthless secular world, the virtuous person continues to be put down, ridiculed, and accused of hypocrisy, arrogance, condescension, and worse. So it is with Catholic-bashing in our time. Evil people can't stand people who try to be virtuous.

The letter of St. James, in one of the most perceptive passages ever written, makes the same point about those who are completely this-worldly. It gives what we today might call a psychological analysis of the motivation of the evil person. Viciousness can arise from our own insecurity. That insecurity in turn results in self-seeking. When people think they're nobodies, they feel somehow compelled to prove that they're somebodies. In addition to attention-getting devices, they try to prove themselves worthwhile by putting others down.

James lists some of the qualities of people with no wise insights: Their pride and guilt give rise to jealousy, ambition, lies, disorder, and an endless variety of foul practices (vv. 14-16). His list shows that a world without God is a cruelly violent world. The truly secure person, such as the Gospel advocates, can afford to take the last place.

James joins all those Jewish writings like the Book of Wisdom which were always of one mind that *true* wisdom is "from above" (v. 17), from God. James's descriptive adjectives for the wise people who are endowed from above contrast sharply with people who are only street-smart. People imbued with God's wisdom are *pure* enough to approach God. Such people are *peaceable*, maintaining a right relationship between person and person and between people and God. They're *gentle*, knowing how to forgive even when strict justice may give the right to condemn. They're *compliant*, allowing themselves to be persuaded, knowing when to yield. They're *full of mercy and good fruits*, giving sympathy to people who are in trouble, even though they may have brought their trouble on themselves. They're *constant*, not hesitating to make decisions. And they're *sincere*, having no trace whatsoever of hypocrisy.

James's passage concludes with a consideration of the root causes of strife in a community, and their remedies. Briefly, the root causes are bound up with the failure to pray properly. People who have only street-smarts but not wisdom can't pray properly because they're bound up with their own pleasure. Pleasure-dominated people can only pray that "my pleasures be satisfied," but the wise way to pray is to conclude, "Thy will be done." Foolish people are the center of their own life, and haven't emptied themselves enough of self-love in order to be filled with God's love.

For almost two thousand years, the disciples of Jesus have gathered together on the first day of the week to hear the wisdom of God

— "words to live by" — and to depart with helpful ideas for the coming day or week. Today God's wisdom gives us many ideas to think about. Between knowledge and wisdom as a way of life, which would we choose? Do we give enough attention to God's wisdom in order to make a good life, or are we satisfied with having enough street knowledge to make a living? Do we spend as much time through the week looking for wisdom as we do for the right television channel? Do we look upon our children as in any way our role models? Do we allow our selfish desires to be so strong that we can't pray properly?

TWENTY-SIXTH SUNDAY IN ORDINARY TIME
Nb 11:25-29 Jm 5:1-6 Mk 9:38-43, 47f.

Social Justice
Tolerance; Openness; The Lord's Thumb Is on the Scales
for the Poor; Thoughtfulness toward Others; Ecumenism;
Cooperation with People of Good Will

The human family now numbers almost six billion people. If all of us were gathered together in one place, with each person standing on a two-by-two-foot patch of ground, we'd cover an area of less than 800 square miles — only about the size of Jacksonville, Florida. Yet scientists are discussing how many more people this planet will hold.

Among the reasons for their discussions are current problems. Over half of us go to bed hungry every night, and slightly less than half of those go to bed not only hungry, but starving. One out of every 114 people in the world — an estimated 75 million — has been uprooted by fighting and forced to move somewhere else, in their own country or elsewhere, in search of protection or food.

More than half of us throughout the world aren't free. In some places of the Western world, on the other hand, there's so great an emphasis on individual rights that it seems to blind people to their obligations to others. In other parts of the world, many people aren't accorded even the minimum requirements for basic human living. We don't seem to have struck the right balance.

Some scientists see the solution to be population control, including some radical methods like abortion. The Catholic Church sees the solution to be proper personal development, and sees part of the solution in three of the lessons of today's liturgy.

Against people whose motto is, "Don't rock the boat," today's first lesson in proper personal development is to decry elitism, that evil wherein some people see themselves as best in the world and diminish the rights of others as inferior. In today's Gospel, the apostles tried to exclude those who were outside their own "in" group. That was nothing new: The Jews had done that from the earliest times. The Book of Numbers, the fourth book of the Pentateuch or Law (Torah), calls to mind the Israelites' wandering from Egypt to the promised land. Among their problems was the fact that the people were complaining about food, and Moses, in his condition of ministerial burnout, was complaining about the people.

God commanded that seventy of the elders come to the Meeting Tent, that holy place in which Moses and the elders of the people came into the presence of God. Although the scene may seem strange to us because it reflects the assumptions of a different culture, it was solemn, and its setting conveys a sense of awe and the sacred. When other leaders wanted to stop two outsiders, Eldad and Medad, who were neither elders nor present at the meeting, from speaking in God's behalf, Moses showed his largeness and his quality of leadership by indicating that the spirit of God was with the outsiders too.

In the Gospel, the one who wanted to stop someone driving out demons in Jesus' name (v. 38) was, of all people, St. John. The incident illustrates the fiery temperament of "the beloved disciple" which may have been responsible for earning for him and his brother James the title "Sons of Thunder." It also illustrates the early Church's problem with exclusivity. The early Church wasn't as hierarchically and organically united as today. Each of the early churches in the towns and cities, while recapitulating the entire Church, was in many ways independent of the others. The community of John seems to have been more exclusive than some.

To understand the incident more fully, we must consider also the thinking of the time. Everyone believed in a world of demons, a malign influence that caused mental and physical illness. *The* way to get rid of them, the people thought, was to get to know the name of a more powerful demon and then command the less powerful demon in that name.

The outsider obviously believed in Jesus, otherwise he wouldn't have succeeded in driving out demons in his name. So the issue wasn't that they were teaching a different doctrine, but that they were members of another community. Jesus said basically the same thing as Moses had of Eldad and Medad. His command that his followers cooperate was a permanent injunction for the members of his Church not to refuse to make common cause with those outside the Church, particularly when it's a question of doing good. To do good is to approach Jesus.

Jesus makes an important emphasis on tolerance: whoever is not against us is for us (v. 40). He doesn't mean a *lazy* or *indifferent* acceptance of *anything*. He wants a realization of the magnitude of truth and the impossibility of any one person grasping it all in its entirety. Intolerance is a sign of both arrogance and ignorance — a sign that you believe there's no truth beyond what you see. We may, of course, disagree with another's beliefs, but we should never despise a person who sincerely holds them.

Then (vv. 41-48) Mark adds collections of sayings of Jesus that Mark remembered, loosely organized by way of word associations. Every word of Jesus is precious, memorable, and significant. Mark preserves striking sayings, out of context at times, but speaking to the needs of our times as well as his.

One of his strong statements is a second lesson for proper personal development to better our human family. Against scandal (from Greek *skandalon*, stumbling-block), the lesson is to accept our responsibility toward others. Scandal doesn't refer only, as some think, to the corruption, disgrace, and dishonor that takes place in notorious circles, but to actions that you and I can commit before impressionable seekers after truth. Compared with the punishment in store for one who leads astray one such (v. 42), it would be better to be encased in concrete and thrown into the sea. The importance which ancient peoples attached to decent burial added to the terror of this punishment.

The figure of Gehenna as a symbol of hell (v. 43) derived from the garbage dump in the dried-up Valley of the Hinnom River below the southwest wall of the city. It had an evil history. Once the site of child-sacrifices to the god Moloch (2 K 23:10), in the time of Jesus it was the city dump, and its smoldering fires and billowing acrid smoke consuming the smelly garbage were a symbol of the punishment of the damned.

Although Jesus didn't mean the cutting off of limbs literally, he used the image to show the seriousness of scandal. He teaches that, while it's never all right to mutilate ourselves, a most precious value is leading others to truth.

O. Henry, the master short-story teller, once wrote a story about a woman whose mother died when she was just a little girl. When her father came home from work, the lonely little girl would ask him to play with her. Her father would tell her he had no time and that she should go out into the street and play; then he would light his pipe, take off his shoes, put his feet up, and read the newspaper. By the time the little girl grew up, she was used to the streets, and made her living there. When she died, St. Peter looked to Jesus and asked, "I suppose we send her to hell?" The Lord said, "No, she deserves heaven. But go down to earth, look for the man who refused to play with her when she needed him, and send *him* to hell!"

Today's Second Reading contains a third lesson in good personal development that can benefit our needful human family. It laments that some people, instead of being prophets as Moses and Jesus had wished — that is, speakers for God — place their trust in money. In this passage, which concludes our extracts from the letter of St. James for this year, we detect allusions to some of the parables of our Lord, to similar denunciations in the prophets, particularly Amos, and to Paul's idea that the love of money is a root of all kinds of evil (1 Tm 6:10). An angry James wants to show the ultimate worthlessness of riches and to show how detestable some who own riches can become.

James condemns the rich who *hoard* their wealth (vv. 2-3), cheat laborers of their just wages (v. 4), and live in a luxurious way that's unmindful of the poor (v. 6). He, like the rest of Scripture, doesn't condemn wealth as such, but insists strenuously upon its responsibilities and on the perils which surround the person who has it. The more you own, the more you're owned; it's good to have money, if money isn't all you have.

James begins picturesquely by commanding the rich to shriek and howl over losing the *really* important things of life. He's suggestive of the lower right-hand corner of Michelangelo's Sistine Chapel painting of the *Last Judgment*, which pictures the wide-eyed face of a man who's just been condemned to hell and realizes for the first time that he's lost everything. James then (vv. 2f.) applies Jesus' advice not to lay up earthly treasures where moths and rust corrode (Mt 6:19). Grain will rot, garments will become food for moths, and even gold and silver — among the most indestructible items on earth — are doomed to be lost.

The desire for possessions can eat at a person like a fire (v. 3). This all-consuming fire can cause a person to be oblivious of the needs and rights of others — even those to whom we have immediate obligations, like employees. In New Testament times the laborer lived on the verge of starvation. He was paid by the day, and if his small wages were withheld even for a day he and his family didn't eat. James insists (v. 4) that one can't be right with God unless one is just with one's fellow human beings.

The *selfish* rich have lived in soft luxury (v. 5). They've used their wealth to gratify their love of comfort and their lusts, and forgotten their duties to their fellow human beings. But what they have really done is to have prepared themselves for the day when they, fattened, will be slaughtered (v. 5).

James and his contemporaries would probably consider most of us rich. At least, most of us are free of the day-to-day worries of the poor of his time. We hope, however, that we aren't among the *selfishly insensitive* rich whom he addresses. They tell a story of a rich but miserly parishioner who consulted a priest about his discontent. The priest led him to the window. "Look out there," he said, "and tell me what you see." "People," answered the rich man. Then the priest led him to a mirror. "What do you see now?" he asked. "I see myself," answered the rich man. The priest said, "In the window there's glass and in the mirror there's glass. But the glass of the mirror is covered with a little silver; no sooner is it added than you stop seeing others and see only yourself."

TWENTY-SEVENTH SUNDAY IN ORDINARY TIME
Gn 2:18-24   Heb 2:9-11   Mk 10:2-16 (or 2-12)

Sex, Marriage, and Divorce
Thank God for Human Love; Marriage Appreciation

Little Nancy quizzed her mother about where she came from, and was given the traditional answer among some parents, "God sent you." "And how did you get here, Mother? Did God send you, too?" "Yes, dear," answered the mother piously. "And grandma?" "Yes, dear." "And great-grandma?" "Yes, dear." The child concluded with, "Do you mean to say, Mother, that there have been no sex relations in this family for over 200 years?"

Despite the reticence of that mother, sexual leniency today is rampant. One of the major obstacles to sexual wrong, though, is Jesus Christ. By what right?

Today's portion of the letter to the Hebrews gives one reason. The letter is important enough to call for excerpts on seven current Sundays; today's portion speaks of the paradox of Jesus' being at the same time God and having to undergo suffering as a human being. While his being God gave him a unique perspective, his suffering is proof that he fully shared our lot as human beings. For him to have been tested in every way that we're tested, as this letter to the Hebrews says elsewhere, includes sex. For at least these reasons, Jesus is uniquely qualified to answer questions on sex, marriage, and divorce.

Today's Gospel shows that. It contains two themes (divorce and children) and three scenes (a public and private one on divorce and one on children).

Despite the Jewish high ideal of marriage, there was a great deal of divorce. Evidently this had been true right from the time of Moses. The Pharisees' question to Jesus concerned whether it was lawful for a husband to divorce his wife (v. 2). Their motives in asking the question could have been any one of many. The matter of divorce was a frequent topic for rabbinic discussion, and they may honestly have wanted Jesus' opinion. Or they may have wanted to trip him up. Or they may have wanted to have Jesus incur the hostility of Herod, who had divorced and remarried. Or they may have wanted Jesus to contradict the law of Moses and thus charge him with heresy.

Jesus asked, "What did Moses command you?" (v. 3). They answered correctly that the Law of Moses permitted a man to write a bill of divorce and dismiss his wife (v. 4). That Law gave the man permission for divorce if he found in his wife "something indecent" (Dt 24:1). The crux of this regulation from Deuteronomy was the interpretation of "something indecent." The school of Rabbi Shammai (a leading scholar during the reign of Herod the Great) favored a narrow interpretation: The words meant a man could divorce his wife for adultery only. On the other hand, the school of Rabbi Hillel, a foremost master of biblical interpretation and commentary, who was like Shammai

roughly Jesus' contemporary, was liberal: The words could mean if a
wife spoiled food, or if she talked to a strange man, or if she spoke ill
of her husband's relatives in his hearing. The liberal school had pre-
vailed, and divorce for the most trivial reasons was tragically common.

Disagreeing with the schools of both Hillel and Shammai, Jesus
asserted that divorce in the Book of Deuteronomy was permitted only
because the hearts of the people had dried up.

Whereas the Pharisees' question had gone back to the Law of
Moses, Jesus' answer went back to the beginning of creation (v. 6).
He referred to today's First Reading. Elaborating on the Book of Genesis, he showed that it was God's intent that marriage be a sacred and
binding union. God completed the creative process of the first man with
woman. When the function of the woman is sometimes translated as
being Adam's "partner" or "helpmate," the Hebrew expression doesn't
have the pejorative sense carried by the English words as though she
held the nails for him while he did the real figuring and the hammer-
ing.

The same Hebrew word is often used to describe God (see Ex
18:4; Dt 33:7; Ps 33:20), and might be expressed better by the word
"companion." The male, whom God created first, needed an associate
for complementation and fulfillment. For God to create animals for this
purpose isn't sufficient: They, having a nature that doesn't correspond
to that of human beings, aren't suitable enough for the human being's
full completion (vv. 19f.) — no matter what pet-lovers say about their
Fido or Tabby.

So God cast a deep sleep on the man (v. 21) — a term suggest-
ing the mysterious and highly meaningful nature of God's activity —
and thus created woman. All the expressions here — rib, bone of my
bone, woman, man — indicate the unity of nature of man and woman,
a unity unlike any other. About the significant term "rib," some rabbis
said that the woman was created not from the man's feet to be beneath
him or stepped on, nor from his head to be above him, but from nearest his heart to be alongside him, equal to him, and loved by him, and
from beneath his arm to be protected by him. Thus, at a time when the
Babylonian culture sold women on their slave market at a price a little
lower than a good cow, the beginnings of the Hebrew tradition proclaimed that woman shared the same nature and dignity as man.

But even as early as Jesus' time a rabbi — Philo of Alexandria
in Egypt — indicated its mythic nature. "For how could anyone ad-

mit," he wrote, "that a woman, or a human being at all, came into existence out of a man's side?" The term "rib" more accurately indicates one of Adam's most intimate parts — his very *life*. In fact, some translations of this text say that God took part of Adam's life and clothed it with flesh.

At the end of the process and Adam and Eve's discovery of the completion of each in the being of the other come the first human words recorded by the Bible — and they're a love song. A most touching part of that song is Adam's joyful exclamation of Eve's equality with him: the words *at last*. Although Adam was surrounded by the wonders of God's creation (everything God made was good), Adam realized all through it that he was incomplete when alone. Especially touching is the three-times repeated term of precious endearment of the man for the woman, "this one": *"This one... is bone of my bones and flesh of my flesh; This one shall be called 'woman,' for out of 'her man' this one has been taken"* (v. 23).

With all that and more in the background, Jesus concluded that what God has joined together, no human being must separate (v. 9). In the divine "joining together," God ratifies the mutual love of persons; their sexual union serves as a pledge of exclusive fidelity to each other. Jesus struck a revolutionary blow for women by recognizing women's preference for intimacy, close relationships, and emotional proximity to persons.

Marriage has always been of interest and importance to everybody, so when they were back in the house the disciples again questioned Jesus about it (v. 10). He answered unswervingly that whoever divorces his wife and marries another commits adultery (v. 11). He reflects his awareness of non-Jewish Roman customs around him when he adds that the woman who divorces her husband and marries another commits adultery (v. 12): Whereas Roman law permitted a woman to seek a divorce, this didn't exist among Jews.

Yet no one may legitimately interpret anything that Jesus said as implying a need for feeling guilt in marriages that have become bitter, disappointing, or sour, and have failed.

After the discussion on marriage St. Mark describes people bringing their little children (who are a primary purpose of marriage) to Jesus to have him touch them (v. 13). Jesus was the kind of person with whom you would do that — he cared for everyone, including children, and, because he radiated sunshine rather than gloom, children cared for him, too.

All of us have experiences analogous to marriage and divorce: the single among us as well as the married, widow and widower, male and female, gay and straight. That analogous experience is with our weakness, the gnawing sorrow that we aren't able to be what we hoped or promised with love. In our brokenness, we all fail one another. All of us to some extent have "hearts dried up." For those who are morally sensitive, all divorce from other people, particularly in a marriage, is sad. But constancy is difficult, and not all interpersonal relationships are able to fully reflect the ideal.

We must take those realities of inadequacy and sin into account even as we realize that in Jesus' vision marriage is made in heaven. While marriage is fundamentally God's work, it's not what's portrayed in celebrity magazine articles where the married couple are awesome lovers, blissful parents of two children, united in common devotion to a dog or cat.

Nevertheless, in the Old Testament, marriage was the symbol of the love of the Lord for his people Israel, and in our New Testament marriage is the sign of the union between Christ and his Church. And in all interpersonal relationships we Christians have what many people don't have: the teachings of God in Jesus to further our understanding and guide our actions.

TWENTY-EIGHTH SUNDAY IN ORDINARY TIME
Ws 7:7-11   Heb 4:12f.   Mk 10:17-30 (or 10:17-27)

Your Choices Define You
Importance of the Word; Wealth and Wisdom in the Scheme of Things;
Value and Worth; Christianity vs. Respectability; Life in the Light of Death

Words can have tremendous effects. Patrick Henry's "Give me liberty, or give me death" galvanized the early American colonists against England. The "Rum, Romanism, and Rebellion" slogan of the 1876 U.S. Presidential campaign ultimately helped lose the presidency for James G. Blaine, the renegade Roman Catholic candidate. Winston Churchill's request for "blood, sweat, and tears" helped solidify the resolve of the British during difficult times in World War II.

Today's portion of the letter to the Hebrews gives some descriptions of God's word, the great mystery of His communicating with us through human language. It begins by telling us that God's word is *living*. Some words are limited by time, either because they become dead to living language, or because of the restricted circle of their interest. God's word, to the contrary, is alive and life-producing for people of all time: Bible sales through history have been proof of that.

The passage then tells us that God's word is *effective*: When people have taken God's word seriously, things begin to happen; if the words of *people* can lead to action, what greater accomplishments can come from the words of *God*, when properly understood and treasured! God's word *penetrates* — like a sword, right down to the very marrow of one's inner spirit. God's word *judges the reflections and thoughts* — of one's whole being. You can run from God, but you can't hide.

Take, as an example, today's Gospel. St. Mark sees in Jesus the Moses-like teacher who proclaims the reign of God, who leads God's people, and whom the people are expected to follow. Jesus, Mark tells us, was setting out on a journey (v. 17). It increases the pathos of the scene to know that this is the journey to Jerusalem, where Jesus must suffer and die.

A rich young aristocrat came running up to Jesus. He must have made quite an impression on the apostolic band: His story occurs in all three synoptic Gospels. Although Mark here refers to him only as a man, St. Matthew tells us that he was young and St. Luke describes him as a ruler. His eagerness is shown by his running to kneel at the feet of Jesus. With youthful idealism and enthusiasm, he called Jesus "Good teacher," a flattering title that approached the Messianic.

Jesus picked up on the word "good". He reminded the young man that no action is morally good except in relation to the One Who Is All Good: God. Then he recounted (v. 19), in a general way, the commandments that were found in the Torah, which the young man had been taught contained the way to wisdom and life.

That the man was intelligent and able to obey, he showed by his dropping the word "Good" when he addressed Jesus the second time (v. 20). The rest of the young man's reply amounted to saying, "I never did anybody any harm!" He was satisfied with the commandments' negatives — avoiding evil — but he hadn't gotten very far with the positive: *doing good* for people. He had interpreted Jesus' words as a command to be *respectable* — one thing he had been for his entire life. But for the follower of Christ respectability isn't enough: One must *do* things for others.

This young man didn't understand that: It was obvious from his whole demeanor that he had a need, but that he just couldn't find the words to describe it adequately. He was among the many educated fools in this world who know many things but not how to put everything together in a unified picture. In our own century, our eyes saw what no human being should have to witness: gas chambers built by learned engineers; children poisoned by educated physicians; infants killed by trained nurses; women and babies shot and burned by high school and college graduates — learned monsters or skilled psychopaths all.

It was touching that Jesus, looking at this young man, loved him (v. 21). It was a look of sadness that this loved one might refuse to be all that he could be. Perhaps St. Peter, one of the sources of Mark's Gospel, was reminded of the look Jesus had given him many times, including Jesus' look when during his last suffering Peter had denied him three times (Lk 22:61). There must have been many things in Jesus' look. It was an appeal, essentially, with no anger, and here it included a challenge to the rich young man to get out of his comfortable and respectable life.

Challenge is what all nature thrives on. The wild duck that joined the domestic ducks and was fed, later couldn't fly above the barn; the gulls that fattened up at a shrimp plant starved when it shut down; the hand-fed squirrels that laid up no nuts for the winter bit the hands that had fed them when they no longer held food. People, too, need challenge. A character in the classic film, *The Third Man,* says something to the effect that, "The Borgias presented challenges and produced Michelangelo and the Renaissance. The Swiss had five hundred years of peace, and what did they come up with? The cuckoo clock!" We need challenge!

Jesus' challenge to the young man was to sell what he had and give the proceeds to the poor, and then return and follow him. This pitched his standard higher. It was a big risk. It demanded radical choices, with no shilly-shallying. In modern terms, it's been said that the middle of the road belongs to yellow stripes and dead little animals. Here, the challenge to accept risk put the man on the verge of becoming great. He was faced with the choices with which all people, before and after Christ, are confronted.

King Solomon faced essentially the same choice. The Book of Wisdom, from which today's First Reading is taken, refers to Solomon's age-old prayer for wisdom. Solomon had felt the pull of many temptations that cast a spell on human consciousness. Power and authority present themselves as escape from our dependencies. Abundance of riches has beckoned empires and conquerors. Health has monuments built to its promise that "if you have health, you have everything." Beauty has its troubadours and marketers. The splendor of intellect impresses many as a way out of insufficiency.

But Solomon came to know that people live in fear of losing their power, that abundance of riches never seems to ease the hunger, that people who are "pictures of health" are often burdened with miserable lives, that beauty, skin-deep, doesn't last long, that there are many disenchanted intellectuals. He realized that what we imagine as security is often somehow bondage. He had become the personification of Hebrew wisdom: a practical reality which, by a combination of good training and experience, enabled people to do their jobs well. It had a characteristic religious slant: Reverence for God is the beginning of wisdom, and is basic to it.

The Book of Wisdom was written about 100 years before Christ, in Greek-dominated Alexandria in Egypt. The Jewish community there, though large in numbers, was in danger of losing its identity because of the twin dangers of Greek philosophy and Greek morals. It was a time when Jews were abandoning their faith in great numbers — for social acceptance, or to follow worldly philosophies, or to acquire material wealth. Many of these "yuppies" wanted to be "with it" — a phenomenon that's intimately connected with today's Gospel and still has a familiar ring.

Solomon was like other people in being not especially disposed by birth toward wisdom. But, realizing that only wisdom can bring true happiness, he prayed for wisdom rather than power, riches, health, or good looks. As a result, he became a legend: for his own time, for Jews thereafter, and for all people. Indeed, even Jesus referred to the wisdom of Solomon (Lk 11:31).

The wealthy young man of today's Gospel, as a good Jew, knew not only about Solomon, but also that he would be responsible for his choice. Could he make the right choice? Heartbreakingly, no: His face fell, and he went away sad, for he had many possessions (v. 22). His lack of outgoing generosity caused him to love *things* more than people, *himself* more than others. Anyone like that will inevitably turn his back on Jesus. This young man was the only person in the entire New Testament who left the presence of Jesus "sad"!

Challenged to return love for love, he couldn't, because he couldn't remove the obstacle of his wealth. Wealth can be a prize to share with others or a prison, and for him it was a prison. Jesus commented (v. 23) on how hard it is for those who have wealth to enter the kingdom of God. "Kingdom of God" here means the willingness to have God rule one's life. If God doesn't rule over a person's life, the person will eventually lose his soul.

To illustrate that, Jesus compared the process to the camel, the largest animal known in Palestine, going through the smallest place in contrast, the eye of a needle (v. 25). This Oriental exaggeration to make a point, a process familiar to Jesus' listeners, has caused a lot of time and ink to be wasted trying to interpret it literally. The apostles, poor men from Galilee who recognized that the young man with his wealth could be of great assistance to their cause, must have been somewhat astounded by Jesus' treatment of him.

One point is clear. Jesus was turning completely upside-down what the apostles and all other good Jews had been taught: that wealth is a proof of character certified by God, a sign of God's favor (Ps 37:25: "Neither in my youth, nor now that I am old, have I seen a just man forsaken nor his descendants begging bread"). Jesus, on the other hand, saw the danger of material possessions: They can fix your heart to this world, and can make you think of everything in terms of *price* rather than *value*.

Not only did Jesus' teaching contradict what the apostles had been taught, but it seemed to make salvation practically impossible. The apostles were understandably overwhelmed (v. 26). So Jesus put the whole of his teaching on that subject in a nutshell by reminding them that God alone saves (v. 27). Grace is God's gift, and only those whose arms are empty of self can stretch out to receive the gift of grace. Peter, though, couldn't help but compare himself and his companions favorably with the poor rich young man (v. 28). It was laughable to think of what they had left to follow Jesus — hovels, some rickety boats, and some old fishermen's nets — but it was, in truth, all they had.

This age-old choice, which Solomon, Paul, and Jesus made in one direction and the rich young man in another, confronts us too — even more, perhaps, in our society which posits the underlying principle that worth really does come from material wealth: from the size of our home, the cost of our car, the amount of our investments. Christianity challenges us to change not only ourselves, but even our capitalist system when it's solely market-driven, heartless, and materialist. What do we want? Wealth, or wisdom? True value, or price? An understanding of the full dimensions of human life, or only of what appears? Before God, we shall be held responsible to return love for love. The words with which we choose will have a tremendous effect: They will define who we are.

TWENTY-NINTH SUNDAY IN ORDINARY TIME
Is 53:10f.   Heb 4:14-16   Mk 10:35-45 (or 42-45)

Ours Is a Different God
Joy in Humble Service; Instructions for Greatness;
Temptations to Power; The Criteria for Success; Ambition

Who we understand God to be is extremely important to the way we live our lives. One of the most popular instructional films on Buddhism shows, amid the confidence-inspiring tones of an announcer and the relaxing pictures of lotuses floating in ponds, that the Buddhist God is no more than only nature and people. So the major obligations on the lives of Buddhists are environmentalism, attempts at supreme illumination, and reaching a state of perfect enlightenment. By way of contrast, in the West Judaism, Christianity, and Islam affirm that their God is the Supreme Being — superior to both the human race and nature, the ultimate Being upon Whom all else depends and Who's dependent on nothing higher.

He's also all-powerful, all-knowing, unchangeable, everywhere present, neither male nor female, and perfectly good. He's simultaneously transcendent and immanent: the Creator of the world, distinct from and superior to it, and at the same time present to us and to every smallest particle of creation, like sparrows. So He makes demands on our lives. Christians believe in addition that God sent His Son into the world to show people a reflection of God's highest attribute, love.

Even with Jesus, though, not everyone understands. Take James and John, who placed before Jesus their ambition to occupy his highest two places of honor (v. 37): to be the chief courtiers who would dispense the patronage. They were uncomfortably close to the mindset of today's corporate structure, in which climbers have no regard for others, self-interestedly proclaim themselves, and want to disregard merit to push themselves to the top. James's and John's prayer, though earnest, was wrong: Prayer is unacceptable when it tells God to "do what I want."

Though James and John believed in Jesus, they certainly didn't yet fully understand him. The timing of their expression was atrocious: It came right after Jesus' third and most detailed forecast of his death. And their petition was dramatic: They declared themselves ready to risk death with Jesus — provided, of course, that he guarantee them the highest positions in a kingdom which they conceived as being powerful even after his death.

With extreme patience, Jesus told them they didn't know what they were asking (v. 38). He asked them bluntly if they could drink the same cup of heartache from which he would drink and be submerged in the same bath of pain. They didn't understand his metaphor. The grand palace and great court that they associated with the Messiah still swimming in their heads, they brashly said they could (v. 39).

Unwittingly, they carried out that promise. About twelve years after Jesus' death, James was the first of the apostles to suffer martyrdom (Ac 12:2): He was beheaded at Jerusalem. In fact, there are traditions that all the other apostles except John were also martyred. Andrew was tied to a cross, where he preached to his persecutors until he died. Bartholomew was skinned alive. Peter was crucified at Rome with his head downward. James son of Alphaeus ("James the Less") was thrown from a lofty pinnacle of the Temple, and then beaten to death with a club. Thomas was run through with a lance in the East Indies. Matthias was stoned and then beheaded. Jude Thaddeus was shot to death with arrows. Philip was hanged at Hieropolis in Phrygia. Barnabas was stoned to death by the Jews at Salonica.

Later John, the only apostle to die a natural death, was put into a cauldron of boiling oil but escaped in a miraculous manner, was scourged (Ac 5:40), and afterwards exiled to Patmos (Rv 1:9). Tradition has it that the other authors of the Scriptures, too, suffered martyrdom. Matthew was run through with a sword at a distant city of

Ethiopia. Mark died by being cruelly dragged through the streets of Alexandria. Luke was hanged on an olive tree in the classic land of Greece. And Paul, after various tortures and persecutions, was at length beheaded at Rome by the Emperor Nero.

Even so, Jesus now said that a place of honor was not his to give (v. 40). He could point the way to glory, but only God the Father can bestow places of honor.

The other ten, overhearing the conversation, became indignant at James and John (v. 41) — unfortunately, not out of disappointment with the ambition of their fellow disciples: The Gospels show elsewhere that they had similar thoughts. The disciples were, after all, shrewd, street-wise people. They included weather-beaten fishermen, a callous tax-collector, and a man always in search of a silver coin or two. More than just having their sins forgiven, they were in the business of discipleship of Jesus because there was something in it for them. But James and John had got there first.

So Jesus called them all together for a much-needed lesson on ambition. Believers in a worldly god, then and now, understand their own criteria for "success." Their criteria formulate certain questions. How many people do you control? How big a budget do you have? How many people can you make do what you want?

For our God, though, the criteria are different. For Him, whoever wishes to be great among us will be the servant (v. 43). Success is judged not by how much you can get out of life, but how much you put into it. To aspire to greatness is to aspire to lowliness. Because the Church is a visible society, however, there must be those who exercise authority — but even they mustn't imitate the pagans. Jesus' mandate of service is good psychology for happiness, common sense for contentment, and excellent business practice for success.

Unfortunately, the surrounding culture influences everyone, even some in the Church. While there are many who have a genuine desire to serve, some people want to be important in a parish in the same way that others are important in a corporation. They're on an ego trip rather than a yearning to be of service. They want to exercise authority as a pastor, or president of a parish society, or chairperson of a committee. The source of *Jesus'* greatness, on the other hand, was that he suffered; only then was he raised up. He had said three times that he must suffer and die; now he would soon give his life to save the many (v. 45).

And that's what today's reading from Isaiah is about. It speaks of God's will that the Suffering Servant give his life as an offering for sin (v. 10). Israel was very sin-conscious, and this Servant is a mysterious, sinless person who suffers for the sins of the people — the "many," whom both the rabbis and the early Church interpreted to mean all other nations as well as Jews. These remarkable descriptions were fulfilled only in Jesus. Isaiah's words about the Suffering Servant have been used frequently ever since they were written in the Sixth Century B.C. The Church, for example, proclaims this Suffering Servant every year on Good Friday.

Today's passage from the letter to the Hebrews gives a more detailed and glorious picture of the Suffering Servant: Jesus in the reality of his manhood and the majesty of his Godhood. Few passages in the New Testament are so packed with meaning as these verses. The passage offers the comforting image of the Son of God who drew near us and invites us to draw near him. The letter's audience was Christian Jews: people who were very proud of their former heritage; a group who weren't always at home in the larger Christian community; people who had experienced persecution, were fearful of more, and were faltering in their allegiance to Christ and his Church. They were partially estranged because they felt a lack of continuity with the past, missed comfort in the present, and lacked security for the future.

They would understand the letter's reference to Jesus as the great High Priest (v. 14). A good priest must be in touch with his people and with God, because he's the intermediary between the two, bringing God to people and people to God. He must know both and love both. Jesus the priest came to us from God Himself. After alluding to the greatness of Jesus as God, the passage shows the greatness of Jesus as human being. Because he came among us and was tested in every way (v. 15), he's able to sympathize with our weaknesses. The Gospels indicate that his temptations didn't occur only once, but were constant in Jesus' life. Through what Jesus did, the throne of God has become the throne of grace (v. 16).

In the person of Jesus, God has drawn close to His people; and Jesus, since his ascension, has come into the living presence of God the Father. Reverent approach to God, once the domain of priests and Levites, is now open to all. And we can approach confidently, because Jesus has sympathy for us and taught us that we have a loving God in heaven. We often forget that the biblical expression of our Father "who art in heaven" doesn't mean a place, but a way of being: It doesn't mean that God is distant, but majestic (*Catechism of the Catholic Church,* 2794).

And we often forget that the ideas about God given us by Jesus are completely new. For the Jews, God was holy — and therefore separate, apart, different. For the Greeks, their gods were even more aloof. We're lucky to have had Jesus teach us about the true God and how we can best live our lives in imitating and serving Him.

THIRTIETH SUNDAY IN ORDINARY TIME
Jr 31:7-9   Heb 5:1-6   Mk 10:46-52

Seeing for the First Time
The Gift of Sight; Our Journey

To watch someone *see* for the first time is very dramatic. While the bandages from microsurgery are being taken off, the suspenseful patient trembles with wonderment over whether the treatment has been a success. With the last bandages, he quivers with disbelief that his eyes are sensitive to light, then sheds incredulous tears of happiness over the realization that he can see. A whole new wonderful world of discovery lays before him. In the Holy Land, the heat and the dust cause frequent and varied eye diseases, and there are even today many eye hospitals. In Our Lord's time, there were no medical cures. So because cures were infrequent, and because Mideastern people are by nature emotional, their reactions when a rare cure took place were accentuated.

Take today's Gospel, for example. Jesus was marching steadily and knowingly toward his suffering and death in Jerusalem. A main road to Jerusalem ran right through Jericho, a bedroom community for the more than 20,000 priests who served at the Temple in Jerusalem. As Jesus was passing through, many of them wouldn't yet have begun the fifteen-mile trip to Jerusalem for Passover, one of the rare feasts when all served at the same time. The Temple priests and the people had their intellectual appetite whetted by this young rebel Jesus, who was going against the Establishment. If Jesus was correct, Temple worship would be a thing of the past. Because this idea would adversely affect the local work force and their families, many of the eyes in the crowd were hostile.

Jericho, like outside a church today, was a perfect place for beggars to seek alms from those on pilgrimage to Jerusalem. Bartimaeus, evidently not only an eager but also an impulsive character, when he discovered that Jesus of Nazareth was passing by, began to cry out (v. 47). He called Jesus "Son of David" — a Messianic title, but with all the usual wrong overtones of power and mastery. But Bartimaeus had a *true faith*, which made up for his mistaken theology (which was at times true even of the saints). He's a model of the way Christianity begins: as a personal reaction to Jesus. Jesus rewarded his persistence by stopping and inviting him over. The crowd, which had been trying to quiet him down, now, fickle as ever, encouraged him.

His enthusiasm inspired him to throw aside his cloak so as to be freer to spring up and come to Jesus (v. 50). Jesus asked him the same question he had put to James and John when they showed their undue ambition (10:36): "What do you want me to do for you?" (v. 51). The question always gave his hearers an opportunity to show their real selves. Bartimaeus knew precisely what he wanted of Jesus: his sight. His certainty is a lesson to all of us not to be sentimental or vague in our following of Jesus, but to be as definite as Bartimaeus was.

Most people's blindness isn't physical, but spiritual. And it happens all the time. The old saying is true that "There are none so blind as those who will not see, and none so deaf as those who will not hear." Although not too many people are spiritually *completely* blind, most of us have some blind spots: social, cultural, political, religious, psychological. We can be blinded by passion, ambition, and unforgiveness. Conservatives see the blind spots of liberals, liberals of conservatives; the poor see the blind spots of the middle classes, the middle classes of the poor and upper classes; and so on. We — especially youth — can be blind to a lack of caring relationships with friends and peers.

Some have a blindness about the Church, seeing what's wrong but not all the things that are right: the sheer wonder of the sacrament of reconciliation, for example, and the beauty of the Mass. Some have a blind spot about other people, seeing faults but not all that is courageous, holy, beautiful, and noble. Unless we've learned to be self-critical, we're likely to have *many* blind spots. On the other hand, we mustn't be blind to our own goodness: Bartimaeus, after all, was not *only* sightless, and his blindness wasn't the *whole* truth of who he was.

Spiritual blindness can happen with entire peoples, as Jesus found in Jerusalem and Jeremiah with the ancient Hebrews. Jeremiah's first 25 chapters represent a message of doom against his people for their dried-up hearts that refused to listen to God's word. But God wanted Jeremiah also "to build and to plant." Today's passage is taken from a section that represents the "sunny side," Jeremiah's "Little Book of Comfort." Jeremiah's warnings had gone unheeded, and the destruction he had foretold had come true. Addressing the people of Judah who were exiled to what is the north of modern Iraq, Jeremiah now optimistically looked to future days when his people would come back to the land (30:3).

Today's central theme is the exuberant joy of the return — of an odyssey from spiritual blindness to sight. Opening with a solemn call to joy, the hymn uses strong words like "shout," "proclaim," and "praise." Jeremiah speaks of "the remnant" (v. 7). In this case the term "remnant" referred to the small number of those who escaped the calamity of defeat and exile and had been purified to constitute the new Israel, faithful to her God. The term has, however, referred ever since to all those small numbers who remain faithful through all calamities.

The returning caravan will consist of the blind, the lame, mothers, those with child, and other physically vulnerable people. The return would be a new exodus, but in a much more glorious form. By saying that they departed in tears (v. 9), Jeremiah begins allusions to the first Exodus. Unlike the incident in the first Exodus, however, in which water came from a rock, the desert will see brooks of water constantly flowing; unlike the rough going of the first Exodus, here God will lead them on a level road, providing an easier march. Today's Responsorial Psalm reflects the delirious joy of displaced persons coming home, of the spiritually blind receiving their sight.

Jeremiah had the mission of leading his people along a journey to God, and Jesus had the same mission. Jesus, however, eclipsed Jeremiah in many ways. Today's portion of the letter to the Hebrews reminds us of one way: Jesus was a priest — *the* priest of the Judeo-Christian faith. Hebrews presents thoughts about three basic requirements for a priest. First is his humanity: A priest is taken from among people (v. 1). The priest is a link between God and people. In ancient Israel, and with us, the priest has the special function of offering gifts and sacrifices for sins. Sin disturbs the relationship between God and people; sacrifice is intended to restore that relationship. Jesus surpassed that requirement: He was himself both completely man and fully God;

he had been tempted but remained without sin; and he underwent the preëminent sacrifice of the cross.

Secondly, the priest is able to deal patiently with the erring (v. 2). The priest's patience is to be a mean between extravagant grief and indifference. Nobody can deal well with other people unless he has the God-given virtue of compassion. The priest's compassion for people must be extraordinary, because he realizes that he himself is beset by weakness. The priest, in other words, shares humanity with his people. Jesus is once again the model of the compassionate person — the compassionate priest.

Finally, no one takes this honor upon himself, but only when called by God (v. 4). The priesthood isn't an office. It's not solely a profession, like medicine or law. It's a privilege to which some, without merit on their part, are called by God. The initiative is God's. Again Jesus went beyond the requirement: He's the very "son" of God.

Recognizing that Jesus was interested in every condition of people, we're to imitate Bartimaeus and come to Jesus. Bartimaeus is a symbol of all who want to come to Christ. He was a blind beggar, with no resources of his own, with only his need to impel him, and with no gift to offer in return; he heard about Jesus through the preaching of the Good News, and called upon him as Lord; he was rebuked by some people, but paid them no mind; he was told by others to come to Jesus and did so, casting his fears aside; he responded instantly; and once he saw who Jesus really was he fell silent. Then, intrigued by the idea of his faith having healed him, the newly liberated Bartimaeus perceived as in a mirror darkly that there was even more to be seen.

Jesus expects us to come to see, and to grow in faith. Some people walk through life with their eyes wide open, yet comprehend little of its meaning because they're inwardly blind or have tunnel vision. The physically blind are well aware of their handicap, the spiritually blind usually not.

After we've come to say the right words about Jesus, our faith must become more personal. Then we need to see ourselves in a more truthful way. For some, this means recognizing their sins in clearer light. The need of others is for the exact opposite: to see themselves more as being loved and beautiful in God's sight. Next we realize that Jesus is the one who can bring us new life. Finally we really set out on the road of true discipleship. For some people this process may occur in their youth; for others full faith develops only over the years, perhaps after much weakness. Until we're involved in that process, we too are blind.

FEAST OF ALL SAINTS
Rv 7:2-4, 9-14   1 Jn 3:1-3   Mt 5:1-12

God's Noblest Creation: the Saints
God's Creation: Actual and Potential; How to Succeed in Holiness with a
Little Trying; True Bliss: Christianity vs. Gloom; What We're Called to Be

In the National Shrine of the Immaculate Conception in Washington,
D.C., under the commanding mosaic of Christ in glory, are six pillars.
Atop each is a statue of a saint. There, side by side, are the figures of a
queen (St. Elizabeth), a vagrant (St. Benedict Joseph Labre), a cook
(St. Zita), a doorman (St. Conrad), a mystic (St. Gemma), and a parish
priest (St. John Vianney). Were all these to come from the same time
and place, they probably would never have met.

Further, just as no two of us are alike, no two saints — being real
people — are alike. For some of them, the road to holiness was easy,
for others very hard. Some saints had gifts of great natural talent; others seemed devoid of it. Some saints were fiery, others gentle. Some
were gregarious, others loners. There are old saints (such as St. An-
thony of the Desert, who lived to be 105) and young saints (such as
Aloysius Gonzaga and Maria Goretti). There were brilliant saints (such
as Thomas Aquinas) and dense saints (such as Joseph Cupertino). There
were tough saints (such as Teresa of Avila) and emotional saints (such
as Thérèse of Lisieux). There were innocent saints (such as Dominic
Savio) and reformed sinners who became saints (such as Augustine).
There are also saints who didn't always agree with each other, such as
Jerome and Augustine, who had a running battle of words for years.
Nevertheless, the saints belong together: They all responded to God's
invitation to sainthood commemorated in today's liturgy.

Today's Feast of All Saints is a feast of encouragement, celebrating that we're all called to be saints. The biblical meaning of "saint" is
a person who's trying to live a life of holiness for the Lord. Our modern idea has restricted the term to those who are in heaven. Just the
same, we still use the term "Communion of Saints" to refer to the union
of all members of Christ in the Church militant here on earth and the

---

Note: This homily is mostly on 1 John; for Matthew, see Cycle A; for Revelation, Cycle C.

Church suffering in purgatory, as well as the Church triumphant in heaven. The "communion" or "fellowship" which we have with each other comes from our union with God. We don't come together to form a community and then begin to worship. Rather, we come to worship, and by that worship we're formed into a community.

And we must always see our Communion of Saints in the context of Christ. Only through, with, and in him do we have communion with each other and with the saints in heaven. So we shouldn't visualize our relationship with the saints as their being so many functionaries through whom we must go to get to the boss. Our relationship with the saints is a circle, not a hierarchical bureaucracy. The saints intercede for us, just as we intercede for each other.

In today's Second Reading, St. John's letter puts forth one of his basic notions: We're all called to be God's children. We're by nature *creatures* of God, because God is our Creator; but it's by grace alone that we become *children* of God. While grace is the term to describe our share in God's life here on earth, our full share in God's life in heaven is called "glory." Only those are children of God who respond to God's initiating grace. We who've been baptized aren't only called to be God's children, but this is our present reality. Inasmuch as we're not gods, however, but only godlike, our being God's children is by adoption, a beautiful privilege mentioned often in the New Testament.

Why, then, doesn't everyone rush to be baptized into rebirth as God's children, and why are all the baptized not zealous to observe the commandments that keep one a child of God? Well, we live in a world that doesn't recognize these categories because it never recognized God's Son upon whom they're based. That's the world from whose influence Jesus prayed at the Last Supper that his disciples would be free. It's a world subject to sin and darkness. That's the world of which Jesus told us that if the world hates us, we must remember that it hated him before us, and that he has overcome the world.

(At the same time we must never forget that the term "world" at times means that which is good, that which comes from the hand of God. It's in this sense that St. John tells us that God so loved the world that He sent his only Son.)

Failing to know the prophetic word of God began with the world of ancient Israel, as St. Stephen said right before his martyrdom when he called the Hebrews a stiff-necked people who always oppose the Holy Spirit; he asked them which of the prophets they didn't persecute (Ac 7:51-53). They repeated their habit of persecution in their rejection of the Word become man. History has testified that the world has continued this rejection, and the world accords the same treatment to Jesus' disciples that it accorded the Master.

Jesus continually spoke of his coming judgment of the world. He told Nicodemus, for example, that his verdict was coming, because when the light came into the world people preferred darkness to the light (Jn 3:19). After Palm Sunday Jesus said that the time of judgment of the world was now: Now the ruler of the world would be driven out (Jn 12:31). The paradox of Jesus' exaltation was that it appeared that he had been defeated by this world, but in reality the power of Satan was broken. Jesus didn't say that Satan would be destroyed, but that he would no longer be the ruler of the world — except, of course, to the extent that people would permit.

Though Christians are children of God, there's a fulfillment toward which we look which hasn't yet been revealed (1 Jn 3:2). This life is only a beginning. At the end, the creation story in which we were made in the image and likeness of God will become completely true. We shall share the life of God and the Christian community — the latter being, as it were, the social incarnation of the Trinity. We shall fulfill the prayer of Jesus at the Last Supper (Jn 17) that we may be one just as the persons of the Trinity are one, that we may be one as Jesus and the Father are one: Jesus in us and God in Jesus.

We need look only at history, or in a mirror, to see how far short we've fallen of the fulfillment of our true destiny. This side of the grave, people can become like Christ and — at least in that way — be like God. In this life, we see our image of God through a mirror medium: that is, faith. The image of God for which the Christian is destined, however, is more immediate and intimate. The life goal of all truly great people like the saints has been the vision of God.

That vision is still a hope. It's a hope that can give life a meaning as well as a great goal. The reality of the hope is shown in the Christian's striving for virtue. All who have this hope based on Jesus make themselves pure, as Jesus is pure (1 Jn 3:3). By imitating him who is pure the Christian is already beginning — but only beginning — to live the rewarding and glorious life with God.

Epitomizing this, as well as the content of the beatitudes, is the well-known prayer attributed to St. Francis of Assisi:

Lord,
> make me an instrument of Your peace.
> Where there is hatred, let me sow love;
> Where there is injury, pardon;
> Where there is doubt, faith;
> Where there is despair, hope;
> Where there is darkness, light; and
> Where there is sadness, joy.

O divine Master,
> Grant that I may not so much
> Seek to be consoled as to console;
> To be understood as to understand;
> To be loved as to love;
> For it is in giving that we receive;
> It is in pardoning that we are pardoned; and
> It is in dying that we are born to eternal life.

All this isn't something only for great spiritual mystics to be incorporated in a shrine's mosaics. It's the life to which we've all been called. It's what made the saints God's noblest creation. It's the way of the privileges of the Christian life and the possibilities of the Christian life to which we're all called. To achieve it means being as single-minded as the saints in pursuing the goals of life. This all the saints have in common, whether they're queens, vagrants, cooks, doormen, mystics, or priests.

THIRTY-FIRST SUNDAY IN ORDINARY TIME
Dt 6:2-6   Heb 7:23-28   Mk 12:28-34

Something New for Your Love
Life Values that Reflect Faith; Back to Basics;
What's New in your Love Life?; The Meaning of Life

At times religion seems unnecessarily complicated. Some Catholics get so tied up in rosaries, novenas, medals, scapulars, votive candles, holy water, statues, and such, that they sometimes lose sight of what's most

important. It would be interesting to ask non-Catholics for their first
impression of Catholics: Many would say "the rosary"; in music, they
might say Schubert's *Ave Maria*. Try the experiment!

The ancient Jews had a similar problem. Their sacred Torah, or
Law, prescribed many different kinds of sacrifices, what kind of food
the people were to eat, how many washings they were to undertake,
and so on. In fact, they had 613 written prescriptions that derived from
the Law, and many more oral ones! The rabbis often discussed what
they called the "heavy" precepts over and against the ones they called
"light."

In St. Mark's Gospel today, one of the scribes came up and asked
Jesus a question that the people asked rabbis often: Which is the first
of all the commandments? (v. 28). It's a question that people ask all
the time: "What's *essentially* required in order to please God?" It's an
honest question.

The first part of Jesus' answer was today's passage from the Book
of Deuteronomy, the final book of the Torah or Pentateuch. This passage was part of Moses' poignant farewell address as he was about to
die, just before the Hebrews entered the Promised Land. He urged
fidelity to God's law for two reasons: It will bring a reward, but also
it's due God in thanks for all the blessings they'd received, including
their current entry into the Promised Land. It was a land "flowing with
milk and honey." To a weary tribe of nomads just come from the arid
southern desert, even the dry hill-country of Judea could well be described in those terms.

Today's portion contains the keynote of Deuteronomy: the great
Jewish prayer, called from its opening word the *Shema*. This prayer
begins with the basic principle of the entire Mosaic law: The Lord alone
is God. Moses had declared — and today's Gospel shows that Jesus
agreed — that, as our God is unique, so the basic human response to
God must also be unique and undivided: "You shall love the Lord your
God with all your heart, with all your soul, with all your mind, and
with all your strength" (v. 30): wholeheartedly, as we might say. The
entire person is to love the God who loves every person entirely.

The *Shema* would become many things to Israel. It would be a
call to worship, beginning the services of prayer. It would be "words
to die by" as well as "words to live by." Hebrew martyrs went to their
death with these words on their lips. The words would be written on
tiny scrolls and put into the prayer-boxes (*phylacteries*) that adorn fore-

heads and wrists while at prayer. The words would be contained in the
mezuzah, a little container to this day affixed to the entrances of the
homes of devout Jews to remind them of the word of God as they come
and go. Christians have adapted this respect for God's word by signing their foreheads, lips, and hearts whenever the Gospel is proclaimed.

So what's new about Jesus' giving this as the first of all the commandments? One aspect of newness was that he added another part:
"You shall love your neighbor as yourself" (v. 31). These words, it's
true, are also not new: They come from the Book of Leviticus (19:18).
What *is* new is that Jesus went further: For him there's an extremely
intimate bond between love of neighbor and love of God. In Christian
charity, people and God aren't merely side by side; they're insepara-
bly one. *That* idea was new.

Another facet of newness was that Jesus gave a completely new
interpretation of "neighbor." In the time of Leviticus it meant Hebrews
only. By the time of Jesus, it included resident aliens as well. For Jesus,
the word has the widest meaning possible: It includes *every member
of the human race*: He died for *all* of us. This was a much greater depth
and breadth than ever before imagined.

Jesus' questioner, like many of his fellow scribes, was a good
man whom Jesus declared to be not far from the kingdom of God (v.
34). One unequivocal sign characterizes those who aren't far from the
kingdom: their service of love to its two inseparable objects, God and
neighbor. Love of God and neighbor must begin with proper love of
self. Love of oneself, though important, is taken for granted. Whereas
in the theological order of priority God and neighbor come first, in the
psychological order unless we have sufficient self-esteem, respect, and
love for ourselves, we can go no further.

Wholehearted love. At first hearing, that may suggest to us, as it
did at the turn of our own century to young Thérèse Martin, a range of
high and mighty acts. She wrote to Jesus of

> all the deeds I long to accomplish for you. I would be a mar-
> tyr, a doctor of the Church. I should like to accomplish the
> most heroic deeds — the spirit of the crusader burns in me. I
> long to die on the battlefield in defense of the Holy Church. I
> would be a missionary. I would choose to be flayed like St.
> Bartholomew, plunged into boiling oil like St. John, or like
> St. Ignatius of Antioch I would be ground by the teeth of wild
> beasts into bread worthy of God. With St. Agnes and St.

Cecilia I would offer my neck to the sword of the executioner, and like St. Joan of Arc, I would murmur the name of Jesus at the stake.

But the young Thérèse Martin, psychologically and physically frail, hidden and protected from the onslaughts of the world, soon realized that her wholehearted love would enable none of those things; her work was to love with whatever heart and mind were given her. Through that, she became St. Thérèse of Lisieux.

In loving, Jesus is the ideal. One of the best statements of that is today's portion of the letter to the Hebrews: Jesus is the perfect high priest, the model mediator between God and human beings sketched in terms of the expectations of the people of the Older Covenant. The Hebrews' High Priest was a combination of our President, Supreme Court, and lawmakers together. In a theocracy — a nation with God Himself as its head — the High Priest was supreme.

Jesus' priesthood is superior even to all of that. For one thing, whereas under the Old Covenant the priests were prevented by death from remaining in office, Jesus, because he remains forever, has a priesthood that doesn't pass away (vv. 23f.). Jesus is precisely the High Priest whom the human race needs (v. 26). He's *holy* — a person who appears before God as well as before his fellow human beings as having the greatest goodness. He's *innocent*, having shown a complete absence of evil. He's *undefiled*, being free from all blemishes which might keep him from approaching God.

He's *separated from sinners*, in that he never gave in to the temptations that assailed him. Whereas Aaron's successors to the Old Testament priesthood, as sinful people, had to offer sacrifice first for their own sins (v. 27), Jesus, the sinless Son of God, made his sacrifice for the sins of others. And, while all of that stresses his being human, he's also God, being *higher than the heavens*: After his ascension, he remains at God's right hand.

Yet in Jewish theology Jesus was a layman. He was born a Jewish layman, conducted his ministry as a Jewish layman, and died a Jewish layman. He was of the tribe of Judah, not the priestly tribe of Levi who inherited the priesthood. In the theology of the letter to the Hebrews, though, Jesus became a priest by undergoing a sacrificial death on the cross and then entering the heavenly sanctuary. According to this letter, Jesus' atoning sacrifice is also his ordination sacrifice.

The word "love" is bandied about so much in our culture that it often loses its full meaning. Love is many beautiful things. It's not only what makes the world go 'round: It's what makes the ride worthwhile. But love is also demanding. To love means to go beyond ourselves, truly to face another person, to rise above our own need, to stretch out to someone, to see the faces of those who desperately need our love, to risk discomfort, to give our time and energy — indeed, ourselves — to others.

Love involves nothing less than everything. I can't love you part-time. I can't love you just when I'm in a good mood. I can't love you just because it makes me feel good. Love has to do with feelings, it's true, but it has far more to do with commitment, challenge, and letting go. Wholehearted loving isn't a matter of "once and for all" and is then done with, or something that happens overnight. It has to do with being there for the other. Furthermore, without being loved it's almost impossible to love.

We sometimes fear that if we offer our all, too much might be asked, something terrible demanded. Rabindranath Tagore, the great Bengali poet, in his *Gitanjali* tells the story of a beggar going from door to door asking for alms. He suddenly sees his celestial king approaching in a chariot, and he dreams of the king showering upon him bountiful gifts. But to his surprise, the king asks him what he has to give. After staring, confused and undecided, he finally peers into his sack of meager possessions, takes out a tiny grain of corn, and gives it to the king. Later he says, "But how great my surprise when at the day's end I emptied my bag on the floor to find a little grain of gold among the poor heap! I bitterly wept and wished that I had had the heart to give my all."

The truth is that we human beings only are truly "human beings" when we give ourselves away in love. Love is central in all moral decisions. Real-life examples go to family, workplace, neighborhood, employer-worker relations, social involvement, school, Church, citizenship, and even the international level. There are in the lives of each of us many examples of how we can do better at our central command of loving — examples that only we ourselves personally know. Let's think of them now.

THIRTY-SECOND SUNDAY IN ORDINARY TIME
1 K 17:10-16   Heb 9:24-28   Mk 12:38-44 (or 41-44)

Love's Total Self-Giving
Solidarity; Altruism; Generosity; Proper Motivation;
Who Is a Practicing Church Member?

Does religion make people good, or is it because people are good that religion can exist?

In today's portion of St. Mark's Gospel, people in the forefront of religious practice don't give a very good example of goodness, while someone less learned in religion gives of herself totally. The opening frame of the Gospel (vv. 38-40) is Jesus' remarks against experts in religion, the scribes. Some of them had found in religion a success route that was similar to the modern corporate ladder.

They liked to go around in long robes (v. 38), using their prayer shawl (*tallith*) outside of prayer time as a showy display of what passed for "piety." They accepted the deep ceremonial bows of the people as marks of respect for their alleged superiority. In addition, they wangled places up front facing the ordinary people in the synagogues, got seats on the dais at banquets (v. 39), and made their public prayers long (v. 40). To Jesus' charges of pride and hypocrisy against them, he added devouring the savings of widows.

Widows are a Bible favorite. Three of the Bible's books bear women's names — Esther, Judith, and Ruth — two of whom are widows. Widows were looked upon as more powerless and unprotected than others, having to stretch and save their resources carefully, without the husband upon whose intimate love they had come to depend.

In today's story of a poor widow (v. 42), we don't even know her name. She sat in one of the Temple courts, where there were many collection boxes and, as with churches in some parts of the world today, each box was labeled for a different need: "For Incense," "For Doves," "For Building Maintenance," and so forth. As in all times, many rich people put in large sums (v. 41). The widow had little to give, but she put in two small coins (v. 42) — the *lepton*, the smallest copper coin made, worth about one-sixty-fourth of the daily wages of a laborer. She gave quietly, from a loving heart.

The widow could have made a good case for not being able to contribute anything at all. Or she could have put in one of the coins and kept the other. But true giving must have sacrifice connected with it — even a certain courageous recklessness. The worth of an offering is in terms of the amount of self-giving involved. Too often the rich expect to be celebrated and commemorated for their giving. The poor, when they let their hearts be touched and share what little they have, often expect nothing in return. This widow's faith meant a great deal to her, she was not casual about it, and her commitment to it called forth generosity of spirit. Jesus said that she put in more than all the other contributors (v. 43).

Today's story from the cycle of stories about Elijah, who lived about 900 years before Christ, is similar. The Jews consider Elijah to be the greatest of the prophets — indeed, one of the most important figures in First Testament history. He and Moses represent the whole of that Testament: Moses, the Torah (Law); and Elijah, the prophets.

Because Elijah is described as having been taken up to heaven in a fiery chariot, to return to earth before the coming of the Messiah, Jews even today at their Passover Seder set an extra place at table should he come during the meal. Today's story is among those which were told in order to enhance the reputation of the prophet and thereby increase the value of his word.

During three years of drought and famine, when Elijah arrived at the entrance to the Baal-worshiping city of Zarephath and saw a widow, he asked for a drink of water (v. 10). The Phoenician woman, a pagan who didn't know Elijah as anything but a fellow human being, obliged. So Elijah went further and asked her for some bread (v. 11).

To this presumptuous request, the woman laid out her situation honestly: She was a widow, she had nothing, and she expected that shortly she and her son — her only child — would die (v. 12). Elijah had the *chutzpah* to ask her to take care of him first (v. 13), and assured her that then the God of Israel would in turn take care of her and her son (v. 14). The desperation of her condition was obvious from her gathering of sticks, her last piece of food and last drop of oil, and her expectation of death for herself and her son.

Nevertheless, with a generosity that was simple, complete, and reckless, she did as Elijah asked: This wonderful woman, who had no religion to make her good but who showed respect for Elijah's religion by referring to "the Lord your God," fed the prophet even before she fed herself and her son (v. 15). Imagination can conjure up for us her feelings of helplessness and powerlessness, and the deep courage behind her act.

Such generous sharing is daily experience — especially of the very poor — around the world: They find in this kind of solidarity with one another an endless source of support and strength. Modern Calcutta, among the world's poorest places, has been called the "City of Joy." And God fulfilled the promises that Elijah had made in His name: Her food didn't run out until the famine was over.

Jesus considered that story of Elijah so impressive that he told it in a synagogue instruction at Nazareth. In fact, it was when, to teach God's care and love of all people, he used the example of this pagan widow and another pagan, Naaman, a leper cured by the prophet Elisha, that the townspeople of Nazareth tried to kill him (Lk 4:20-30).

Today's portion of the letter to the Hebrews again makes comparisons between First Testament prefigurements and the excellence of Jesus. To appreciate the comparisons fully, one has to understand something of First Testament religious practices. The most sacred part of the Hebrews' Temple was the innermost building, consisting of the Holy Place and the Holy of Holies. Their Holy Place is our sanctuary, their Holy of Holies our tabernacle. Their Holy Place was separated from the Holy of Holies by a veil — the veil whose tearing apart at the moment of Jesus' death would signify the end of the Old Covenant.

Their Holy of Holies represented the dwelling-place of God on earth; only once a year only one person was allowed to enter it. That day was the Day of Atonement (Yom Kippur) and the one person was the High Priest. As the High Priest was performing the sacred ritual in the Holy of Holies, the people would suspensefully wait. The High Priest would finally emerge: fresh, and shining like a vessel of gold (Si 50:5). The ceremony was solemn, majestic, awe-inspiring.

In contrast, Jesus didn't offer sacrifices daily or annually, but once. That sacrifice was the total self-giving of his life. He took away the sins of all people by taking those sins upon himself (v. 28). The blood of the sacrifice was his own — ineffably more effective by reason of his worth than the previous sacrifices of animals (v. 23). Rather than entering the sanctuary of the Temple, which was only a man-made construction (v. 24), he entered heaven itself that he might now appear before God on our behalf.

In answer to the question with which we began, the pagan widow at Zarephath teaches us that goodness is not confined to people who profess to be religious. Indeed, all people appreciate the truth of Shakespeare's observation that any work of kindness and mercy "is twice blessed: It blesses him that gives and him that takes."

A man named Paul received an automobile from his brother as a Christmas present. When he came out of his office, a street urchin was walking around the shiny new car, admiring it. "Is this your car, Mister?" he asked. Paul nodded. "My brother gave it to me for Christmas." The boy was astounded. "You mean your brother gave it to you and it didn't cost you nothing? Boy, I wish. ..."

Paul knew what he was going to wish for. He was going to wish he had a brother like that. But what the boy said jarred Paul down to his heels. "I wish," the boy went on, "that I could be a brother like that."

Paul looked at the boy in astonishment, then impulsively added, "Would you like to take a ride in my automobile?"

"Oh yes, I'd love that."

Paul smiled. He thought he knew what the boy wanted: to show his neighbors that he could ride home in a big automobile. But Paul was wrong again. "Will you stop where those two steps are?" the boy asked.

He ran up the steps. In a few moments Paul heard him coming back, but he wasn't coming fast. He was carrying his little crippled brother. He sat him down on the bottom step, then sort of squeezed up against him and pointed to the car.

"There she is, Buddy, just like I told you. His brother gave it to him for Christmas and it didn't cost him a cent. And some day I'm gonna give you one just like it... then you can see for yourself all the pretty things in the Christmas windows that I've been trying to tell you about."

Paul got out and lifted the crippled boy to the front seat of his car. The shining-eyed older brother climbed in beside him and the three of them began a memorable holiday ride.

That Christmas Eve, Paul learned what Jesus meant when he said, "It's more blessed to give. ..."

True religion can inspire new heights and depths and breadths of such aspects of goodness as generosity, altruism, and compassion, as with the widow Jesus observed in the Temple. Certainly the true practice of religion helps further motivate good people to best practice love's self-giving.

Consonant with our religion, let's face our difficulties — at work, within our family, and in our community — with religious faith, courage, and generosity. Let's try to be a giver rather than a taker; to help and not to hinder; to build up and not tear down; to encourage, and not to criticize; to be thoughtful and kind, a ready listener to the troubles of others, and motivated by the genuine caring taught and exemplified by the good Lord of our religion.

THIRTY-THIRD SUNDAY IN ORDINARY TIME
Dn 12:1-3   Heb 10:11-14, 18   Mk 13:24-32

Readiness for the Lord's Coming
Serving God in Faith and Love

Time is so basic to our way of life that we forget that it's a human invention and, in some respects, arbitrary. The experts believe that time reckoning began with the invention of agriculture 10,000 years ago. Farming made it important to know when to plant, and that required a calendar. Agriculture led to the development of towns and the division of labor, which in turn led to commerce. Commerce led to hours divided into minutes and minutes into seconds: You can't pay employees by the hour if there's no such thing as an hour.

When medieval monks conceived an obligation to pray at fixed hours of the night, their need spurred the invention of a mechanical clock that replaced the sundial and worked even in the dark. From the 14th-century clock came the 15th-century navigational instruments that could guide mariners across an uncharted ocean. Now a sense of an extended future began to be part of the equation. Only after that could such important institutions as savings banks and insurance agencies become viable.

So time is precious. Queen Elizabeth I, with her dying breath in 1603, said, "All my possessions for a moment of time." In our age, with so many activities crowded into our day, time may have become the most precious commodity in our land. With technological improvements like going to other planets, optimists say we're at the dawn of a new age, while some pessimists look to Scripture to back up their analysis that civilization as we've known it is doomed.

But the Scriptures were never intended for this purpose. The apocalyptic writings, as this genre is called, are somewhat like unraveling poetry. Outside time, their focus is on the timeless and eternal, the *ultimate realities* which underpin day-to-day events.

Jesus knew the way his people thought, and he used their images as well as prophetic apocalyptic literature to reach them. In today's Gospel, one of the most Jewish sections in the New Testament, Jesus adopted the language of apocalyptic: trials, darkened sun, moon without light, stars falling, the shaking of "the heavenly hosts," and the glorious coming of the Son of Man.

That was the language of Jesus' day. Today, it's *science* that prognosticates the end-time, and if Jesus were addressing modern audiences he would probably use scientific terminology to get his ideas across. The fantastic theories of science aren't inconsistent with the equally fantastic Scriptures.

In today's language, cosmologists say that, if the universe keeps rushing off into space as it is now, it will eventually become so cold as to make life as we know it impossible. If on the other hand our universe loses the momentum of its expansion into space, reverses its direction, and contracts in what is described as the Big Crunch, there will come a point when the heat will burn everything up. Thus the end of our universe will take place by either fire or ice.

That's except for other recently-discovered possibilities. One theory is that a flood of all but undetectable subnuclear particles spawned by silent collapsing stars every 100 million years surges through the earth, producing a blast of cosmic rays that would destroy the earth's protective ozone layer. This could cause an epidemic of fatal cancers and genetic mutations with dire results for many species. Scientists assume that great numbers of such neutrinos constantly stream through human beings and everything else on earth, causing neither sensation nor discernible injury. But the astronomical numbers of high-energy neutrinos produced by the quick collapse of massive stars are a more serious matter.

And there are other possible catastrophes to bring about the end of our planet before all that, such as human nuclear explosions and asteroids. The human race is more in control of the nuclear explosions, whose dangers we've already seen, than of asteroids. Revolving around the sun, asteroids are dark, craggy rubble from the creation of the so-lar system, some being remnants of planets that failed to form, others parts of larger bodies that disintegrated in collisions. Most of them, like Gaspra out beyond Mars, are believed to be composed of a mixture of rocky and metallic minerals.

Serious collisions with earth have occurred as recently as 1908, when a celestial object exploded in Siberia with the force of 12 mega-tons of TNT. Forests were leveled for dozens of miles around, and horses 400 miles away were reportedly knocked down. The largest crater found so far, measuring 124 miles from rim to rim, is in Ontario. A three-quarter-mile crater in northern Arizona was created by a 150-foot-wide asteroid that slammed into the earth 50,000 years ago. The total of confirmed asteroid craters now stands at about 140, the list growing by five or six a year.

Experts say there are probably 500 asteroids that cross through the earth's orbit with diameters of roughly a mile, and perhaps a dozen that are three or more miles wide. The largest current asteroid known by science to be out there, Ceres, is about 570 miles wide. If one like that hit, the explosion would be a billion times bigger than the bomb at Hiroshima.

Scientists, extrapolating from craters observed on the moon and from a partial survey of earth-crossing asteroids, calculate that one slams into this planet once every 300,000 to one million years. The theories, once pooh-poohed as paranoid, have grown in respectability. In 1990, the United States Congress called for a series of detailed studies after a half-mile-wide asteroid crossed our planet's path at an uncom-fortably close distance in 1989.

Although no asteroid found so far is expected to hit the earth soon, somewhere in space at this moment, hurtling toward earth at roughly 16 miles a second, is an asteroid dubbed by scientists the "doomsday rock." This is an asteroid large enough to severely disrupt life on earth upon impact, lofting pulverized rock and dust that would block most sunlight. Agriculture would virtually end, and civilization could wither and die. This killer asteroid by definition would be a mile wide or larger.

Astronomers declare that a threatening asteroid could be observed while it was as much as a year away, and talk about ways to dodge the threat. One is nuclear-tipped interceptor rockets to fragment the aster-oid; some scientists fear that this procedure might result in the pieces doing as much damage as the impact of the whole asteroid. Another idea is to use a nuclear interceptor to deflect it from its collision course with the earth. Still another suggestion is to trap asteroids in earth orbit and mine them for precious metals.

It's in the light of these current speculations that we read today's portion of the Book of Daniel as well as today's Gospel. The ultimate truth they express is that when God comes to arbitrate the course of human events, the record will be set straight. The Book of Daniel was written to console God's people who were suffering persecution for their religion 165 years before Christ. The mood of the passage is one of reassurance: Despite the fact that the end-time will be a period of great distress, the virtuous will shine like the stars.

The Pacific Ocean in the Solomon Islands is fickle. A calm sunny day can quickly turn into one of surging rollers, which in a frail canoe is an alarming experience. So in every village there is someone who can read the sea — a man or a woman with the gift of discernment. Before anyone goes to sea, they say to the discerner something like, "I want to go to Gizo tomorrow." The discerners, before offering advice, carefully observe the behavior of the land crabs, gaze at the tops of certain trees, and go to the edge of the sea. Their advice, something like "Leave before six in the morning," is invariably correct.

We're all to be discerners. What we're sure of from today's liturgy is that the world as we know it will come to an end, that Christ will come in his glory, that the dead will rise, and that there will be a final judgment. Further, the unity toward which all time is tending isn't solely a property of a future event, but takes place just as absolutely in the present, certainly for each of us when we die. The message of forgiveness in the letter to the Hebrews begets an underlying consolation and peace.

In the final analysis, none of the picturesque end-time displays of fireworks or deep-freeze, nuclear explosions or asteroids, has any importance. What is important is today's challenge to judge the times of our lives in terms of God's ultimate realities. We're to take part in an aspect of *on-going creation*: the bringing of God's justice, love, and mercy to all the human race. With a sense of urgency, we're to prepare for death — or for the end of the world, whichever comes first — by working toward the realization of God's plan. To prepare for this, we're to serve God in faith and love. Because next Sunday, the last Sunday of the Church year, we celebrate Jesus Christ as Universal King, on this next-to-last Sunday (the last Sunday with green vestments until after Epiphany) the Church wants us to look to those things that are last in the order of time, but first in the order of importance.

SOLEMNITY OF CHRIST THE KING
Dn 7:13f.   Rv 1:5-8   Jn 18:33-37

Properly High Estimation of Both God and Yourself
The Kingship of Christ

Many people of our time underestimate both God and themselves. Some say they don't believe in God, when the truth is that they don't believe in the image of God presented to them, which is often too low. If the most ardent believers thought that that low concept was who God is, they wouldn't believe either. And one of the reasons why we treat other people as badly as we do is that we don't think highly enough of one another. Today's solemnity of Christ the King addresses the greatness of God and the dignity He's given to people.

In trying to come to a judgment about God and others, we too often act like Pilate confronting Christ in today's Gospel. We begin by trying to lay the responsibility on someone else: Pilate began by telling the people that a judgment about Jesus wasn't his affair, and they should judge him themselves. That didn't work, so he tried to find an escape: to use the custom of releasing a prisoner each year in celebration of Passover. If he'd gotten away with that, it would have meant no harm to anyone — except the other person who might otherwise have been released. When that too didn't work, Pilate tried still another tack — an appeal to people's mercy: He had Jesus scourged. Like all weak people, he tried to salve his conscience by not facing the issues squarely and making a proper decision.

In contrast, look at Jesus before Pilate. Despite the night-long taunts of the soldiers and his scourging that morning, he had a regal majesty. He gives the impression not that this is the story of a man who was to be killed, but of one whose last days were a triumphant procession. It doesn't seem to be Jesus who's really on trial here, but Pilate and the rest.

The pitiful Pilate's question about Jesus' being a king wasn't far-fetched. But because Pilate's mind connected kingship with splendor and power and that wasn't what Jesus had in mind, Jesus had to answer his question in the negative. A kingdom not of this world? That was beyond Pilate's power to comprehend. At the time, Rome was doing all in its might to keep the lid on its power in the world. Jerusalem was a good example: In its explosive atmosphere, if Jesus had wanted to establish a kingdom he certainly had the opportunity, and this Passover time with its crowds would be ideal. Pilate knew that as well as Jesus. Jesus had close followers and was extremely popular among the masses.

But the nature of Jesus' kingdom was different from any other before or since. The Kingdom of God is the center of Jesus' teaching. The phrase "Kingdom of God" occurs 122 times in the Gospels, 90 of which are on the lips of Jesus. It's therefore important to look very closely at Jesus' proclamation of his Kingdom and to become aware of its uniqueness.

The phrase "Kingdom of God" can be misleading to anyone who doesn't know its biblical background. "Kingdom of God" is a vague and abstract-sounding locution that, if it conveys anything, conveys the idea of a set territory or realm over which God rules. Both connotations — abstractness and emphasis on territory — create a false impression. The truth is that "Kingdom of God" is meant to conjure up the dynamic notion of God powerfully ruling over his creation, over his people, and over the history of both. God's action upon and his dynamic relationship to those ruled, rather than any delimited territory, is what is primary.

The truth encapsulated by the phrase "the Kingdom of God" stretches from the first page of the Bible to its last. If we were to construct an artificial summary of the story of the Kingdom, it would include God's creation of His good and ordered universe, creation's corruption by human sin and rebellion, God's gracious choice of the people Israel to be His very own, His liberating them from slavery in Egypt, the experiences of sin and salvation at the Reed Sea and Mt. Sinai, the desert journey, and entrance into the promised land. The story might include the kingdom of the all-too-human-but-later-idealized King David, God's choice of Jerusalem and Mt. Zion for His dwelling place, the disasters caused by David's less than ideal successors, the descent of Israel into every greater idolatry and sin, Israel's rejection of the prophets' warnings, the destruction of Jerusalem and the Babylonian exile, the promise of future restoration that would include a rebuilt Jerusalem and a new, purified Temple, the subjection of the hostile Gentiles, and the establishment among human beings of God's eternal Kingdom of peace and justice.

There are many things the Kingdom isn't: It isn't, for example, some kind of extraterrestrial entity that will be superimposed on this world, nor is it a process of spiritual or internal change that leaves the outer realities looking pretty much the same. And it isn't to be in another world: The Kingdom of God is the liberation of this world we live in, know, touch, smell, and suffer, from all that corrupts it. The Kingdom is a total, global, and structural transfiguration and revolution of the reality of human beings; it means the cosmos purified of all evils and full of the reality of God.

To paraphrase today's Preface, his was a Kingdom that was confined to no time in history such as Pilate's was, but is eternal; a Kingdom that knew no national boundaries such as Pilate knew, but is universal; a Kingdom that wasn't to provide only convenience and protection, but holiness and grace; and a Kingdom that's to be ruled not by power, but by justice, love, and peace.

The Kingdom defined in a short formula is nothing else than justice, peace, and joy in the Holy Spirit. *Justice* as a biblical concept could best be translated as *right relations* in a threefold way: to one's self, to one's neighbor (individually and socially), and to God. *Peace*, the Hebrew *shalom*, means *reconciliation* with self, neighbor, and God. *Joy* in the biblical sense is the expression of *fullness*, *life*, and *love* in abundance. After all, the image of what's meant by heaven in the Bible is the *wedding feast* where the happiness and joy of all are guaranteed. As the old Quaker hymn reminds us: "When Love is Lord of heaven and earth, how can I keep from singing?" *In the Holy Spirit* is the most important aspect. Since the Kingdom on earth now is an anticipation of the New Heaven and the New Earth, it can only be a creation of the Holy Spirit because it's only he who will bring forth the New Creation.

Jesus' "growth parables" (Mt 13; Mk 4) are of the highest importance for an adequate understanding of the Kingdom message: his stories of the sower, the growing corn, the double parable of the mustard seed and the leaven, the weeds among the wheat, and the net full of fish.

When is the Kingdom to come? Perhaps a metaphor from warfare may help. The decisive battle in a war may have occurred in a relatively early stage of the war. Although the definitive effect of that battle is perhaps not recognized by all, it nevertheless already means victory, even though the war still continues. In the ministry of Jesus the decisive battle has been fought and won, Satan has fallen (Lk 10:18), and the power of the evil spirits is broken. Yet the battle still goes on.

That's the kind of kingdom of which Jesus is King — whatever "king" means to us in a time when there are very few left, and those who remain are largely ceremonial figureheads from a different past. We call today's celebration the "Solemnity of Christ the King" because, when this feast was instituted, there was no higher designation with which to honor a person than to call him "king." The Scriptures suggest the inadequacy of other words like leader, president, master, guide, mentor, hero, chief, or commander. Yet "king" is inadequate, too.

St. John in his Book of Revelation — today's Second Reading — approaches the *cosmic* dimensions of Jesus by calling him the "ruler of the kings of earth." Even today, we have no other word than "king" that will encapsulate all the things we want to say about Jesus, except perhaps "Lord." Yet there are many contrasts between the ways of ordinary kings and Jesus. Even in better times for royalty than today, kings have been associated with opulence and reckless appetites. They've been unapproachable, high and mighty, surrounded by sycophants and jesters, decked in finery, and decorated with trimmings of lordliness. Jesus, on the other hand, as he told Pilate, came into the world to witness to the *truth*: about God, about people, and about life. He will not kill for the truth; he will die for it. He will win, not by spilling the blood of others, but by offering his own. He doesn't dominate, muster armies, or amass territories; he just invites and serves, reliant on nothing other than the response of hearts.

John took as his picture of Christ's Kingdom a vision in the Book of Daniel (7:1-14). Despite the fact that some of the grand associations of kingship preoccupy Daniel's dream, the verses in today's First Reading take up the question that faces all people, such as faced the faithful Jews in the midst of horrible persecution by Antiochus IV Epiphanes around 165 B.C. when this book was written: Would the forces of evil ultimately triumph or would God's people finally win out? In a vision, Daniel saw "one like a son of man." The "son of man" in Daniel appears in the majestic presence of God, trailing clouds, and given the prerogatives of a king. It was a scene of great majesty.

Who was that "son of man"? The personification of the people of Israel? An angel in human form? An ethereal human being some-how glowing with the divine? People have said all those things, but the Book of Revelation sees him as Jesus: a human being to whom God grants dominion, glory, and kingship, served by nations of every lan-guage (v. 14). Jesus referred to himself as "son of man," perhaps for the very reason that the term is ambiguous.

Today's portion of the Book of Revelation concludes by telling us (v. 8) that God's personification on earth, Jesus, is the Alpha and the Omega. In the Greek language in which that was written, Alpha is the first letter of the alphabet and Omega the last. Jesus is the begin-ning and the end, the one who's not up in the sky controlling the world by concealed strings or invisible ray guns, and not distant and removed from human affairs — but intertwined with everything we do and think and with every moment of our being.

Today, at the end of the current Church year and before the be-ginning of the new Church year next Sunday, we conclude with two observations. In our pluralistic society, it's well-nigh impossible for us to have a form of government with God as its head. Nevertheless, behind everything must be our wish to acknowledge the kingship of Christ. He and his values must be at the core of our private and public life, our individual and social life, our economic and political life. And that means not merely sentiment, but by way of principle.

Second, we remind ourselves from the Book of Revelation that Jesus offers his priestly royalty to all of us. If we accept it, we're to demonstrate our royal dignity in all situations of life. We're to show that we're caring persons by the witness of our actions: by a preferen-tial option for the poor and underprivileged, by supporting campaigns for human development, and by participating in such critical areas as social and economic development, housing, health care, and education. If we reject it, or accept it only in part, it's in some measure because we don't sufficiently see either the greatness of God or the high dig-nity to which we've been called.